China-India Border Conflict : Recent Perspective

China-India Border Conflict

Recent Perspective

Mohd. Wasim
Commandant (Retd.)

Prashant Publishing House
DELHI - 110094 (INDIA)

PRASHANT PUBLISHING HOUSE
C-34, 28 Foota Road, Gali No. 3
West Karawal Nagar, Delhi-110094
Phone : 9810396373, 22963970

China-India Border Conflict : Recent Perspective

First Published : 2010

ISBN : 978-93-80565-01-9

PRINTED IN INDIA

Published by Mr. R. K. Jha M/s. Prashant Publishing House, Delhi and Printed at H.S. Offset Press, Delhi.

Preface

The 1940s saw huge change in South Asia with the Partition of India in 1947 (resulting in the establishment of the two new states of India and Pakistan), and the establishment of the People's Republic of China in 1949. One of the most basic policies for the new Indian government was that of maintaining cordial relations with China, reviving its ancient friendly ties. India was among the first nations to grant diplomatic recognition to the newly-created PRC. At the time, Chinese officials issued no condemnation of Nehru's claims or made any opposition to Nehru's open declarations of control over Aksai Chin.

In 1956, Chinese Premier Zhou Enlai stated that he had no claims over Indian controlled territory. He later argued that Aksai Chin was already under Chinese jurisdiction, implying that there was therefore no contradiction with his earlier statement since China did not regard the region as "Indian controlled", and that since the British hand-over China had regarded the McCartney MacDonald Line as the relevant border. Zhou later argued that as the boundary was undemarcated and had never been defined by treaty between any Chinese or Indian government, the Indian government could not unilaterally define Aksai Chin's borders. However, within a short time the PRC announced its intention to reclaim Tibet from the British, and later extended its influence by placing border posts within the Indian-claimed territory of Aksai Chin. India protested against these moves and decided to look for a diplomatic solution to ensure a stable Sino-Indian border. To resolve any doubts about the Indian position, Prime Minister Jawaharlal Nehru declared in parliament that India regarded the McMahon Line as its official border. The Chinese expressed no concern at this statement, and in 1951 and 52, the government of China asserted that there were no frontier issues to be taken up with India. In 1954, Prime Minister Nehru wrote a memo calling for India's borders to be clearly defined and demarcated: in line with previous Indian philosophy, Indian maps showed a border that, in some places, lay north of the McMahon Line. Chinese Premier Zhou Enlai, in November 1956, again repeated Chinese assurances that the People's Republic had no claims on Indian territory, although official Chinese maps showed 120,000 square kilometres of territory claimed by India as Chinese.

The China-Indian War, also known as the China-Indian Border Conflict, was a war between China and India that took place in 1962. A disputed Himalayan border was the main pretext for war, but other issues played a role. There had been a series of violent border incidents after the 1959 Tibetan uprising, when India had granted asylum to the Dalai Lama. In response to Chinese incursions, India initiated a Forward Policy in which it placed outposts along the border, including several north of the McMahon Line, the eastern portion of a Line of Actual Control proclaimed by Chinese Premier Zhou Enlai in 1959. The Chinese launched simultaneous offensives in Laddakh and across the McMahon Line on 20 October 1962, coinciding with the Cuban Missile Crisis. Chinese troops advanced over Indian forces in both theatres, capturing Rezang la in Chushul in the western theatre, as well as Tawang in the eastern theatre. The war ended when the Chinese declared a ceasefire on 20 November 1962, and later withdrew from the disputed area. The Sino-Indian War is notable for the harsh conditions under which much of the fighting took place, entailing large-scale combat at altitudes of over 4,250 metres (14,000 feet). This presented enormous logistics problems for both sides. The Sino-Indian War was also noted for the non-deployment of navy or air force by either the Chinese and Indian sides.

—Author

Contents

1 Origin of China-India Border Conflict: Historical Perspective

INTRODUCTION

The China-Indian War, also known as the China-Indian Border Conflict, was a war between China and India that took place in 1962. A disputed Himalayan border was the main pretext for war, but other issues played a role. There had been a series of violent border incidents after the 1959 Tibetan uprising, when India had granted asylum to the Dalai Lama. In response to Chinese incursions, India initiated a Forward Policy in which it placed outposts along the border, including several north of the McMahon Line, the eastern portion of a Line of Actual Control proclaimed by Chinese Premier Zhou Enlai in 1959.

The Chinese launched simultaneous offensives in Laddakh and across the McMahon Line on 20 October 1962, coinciding with the Cuban Missile Crisis. Chinese troops advanced over Indian forces in both theatres, capturing Rezang la in Chushul in the western theatre, as well as Tawang in the eastern theatre. The war ended when the Chinese declared a ceasefire on 20 November 1962, and later withdrew from the disputed area. The Sino-Indian War is notable for the harsh conditions under which much of the fighting took place, entailing large-scale combat at altitudes of over 4,250 metres (14,000 feet). This presented enormous logistics problems for both sides. The Sino-Indian War was also noted for the non-deployment of navy or air force by either the Chinese and Indian sides.

Situation

China and India share a long border, sectioned into three

stretches by Nepal and Bhutan, which follows the Himalayan mountains between Burma and what was then West Pakistan. A number of disputed regions lie along this border.

At its western end is the Aksai Chin region, an area the size of Switzerland, that sits between the Chinese autonomous region of Xinjiang, and Tibet (which China declared as autonomous regions in 1965). The eastern border, between Burma and Bhutan, comprises the present Indian state of Arunachal Pradesh (formerly the North East Frontier Agency). Both of these regions were overrun by China in the 1962 conflict. Most combat took place at high altitudes. The Aksai Chin region is a vast desert of salt flats around 5,000 metres above sea level, and Arunachal Pradesh is extremely mountainous with a number of peaks exceeding 7000 metres.

According to military doctrine, to be successful an attacker generally requires a 3:1 ratio of numerical superiority over the defender; in mountain warfare this ratio should be considerably higher as the terrain favours defence. China was able to take advantage of this: the Chinese Army had possession of the highest ridges in the regions. The high altitude and freezing conditions also cause logistical and welfare difficulties; in past similar conflicts (such as the Italian Campaign of World War I) more casualties have been caused by the harsh conditions than enemy action. The Sino-Indian War was no different, with many troops on both sides dying in the freezing cold.

Cause of War

The cause of the war was a dispute over the sovereignty of the widely-separated Aksai Chin and Arunachal Pradesh border regions. Aksai Chin, claimed by India to belong to Kashmir and by China to be part of Xinjiang, contains an important road link that connects the Chinese regions of Tibet and Xinjiang. China's construction of this road was one of the triggers of the conflict. Arunachal Pradesh (called South Tibet by China) is also claimed by both nations—although it is roughly the size of Austria, it is sparsely inhabited (by numerous local tribes) due to its mountainous terrain. The Indian state Arunachal Pradesh has a population of over one million as of today.

The Johnson Line

The western portion of the Sino-Indian boundary originates in 1834, with the Sikh Confederation's conquest of Laddakh. In 1842 the Sikh Confederacy, which at the time ruled over much of Northern India (including the frontier regions of Jammu and Kashmir), signed a treaty which guaranteed the integrity of its existing borders with its neighbours. The British defeat of the Sikhs in 1846 resulted in transfer of sovereignty over Laddakh, part of the Jammu and Kashmir region, to the British, and British commissioners contacted Chinese officials to negotiate the border. The boundaries at its two extremities, Pangong Lake and Karakoram Pass, were well-defined, but the Aksai Chin area in between lay undefined. In 1865, British surveyor W H Johnson came to an agreement with the Maharaja of Kashmir, in whose service he was employed, on a proposed "Johnson Line" which placed Aksai Chin in Kashmir. China rejected the arrangement, and the British government also harboured doubts, so decided to take up the issue in an attempt to reach a settlement.

However in 1892, before the issue had been resolved, China erected boundary markers at Karakoram Pass on the ancient caravan route between Xinjiang and Laddakh (which were disputed by the British Indian Government). Throughout most of the 19th century Great Britain and the expanding Russian Empire were jockeying for influence in Central Asia, and Britain decided to hand over Aksai Chin to Chinese administration as a buffer against Russian invasion.

The newly-created border was known as the MacCartney-MacDonald Line, and both British-controlled India and China now began to show Aksai Chin as Chinese. In 1911 the Xinhai Revolution resulted in power shifts in China, and by 1918 (in the wake of the Russian Bolshevik Revolution) the British no longer saw merit in China's continuing possession of the region. On British maps the border was redrawn as the original Johnson Line, but despite this reversion the new border was left unmanned and undemarcated. According to Neville Maxwell, the British had used as many as 11 different boundary lines in the region, as their claims shifted with the political situation.

By the time of Indian independence in 1947, the Johnson Line had become India's official western boundary. On 1 July 1954, Indian Prime Minister Jawaharlal Nehru definitively stated the Indian position. He claimed that Aksai Chin had been part of the Indian Laddakh region for centuries, and that the border (as defined by the Johnson Line) was non-negotiable. According to George N. Patterson, when the Indian government finally produced a report detailing the alleged proof of India's claims to the disputed area, "the quality of the Indian evidence was very poor, including some very dubious sources indeed". During the 1950s, China constructed a road through Aksai Chin, connecting Xinjiang and Tibet, which ran south of the Johnson Line in many places. Aksai Chin was easily accessible to the Chinese, but access from India, which meant negotiating the Karakoram mountains, was more problematic. Consequently India did not even learn of the existence of the road until 1957 — finally confirmed when the road was shown in Chinese maps published the following year.

The McMahon Line

In 1826 India and China gained a common border, including the area of what is now called Myanmar, following British annexations in the Anglo-Burmese Wars. In 1847, Major J. Jenkins, Agent for the North East Frontier, reported that the Tawang was part of Tibet. In 1872, four monastic officials from Tibet arrived in Tawang and supervised a boundary settlement with Major R. Graham, NEFA official, which included the Tawang Tract as part of Tibet. Thus, in the last half of the 19th century, it was clear that the British treated the Tawang Tract as part of Tibet. This boundary was confirmed in a June 1, 1912 note from the British General Staff in India, stating that the "present boundary (demarcated) is south of Tawang, running westwards along the foothills from near Ugalguri to the southern Bhutanese border." A 1908 map of The Province of Eastern Bengal and Assam (32 miles to the inch), prepared for the Foreign Department of the Government of India, showed the international boundary from Bhutan continuing to the Baroi River, following the Himalayas foothill alignment. In 1913, representatives of Great Britain, China and Tibet attended a conference in Simla regarding the borders between Tibet, China and British India. Whilst all three representatives initialed the agreement, Beijing later objected to the proposed boundary between the regions of *Outer Tibet* and *Inner Tibet* and did not ratify it. The details of the Indo-Tibetan boundary was not revealed to China at the time. The foreign secretary of the British Indian government, Henry McMahon, who drew up the proposal, decided to bypass the Chinese (although instructed not to by his superiors) and settle the border bilaterally by negotiating directly with Tibet. According to later Indian claims, this border was intended to run through the highest ridges of the Himalayas, as the areas south of the Himalayas were traditionally Indian. However, the McMahon Line lay south of the boundary India claims. India's government held the view that the Himalayas were the ancient boundaries of the Indian subcontinent, and thus should be the modern boundaries of India while it is the position of the Chinese government that the disputed area in the Himalayas have been geographically and culturally part of Tibet since ancient times. Months after the Simla agreement, China set up boundary markers south of the McMahon Line. T O'Callaghan, an official in the Eastern Sector of the North East Frontier, relocated all these markers to a location slightly south of the McMahon Line, and then visited Rima to confirm with Tibetan officials that there was no Chinese influence in the area. The British-run Government of India initially rejected the Simla Agreement as incompatible with the Anglo-Russian Convention of 1907, which stipulated that neither party was to negotiate with Tibet "except through the intermediary of the Chinese government".

The British and Russians cancelled the 1907 agreement by joint consent in 1921. It was not until the late 1930s that the British started to use the McMahon Line on official maps of the region. China took the position that the Tibetan government should not have been allowed to make a such a treaty, rejecting Tibet's claims of independent rule. For its part, Tibet did not object to any section of the McMahon Line excepting the demarcation of the trading town of Tawang, which the Line placed under British-Indian jurisdiction. However, up until World War II, Tibetan officials were allowed to administer Tawang with complete authority. Due to the increased threat of Japanese and Chinese expansion during this period, British Indian troops secured the town as part of the defence of India's eastern border. In the 1950s India began actively patrolling the region. It found that, at multiple locations, the highest ridges actually fell north of the McMahon Line.

Given India's historic position that the original intent of the Line was to separate the two nations by the highest mountains in the world, in these locations India extended its forward posts northward to the ridges, regarding this move as compliant with the original border proposal, although the Simla Convention did not explicitly state this intention. On Oct. 29, 2008, David Miliband, the British foreign secretary, announced that the previous British actions including the Simla Accord (1913) and thus the McMahon Line had been an anachronism and a colonial legacy. He apologized to China for not having renounced those actions earlier. He was supported by Chris Patten, the last British governor of Hong Kong, who called the British position embodied in the Simla Accord (1913) a "quaint eccentricity".

FACTORS RESPONSIBLE FOR WAR

Tibet Controversy

The 1940s saw huge change in South Asia with the Partition of India in 1947 (resulting in the establishment of the two new states of India and Pakistan), and the establishment of the People's Republic of China in 1949. One of the most basic policies for the new Indian government was that of maintaining cordial relations with China, reviving its ancient friendly ties. India was among the first nations to grant diplomatic recognition to the newly-created PRC. At the time, Chinese officials issued no condemnation of Nehru's claims or made any opposition to Nehru's open declarations of control over Aksai Chin.

In 1956, Chinese Premier Zhou Enlai stated that he had no claims over Indian controlled territory. He later argued that Aksai Chin was already under Chinese jurisdiction, implying that there was therefore no contradiction with his earlier statement since China did not regard the region as "Indian controlled", and that since the British hand-over China had regarded the McCartney MacDonald Line as the relevant border. Zhou later argued that as the boundary was undemarcated and had never been defined by treaty between any Chinese or Indian government, the Indian government could not unilaterally define Aksai Chin's borders. However, within a short time the PRC announced its intention to reclaim Tibet from the British, and later extended its influence by placing border posts within the Indian-claimed territory of Aksai Chin. India protested against these moves and decided to look for a diplomatic solution to ensure a stable Sino-Indian border.

To resolve any doubts about the Indian position, Prime Minister Jawaharlal Nehru declared in parliament that India regarded the McMahon Line as its official border. The Chinese expressed no concern at this statement, and in 1951 and 52, the government of China asserted that there were no frontier issues to be taken up with India. In 1954, Prime Minister Nehru wrote a memo calling for India's borders to be clearly defined and demarcated: in line with previous Indian philosophy, Indian maps showed a border that, in some places, lay north of the McMahon Line. Chinese Premier Zhou Enlai, in November 1956, again repeated Chinese assurances that the People's Republic had no claims on Indian territory, although official Chinese maps showed 120,000 square kilometres of territory claimed by India as Chinese.

CIA documents created at the time revealed that Nehru had ignored Burmese premier Ba Swe when he warned Nehru to be cautious when dealing with Zhou. They also allege that Zhou purposefully told Nehru that there were no border issues with India. In 1950 the Chinese People's Liberation Army invaded Tibet. Four years later, in 1954, China and India negotiated the Five Principles of Peaceful Coexistence by which the two nations agreed to abide in settling their disputes. India presented a frontier map which was accepted by China, and the Indian government under Prime Minister Nehru promoted the slogan *Hindi-Chini bhai-bhai* (Indians and Chinese are brothers). According to Georgia Tech political analyst John W Garver, Nehru's policy on Tibet was to create a strong Sino-Indian partnership which would be catalyzed through agreement and compromise on Tibet. Garver believes that Nehru's previous actions had given him confidence that China would be ready to form an "Asian Axis" with India.

This apparent progress in relations suffered a major setback when, in 1959, Nehru accommodated the Tibetan religious leader, the Dalai Lama, who was fleeing Lhasa after a failed Tibetan uprising against Chinese rule.

The Chairman of the Chinese Communist Party, Mao Zedong, was enraged and asked the Xinhua News Agency to produce reports on Indian expansionists operating in Tibet. Border incidents continued through this period. In August 1959, the PLA took an Indian prisoner at Longju, which had an ambiguous position in the McMahon Line, and two months later in Aksai Chin a clash led to the death of nine Indian frontier policemen. On 2 October, Soviet Premier Nikita Khrushchev defended Nehru in a meeting with Mao.

This action reinforced China's impression that the Soviet Union, the United States and India all had expansionist designs over China. The PLA (People's Liberation Army) went so far as to prepare a self-defensive counterattack plan. Negotiations were restarted between the nations, but no progress was made. As a consequence of their non-recognition of the McMahon Line, China's maps showed both the North East Frontier Area (NEFA) and Aksai Chin to be Chinese territory.

In 1960, Zhou Enlai unofficially suggested that India drop its claims to Aksai Chin in return for a Chinese withdrawal of claims over NEFA. Adhering to his stated position, Nehru believed that China did not have a legitimate claim over either of these territories, and thus was not ready to concede them. This adamance was perceived in China as Indian opposition to Chinese rule in Tibet. Nehru declined to conduct any negotiations on the boundary until Chinese troops withdrew from Aksai Chin; a position supported by the international community. India produced numerous reports on the negotiations, and translated Chinese reports into English to help inform the international debate.

China believed that India was simply securing its claim lines in order to continue its "grand plans in Tibet". India's stance that China withdraw from Aksai Chin caused continual deterioration of the diplomatic situation to the point at which internal forces were pressurizing Nehru to take a military stance against China.

The Forward Policy

At the beginning of 1961, Nehru appointed General B M Kaul as army Chief of General Staff, but he refused to increase military spending and prepare for a possible war. That summer, China's continuing patrols south of the McMahon Line provoked an Indian response known as the "Forward Policy". According to James Barnard Calvin of the U.S. Navy, in 1959, India started sending Indian troops and border patrols into disputed areas. This program created both skirmishes and deteriorating relations between India and China. The aim of this policy was to create outposts behind advancing Chinese troops to interdict their supplies, forcing their return to China. There were eventually 60 such outposts, including 43 north of the McMahon Line. China viewed this as further confirmation of Indian expansionist plans directed towards Tibet. According to the Indian official history, implementation of the Forward Policy was intended to provide evidence of Indian occupation in the previously unoccupied region through which Chinese troops had been patrolling. Kaul was confident, through contact with Indian Intelligence and CIA information, that China would not react with force. Indeed at first the PLA simply withdrew, but eventually Chinese forces began to counter-encircle the Indian positions. This led to a tit-for-tat Indian reaction, with both forces attempting to outmanoeuver each other. However, despite the escalating nature of the dispute, the two forces withheld from engaging each other directly.

Chinese attention was diverted for a time by the military activity of the Nationalists on Taiwan, but on 23 June the U.S. assured China that a Nationalist invasion would not be permitted. China's heavy artillery facing Taiwan could then be moved to Tibet. It took China six to eight months to gather the resources needed for the war, according to Anil Athale, author of the official Indian history. The Chinese sent a large quantity of non-military supplies to Tibet through the Indian port of Calcutta.

Early Incidents

Various border conflicts and "military incidents" between India and China flared up throughout the summer and autumn of 1962. In May, the Indian Air Force was told not to plan for close air support, although it was assessed as being a feasible way to repel the unbalanced ratio of Chinese to Indian troops. In June, a skirmish caused the deaths of dozens of Chinese troops. The Indian Intelligence Bureau received information about a Chinese buildup along the border which could be a precursor to war.

During the period of June–July 1962, the Indian military planners began advocating "probing actions" against the Chinese, and accordingly, moved mountain troops forward to cut off Chinese supply lines. According to Patterson, the Indian motives were threefold:

1. Test Chinese resolve and intentions regarding India.
2. Test whether India would enjoy Soviet backing in the event of a Sino-Indian war.
3. Create sympathy for India within the US, with whom relations had deteriorated after the Indian annexation of Goa.

On 10 July 1962, 350 Chinese troops surrounded an Indian post in Chushul but withdrew after a heated argument via loudspeaker. On 22 July, the Forward Policy was extended to allow Indian troops to push back Chinese troops already established in disputed territory. Whereas Indian troops were previously ordered to fire only in self-defence, all post commanders were now given discretion to open fire upon Chinese forces if threatened. In August, the Chinese military improved its combat readiness along the McMahon Line and began stockpiling ammunition, weapons and gasoline.

Confrontation at Thag La

In June 1962, Indian forces established an outpost at Dhola, on the southern slopes of the Thag La Ridge. Dhola lay north of the McMahon Line but south of the ridges India maintains the McMahon Line was supposed to represent. In August, China issued diplomatic protests and began occupying positions at the top of Thag La. On 8 September, a 60-strong PLA unit descended to the south side of the ridge and occupied positions that dominated one of the Indian posts at Dhola. Fire was not exchanged but

Nehru said to the media that the Indian Army had instructions to "free our territory" and the troops had been given discretion to use force. On 11 September, it was decided that "all forward posts and patrols were given permission to fire on any armed Chinese who entered Indian territory".

However, the operation to occupy Thagla was flawed in that Nehru's directives were unclear and it got underway very slowly because of this. In addition to this, each man had to carry 35 kg of luggage over the long trek and this severely slowed down the reaction. By the time the Indian battalion reached the point of conflict, Chinese units controlled both banks of the Namka Chu River. On 20 September, Chinese troops threw grenades at Indian troops and a firefight developed, triggering a long series of skirmishes for the rest of September.

Some Indian troops, including Brigadier Dalvi who commanded the forces at Thag La, were also concerned that the territory they were fighting for was not strictly territory that "we should have been convinced was ours". According to Neville Maxwell, even members of the Indian defence ministry were categorically concerned with the validity of the fighting in Thag La.

On 3 October, a week before the triggering of the war, Zhou Enlai visited Nehru in New Delhi promising there would be no war. On 4 October, Kaul assigned some troops with securing regions south of the Thagla Ridge. Kaul decided to first secure Yumtso La, a strategically important position, before re-entering the lost Dhola post. Kaul had then realised that the attack would be desperate and the Indian government tried to stop escalation into an all-out war. Indian troops travelling to Thagla had suffered in the previously unexperienced conditions, two Gurkha troops died of pulmonary edema.

On 10 October, an Indian Punjabi patrol of 50 troops to Yumtso La were met by an emplaced Chinese position of some 1,000 soldiers. Indian troops were in no position for battle, as Yumtso La was 16,000 feet (4,900 m) above sea level and Kaul did not plan on having artillery support for the troops. The Chinese troops opened fire on the Indians under their belief that they were north of the McMahon Line. The Indians were surrounded by Chinese positions which used mortar fire. However, they managed to hold off the first Chinese assault, inflicting heavy casualties.

At this point, the Indian troops were in a position to push the Chinese back with mortar and machine gun fire. However, Brigadier Dalvi opted not to fire, as it would mean decimating the Rajput who were still in the area of the Chinese regrouping. They helplessly watched the Chinese ready themselves for a second assault. In the second Chinese assault, the Indians began their retreat, realising the situation was hopeless. The Indian patrol suffered 25 casualties, with the Chinese suffering 33. The Chinese troops held their fire as the Indians retreated, and then buried the Indian dead with military honours, as witnessed by the retreating soldiers. This was the first occurrence of heavy fighting in the war.

This attack had grave implications for India and Nehru tried to solve the issue, but by 18 October it was clear that the Chinese were preparing for an attack on India, with massive troop buildups on the border. A long line of mules and porters had also been observed supporting the buildup and reinforcement of positions south of the Thagla ridge.

WAR PREPARATIONS

Objectives

Two of the major factors leading up to China's eventual conflicts with Indian troops were India's stance on the disputed borders and perceived Indian subversion in Tibet. There was "a perceived need to punish and end perceived Indian efforts to undermine Chinese control of Tibet, Indian efforts which were perceived as having the objective of restoring the pre-1949 status quo ante of Tibet". The other was "a perceived need to punish and end perceived Indian aggression against Chinese territory along the border". John W. Garver argues that the first perception was incorrect based on the state of the Indian military and polity in the 1960s, it was, nevertheless a major reason for China's going to war. However, he argues the Chinese perception of aggression to be "substantially accurate". The CIA's recently declassified POLO documents reveal contemporary American analysis of

Chinese motives during the war. According to this document, "Chinese apparently were motivated to attack by one primary consideration—their determination to retain the ground on which PLA forces stood in 1962 and to punish the Indians for trying to take that ground".

Another factor which affected China's decision for war with India was a perceived need to stop a Soviet-US-India encirclement and isolation of China. India's relations with the Soviet Union and United States were both strong at this time, but the Soviets were preoccupied by the Cuban Missile Crisis and would not interfere with the Sino-Indian War. P.B. Sinha suggests that China timed the war exactly in parallel with American actions so as to avoid any chance of American or Soviet involvement. American buildup of forces around Cuba occurred on the same day as the first major clash at Dhola while China's buildup between the 10th and 20th of October coincided exactly with the United States establishment of a blockade against Cuba which began on the 20th of October.

Garver argues that the Chinese correctly assessed Indian border policies, particularly the Forward Policy, as attempts for incremental seizure of Chinese-controlled territory. On Tibet, Garver argues that one of the major factors leading to China's decision for war with India was a common tendency of humans "to attribute others behaviour to interior motivations, while attributing their own behaviour to situational factors". Studies from China published in the 1990s confirmed that the root cause for China going to war with India was the perceived aggression in Tibet, with the forward policy simply catalyzing the aggressive Chinese reaction.

Neville Maxwell and Allen Whiting argue that the Chinese leadership believed they were defending territory they believed to be legitimately Chinese, and which was already under de facto Chinese occupation prior to Indian advances, and regarded the Forward Policy as an Indian attempt at creeping annexation. Mao Zedong himself compared the Forward Policy to a strategic advance in Chinese chess:

Their [India's] continually pushing forward is like crossing the Chu Han boundary. What should we do? We can also set out a few pawns, on our side of the river. If they don't then cross over, that's great. If they do cross, we'll eat them up [chess metaphor meaning to take the opponent's pieces]. Of course, we cannot blindly eat them. Lack of forbearance in small matters upsets great plans. We must pay attention to the situation.

The motive for the Forward Policy was to cut off the supply routes for Chinese troops posted in NEFA and Aksai Chin. According to the official Indian history, the forward policy was continued because of its initial success, as Chinese troops withdrew when they encountered areas already occupied by Indian troops. The Forward Policy was having success in cutting out supply lines of Chinese troops who had advanced South of the McMahon Line. However, the Forward Policy rested on the assumption that Chinese forces "were not likely to use force against any of our posts, even if they were in a position to do so". No serious reappraisal of this policy took place even when Chinese forces ceased withdrawing.

By early 1962, the Chinese leadership began to fear that India's intentions were to launch a massive attack against Chinese troops, and that the Indian leadership wanted a war. In 1961, the Indian army had been sent into Goa, a small region without any other international borders apart from the Indian one, after Portugal refused to surrender the exclave colony to the Indian Union. Although this action met little to no international protest or opposition, China saw it as an example of India's expansionist nature, especially in light of heated rhetoric from Indian politicians. India's Home Minister declared, "If the Chinese will not vacate the areas occupied by it, India will have to repeat what she did in Goa. India will certainly drive out the Chinese forces", while another member of the Indian Congress Party pronounced, "India will take steps to end [Chinese] aggression on Indian soil just as she ended Portuguese aggression in Goa".

By mid-1962, it was apparent to the Chinese leadership that negotiations had failed to make any progress, and the Forward Policy was increasingly perceived as a grave threat as Delhi increasingly sent probes deeper into border areas and cut off Chinese supply lines. Foreign Minister Marshal Chen Yi commented at one high-level meeting, "Nehru's forward policy is a knife. He wants to put it in our heart. We cannot close our eyes and await death." The Chinese leadership believed that their restraint on the issue was being perceived by India as weakness, leading to continued provocations, and that a major counterblow was needed to stop perceived Indian aggression. Xu Yan, prominent Chinese military historian and professor at the PLA's National Defence University, gives an account of the Chinese leadership's decision to go to war. By late September 1962, the Chinese leadership had begun to reconsider their policy of "armed coexistence", which had failed to address their concerns with the forward policy and Tibet, and consider a large, decisive strike.

The Chinese leadership initially held a sympathetic view towards India as the latter had been ruled by British colonial masters for centuries. However, Nehru's forward policy convinced PRC leadership that the independent Indian leadership was a reincarnation of British imperialism. Thus, the Indian government must be taught an unforgettable lesson. Mao Zedong stated: "Rather than being constantly accused of aggression, it's better to show the world what really happens when China indeed moves its muscles."

Military Planning

The Indian side was confident war would not be triggered and made little preparations. India had only two divisions of troops in the region of the conflict. In August 1962, Brigadier D.K. Palit claimed that a war with China in the near future could be ruled out. Even in September 1962, when Indian troops were ordered to "expel the Chinese" from Thag La, Maj. General J.S. Dhillon expressed the opinion that ""experience in Laddakh had shown that a few rounds fired at the Chinese would cause them to run away." Because of this, the Indian army was completely unprepared when the attack at Yumtso La occurred.

Recently declassified CIA documents which were compiled at the time reveal that India's estimates of Chinese capabilities made them neglect their military in favour of economic growth. It is claimed that if a more military-minded man had been in place instead of Nehru, India would have been more likely to have been ready for the threat from China.

On 6 October 1962, the Chinese leadership convened. Lin Biao reported that PLA intelligence units had determined that Indian units might assault Chinese positions at Thag La on 10 October (Operation Leghorn). The Chinese leadership and the Central Military Council decided upon war to launch a large-scale attack to punish perceived military aggression from India. In Beijing, a larger meeting of Chinese military was convened in order to plan for the coming conflict.

The Mao and the Chinese leadership issued a directive laying out the objectives for the war. A main assault would be launched in the eastern sector, which would be coordinated with a smaller assault in the western sector. All Indian troops within China's claimed territories in the eastern sector would be expelled, and the war would be ended with a unilateral Chinese ceasefire and withdrawal to prewar positions, followed by a return to the negotiating table. India led the Non-Aligned Movement, Nehru enjoyed international prestige, and China, with a larger military would be portrayed as an aggressor. However, he said that a well-fought war "will guarantee at least thirty years of peace" with India, and determined the benefits to offset the costs. On 8 October, additional veteran and elite divisions were ordered to prepare to move into Tibet from the Chengdu and Lanzhou military regions.

On October 12, Nehru declared that he had ordered the Indian army to "clear Indian territory in the NEFA of Chinese invaders" and personally met with Kaul, issuing instructions to him.

On October 14, an editorial on People's Daily issued China's final warning to India: "So it seems that Mr. Nehru has made up his mind to attack the Chinese frontier guards on an even bigger scale....It is high time to shout to Mr. Nehru that the heroic Chinese troops, with the glorious tradition of resisting foreign aggression, can never be cleared by anyone from their own territory... If there are still some maniacs who are reckless enough to ignore our well-intentioned advice and insist on having another try, well, let them do so. History will pronounce its inexorable verdict... At this critical moment...we still want to appeal once more to Mr. Nehru:

better rein in at the edge of the precipice and do not use the lives of Indian troops as stakes in your gamble." Marshal Liu Bocheng headed a group to determine the strategy for the war. He concluded that the opposing Indian troops were among India's best, and to achieve victory would require deploying crack troops and relying on force concentration to achieve decisive victory. On 16 October, this war plan was approved, and on the 18th, the final approval was given by the Politburo for a "self defensive counter-attack", scheduled for 20 October.

Chinese Offensive

On 20 October 1962, the Chinese People's Liberation Army launched two attacks, 1000 kilometres apart. In the western theatre, the PLA sought to expel Indian forces from the Chip Chap valley in Aksai Chin while in the eastern theatre, the PLA sought to capture both banks of the Namka Chu river. Some skirmishes also took place at the Nathula Pass, which is in the Indian state of Sikkim (an Indian protectorate at that time). Gurkha rifles travelling north were targeted by Chinese artillery fire. After four days of fierce fighting, the three regiments of Chinese troops succeeded in securing a substantial portion of the disputed territory.

Eastern Theatre

Chinese troops launched an attack on the southern banks of the Namka Chu River on 20 October. The Indian forces were undermanned, with only an understrength battalion to support them, while the Chinese troops had three regiments positioned on the north side of the river. The Indians expected Chinese forces to cross via one of five bridges over the river and defended those crossings. However their strategy was wrong. As the Indian troops settled for the night on the banks of the river, the PLA crossed over the shallow October river and made their way to the other side. They gathered themselves up into battalions on the Indian-held south side of the river in the camouflage of the night, with each battalion assigned against a separate group of Rajputs.

At 5:14 am, Chinese mortar fire began attacking the Indian positions. Simultaneously, the Chinese cut the Indian telephone lines so that the Indians could not make contact with CHQ. At about 6:30 am, the Chinese infantry, who had been positioned behind the Indians in the night, made their surprise attack and forced the Indians to leave their trench positions. The Chinese troops overwhelmed the Indians. Proceeding attacks from flanking positions south of the McMahon Line overwhelmed the Indian troops and caused withdrawal from Namka Chu. Fearful of continued losses, Indian troops escaped into Bhutan. However, Chinese forces respected the border and ignored Tsang Le. Now the Chinese troops had occupied the area which was under dispute in the confrontations at Thag La, but they continued to advance into the rest of NEFA.

On 22 October, at 12:15 am, the PLA launched a mortar attack on Walong, on the McMahon line. 400 troops proceeded to launch fire on the Indians posted there. Lights fired by Indian troops on 23 October showed the presence of numerous Chinese milling around the valley. The Indians tried to use their mortars against the Chinese but the PLA then lit a bushfire to create great confusion amongst the enemy troops. The Chinese eventually captured Walong at the cost of more than 200 dead or wounded, while Indian casualties were also heavy.

On 23 October, Chinese troops launched a three-pronged attack on Tawang, which the Indians evacuated without any resistance.

Western Theatre

On the Aksai Chin front, China already controlled most of the disputed territory. China quickly and efficiently got rid of remnants of Indian troops. On 20 October, operations in the Chip Chap Valley, Galwan Valley, and Pangong Lake were successful for the PLA. Many outposts and garrisons comprised were unable to defend against the surrounding Chinese troops. Most Indian troops positioned in these posts fought and were either killed or taken prisoner. India did not support its troops, as the Galwan post had been surrounded by China in August and had received no land support from India since then. After the 20 October attack, this post was not heard from again.

Late on 19 October, Chinese troops launched various attacks

throughout the western theatre. By 22 October, all posts north of Chushul had been cleared. Later on 24 October, there was a battle on the Rezang La Ridge to defend an air strip from impending Chinese takeover.

After realizing the magnitude of the attack, Indian Western Command withdrew many of the isolated outposts to the southeast. Daulet Beg Oldi was also evacuated, but it was south of the Chinese claim line and was not approached by Chinese forces. Indian troops were withdrawn so that they could regroup and be ready if China probed south of their claim line.

Indian forces were hampered by their significant inferiority in numbers and lack of combat readiness. The Indian deployment was sparsely put and needed new commanders in the second phase of the war.

Three Week Lull

By 24 October, the PLA had entered territory previously administered by India to give the PRC a diplomatically strong position over India. The majority of Chinese forces had advanced sixteen kilometres south of the border. Four days of fighting were followed by a three-week lull. Zhou ordered the troops to stop advancing as he attempted to negotiate with Nehru. The Indian forces had retreated into more heavily fortified positions around Se La and Bombdi La which would be difficult to assault. Zhou sent Nehru a letter, proposing

1. A negotiated settlement of the boundary
2. That both sides disengage and withdraw twenty kilometres from present lines of actual control
3. A Chinese withdrawal north in NEFA
4. That China and India not cross lines of present control in Aksai Chin.

Nehru's 27 October reply expressed interest in the restoration of peace and friendly relations and suggested a return to the "boundary prior to 8 September 1962". He was categorically concerned about a mutual twenty kilometre withdrawal after "40 or 60 kilometres of blatant military aggression". He wanted the creation of a larger immediate buffer zone and thus resist the possibility of a repeat offensive. Zhou's 4 November reply repeated his 1959 offer to return to the McMahon Line in NEFA and the Chinese traditionally claimed MacDonald Line in Aksai Chin. Facing Chinese forces maintaining themselves on Indian soil and trying to avoid political pressure, the Indian parliament announced a national emergency and passed a resolution which stated their intent to "drive out the aggressors from the sacred soil of India". The United States and the United Kingdom supported India's response, however the Soviet Union was preoccupied with the Cuban Missile Crisis and did not offer the support it had provided in previous years.

With the backing of other great powers, a 14 November letter by Nehru to Zhou once again rejected his proposal. Neither side declared war, used their air force, or fully broke off diplomatic relations; however, the conflict is commonly referred to as a war. This war coincided with the Cuban Missile Crisis and was viewed by the western nations at the time as another act of aggression by the Communist bloc. According to Calvin, the Chinese side evidently wanted a diplomatic resolution and discontinuation of the conflict.

Resumption of War

After Zhou received Nehru's letter, the fighting resumed on the eastern theatre on 14 November (Nehru's birthday), with an Indian attack on Walong, claimed by China, launched from the defensive position of Se La and inflicting heavy casualties on the Chinese. The Chinese resumed military activity on Aksai Chin and NEFA hours after the Walong battle.

Eastern Theatre

On the eastern theatre, the PLA attacked Indian forces near Se La and Bomdi La on 17 November. These positions were defended by the Indian 4th Division. Instead of attacking by road as expected, PLA forces approached via a mountain trail, and their attack cut off a main road and isolated 10,000 Indian troops. Se La was very high, and faced with this strategic problem, the Chinese captured Thembang, which was a supply route to Se La.

Western Theatre

On the western theatre, PLA forces launched a heavy infantry attack on 18 November near Chushul. Their attack started at 4:35 am, despite a mist surrounding most of the areas in the region. At 5:45 the Chinese troops advanced to attack 2 platoons of Indian troops at Gurung Hill. The Indians did not know what was happening, as communications were dead. As a patrol was sent, China attacked with greater numbers. Indian artillery could not hold off against superior Chinese forces. By 9:00 am, Chinese forces attacked Gurung Hill directly and Indian commanders withdrew from the area.

The Chinese had been simultaneously attacking Rezang La which was held by 118 Indian troops. At 5:05 am, Chinese troops launched their attack audaciously. Chinese medium machine gun fire pierced through the Indian tactical defences.

At 6:55 am the sun rose and the Chinese attack on the 8th platoon began in waves. Fighting continued for the next hour, until the Chinese signaled that they had destroyed the 7th platoon. Indians tried to use light machine guns on the medium machine guns from the Chinese but after 10 minutes the battle was over. Logistical inadequacy once again hurt the Indian troops. The Chinese gave the Indian troops a respectful military funeral. The battles also saw the death of Major Shaitan Singh of the Kumaon Regiment, who had been instrumental in the first battle of Rezang La. The Indian troops were forced to withdraw to high mountain positions. Indian sources believed that their troops were just coming to grips with the mountain combat and finally called for more troops. However, the Chinese declared a ceasefire, ending the bloodshed.

Indians suffered heavy casualties, with dead Indian troops' bodies being found in the ice, frozen with weapons in hand. Chinese forces also suffered heavy casualties, especially at Rezang La. This signalled the end of the war in Aksai Chin as China had reached their claim line-many Indian troops were ordered to withdraw from the area. China claimed that the Indian troops wanted to fight on until the bitter end. However, the war ended with their withdrawal, so as to limit the amount of casualties.

The PLA penetrated close to the outskirts of Tezpur, Assam, a major frontier town nearly fifty kilometres from the Assam-North-East Frontier Agency border. The local government ordered the evacuation of the civilians in Tezpur to the south of the Brahmaputra River, all prisons were thrown open, and government officials who stayed behind destroyed Tezpur's currency reserves in anticipation of a Chinese advance.

Ceasefire

China had reached its claim lines so the PLA did not advance farther, and on 19 November it declared a unilateral cease-fire. Zhou Enlai declared a unilateral ceasefire to start on midnight, 21 November. Zhou's ceasefire declaration stated, Beginning from 21 November 1962, the Chinese frontier guards will cease fire along the entire Sino-Indian border. Beginning from 1 December 1962, the Chinese frontier guards will withdraw to positions 20 kilometres behind the line of actual control which existed between China and India on 7 November 1959. In the eastern sector, although the Chinese frontier guards have so far been fighting on Chinese territory north of the traditional customary line, they are prepared to withdraw from their present positions to the north of the illegal McMahon Line, and to withdraw twenty kilometres back from that line. In the middle and western sectors, the Chinese frontier guards will withdraw twenty kilometres from the line of actual control.

Zhou had first given the ceasefire announcement to Indian chargé d'affaires on 19 November, (before India's request for United States air support) but New Delhi did not receive it until 24 hours later. The aircraft carrier was ordered back after the ceasefire and thus American intervention on India's side in the war was avoided.

Retreating Indian troops, who hadn't come into contact with anyone knowing of the ceasefire, and Chinese troops in NEFA and Aksai Chin, were involved in some minor battles but for the most part the ceasefire signalled an end to the fighting. The United States Air Force flew in supplies to India in November 1962, but neither side wished to continue hostilities.

Toward the end of the war India increased her support for Tibetan refugees and revolutionaries, some of them having settled in India, as they were fighting the same common enemy in the region. The Nehru administration ordered the raising of an elite Indian-trained "Tibetan Armed Force" composed of Tibetan refugees. The CIA had already begun operations in bringing about change in Tibet.

World View

The Chinese military action has been viewed by the United States as part of the PRC's policy of making use of aggressive wars to settle its border disputes and to distract from its internal issues. According to James Calvin from the United States Marine Corps, western nations at the time viewed China as an aggressor during the China-India border war, and the war was part of a monolithic communist objective for a world dictatorship of the proletariat. This was further triggered by Mao Zedong's views that: "The way to world conquest lies through Havana, Accra, and Calcutta". Calvin believes that Chinese actions show a "pattern of conservative aims and limited objectives, rather than expansionism" and blames this particular conflict on India's provocations towards China. However, Calvin also expresses that China, in the past, has been adamant to gain control over regions to which it has a "traditional claim", which triggered the dispute over NEFA and Aksai Chin and indeed Tibet. Calvin's assumption, based on the history of the Cold War and the Domino Effect, assumed that China might ultimately try to regain control of everything that it considers as "traditionally Chinese" which in its view includes the entirety of South East Asia.

The Kennedy administration was disturbed by what they considered "blatant Chinese communist aggression against India". In a May 1963 National Security Council meeting, contingency planning on the part of the United States in the event of another Chinese attack on India was discussed. Defence Secretary Robert McNamara and General Maxwell Taylor advised the president to use nuclear weapons should the Americans intervene in such a situation. Kennedy insisted that Washington defend India as it would any ally, saying, "We should defend India, and therefore we will defend India". The Johnson Administration considered and then rejected giving nuclear weapons technology to the Indians.

The non-aligned nations, perhaps unsurprisingly, remained non-aligned, and only the United Arab Republic openly supported India. Of the non-aligned nations, six, Egypt, Burma, Cambodia, Sri Lanka, Ghana and Indonesia, met in Colombo on 10 December 1962. The proposals stipulated a Chinese withdrawal of 20 km from the customary lines without any reciprocal withdrawal on India's behalf. The failure of these six nations to unequivocally condemn China deeply disappointed India.

In 1972, Chinese Premier Zhou explained the Chinese point of view to President Nixon of the US. As for the causes of the war, Zhou asserted that China did not try and expel Indian troops from south of the McMahon line and that three open warning telegrams were sent to Nehru before the war. However, Indian patrols south of the McMahon line were expelled and suffered casualties in the Chinese attack. Zhou also told Nixon that Chairman Mao ordered the troops to return to show good faith. The Indian government maintains that the Chinese military could not advance further south due to logistical problems and the cut-off of resource supplies.

While Western nations did not view Chinese actions favourably because of fear of the Chinese and competitiveness, Pakistan, which had a turbulent relationship with India ever since the Indian partition, improved its relations with China after the war. Prior to the war, Pakistan also shared a disputed boundary with China, and had proposed to India that the two countries adopt a common defence against "northern" enemies (ie China), which was rejected by India. However, China and Pakistan took steps to peacefully negotiate their shared boundaries, beginning on 13 October 1962, and concluding in December of that year. Pakistan also expressed fear that the huge amounts of western military aid directed to India would allow it to threaten Pakistan's security in future conflicts. Mohammed Ali, External Affairs Minister of Pakistan, declared that massive Western aid to India in the Sino-Indian dispute would be considered an unfriendly act towards Pakistan. As a result Pakistan made efforts to improve its relations with China. The following year, China and Pakistan peacefully settled disputes on their shared border, and negotiated the China-Pakistan Border Treaty in 1963, as well as trade, commercial, and barter treaties. On 2 March 1963, Pakistan conceded its northern claim line in Pakistani-controlled Kashmir to China in favour of a more southerly boundary along the Karakoram Range. The border treaty largely set the border along the MacCartney-Macdonald Line. Because of India's failure against China, Pakistan triggered the Second Kashmir War with India. However, it effectively ended in a stalemate as Calvin states that the Sino-Indian War had caused the previously passive government to take a stand on actively modernizing India's military. China offered diplomatic support to Pakistan in this war but did not offer military support. In January 1966, China condemned the Tashkent Agreement between India and Pakistan as a Soviet-US plot in the region. In the Indo-Pakistani War of 1971, Pakistan expected China to provide military support, but it was left alone as India successfully helped the rebels in East Pakistan to found the new nation-state of Bangladesh.

On Oct. 29, 2008, Britain for the first time recognised Chinese sovereignty over Tibet, in a parliamentary statement by the British Foreign Secretary David Miliband.

'Our ability to get our points across has sometimes been clouded by the position the UK took at the start of the 20th century on the status of Tibet, a position based on the geo-politics of the time. Our recognition of China's "special position" in Tibet developed from the outdated concept of suzerainty. Some have used this to cast doubt on the aims we are pursuing and to claim that we are denying Chinese sovereignty over a large part of its own territory. We have made clear to the Chinese Government, and publicly, that we do not support Tibetan independence. Like every other EU member state, and the United States, we regard Tibet as part of the People's Republic of China. Our interest is in long term stability, which can only be achieved through respect for human rights and greater autonomy for the Tibetans.'

Tibetologist Robert Barnett thinks that the decision has wider implications. India's claim to a part of its northeast territories, for example, is largely based on the same agreements — notes exchanged during the Simla convention of 1914, which set the boundary between India and Tibet — that the British appear to have just discarded.

POSTWAR PERIOD

China

According to the China's official (communist) military history, the war achieved China's policy objectives of securing borders in the western sector, as China retained de facto control of the Aksai Chin. After the war, India abandoned the Forward Policy, and the de facto borders stabilized along the Line of Actual Control. However according to James Calvin even though China had won a military victory it may have lost in terms of its international image. Western nations, especially the United States, were already suspicious of Chinese attitudes, motives and actions. These nations saw China's goals as world conquest, and clearly viewed China as the aggressor in the Border War. China's first nuclear weapon test in October 1964, and her support of Pakistan in the 1965 India-Pakistan Border War tended to confirm the American view of communist world objectives, including Chinese influence over Pakistan.

India

The aftermath of the war saw sweeping changes in the Indian military to prepare it for similar conflicts in the future, and placed pressure on Indian prime minister Jawaharlal Nehru, who was seen as responsible for failing to anticipate the Chinese attack on India. Indians reacted with a surge in patriotism and memorials were erected for many of the Indian troops who died in the war. Arguably, the main lesson India learned from the war was the need to strengthen its own defences and a shift from Nehru's foreign policy with China based on his stated concept of "brotherhood". Because of India's inability to anticipate Chinese aggression, Prime Minister Nehru faced harsh criticism from government officials, for having promoted pacifist relations with China. Indians in general became highly skeptical of China and its military. Many Indians view the war as a betrayal of India's attempts at establishing a long-standing peace with China and started to question Nehru's usage of the term "Hindi-Chini bhai-bhai" (meaning "Indians and Chinese are brothers"). The war also put an end to Nehru's earlier hopes that India and China would form a strong Asian Axis to counteract the increasing influence of the Cold War bloc superpowers. The Indian role in international affairs after the border war was also greatly reduced after the war and India's standing in the non-aligned movement suffered.

The unpreparedness of the army was blamed on Defence Minister Menon, who resigned his government post to allow for someone who might modernize India's military further. India's policy of weaponisation via indigenous sources and self-sufficiency was thus cemented. Sensing a weakened army, Pakistan, a close ally of China, initiated the Second Kashmir War with India in 1965, however, India had set up the Henderson-Brooks-Bhagat Report to determine what the reason was behind India's unpreparedness in the war, and, when Pakistan attacked, India was prepared. The result was inconclusive, since sources were divided on what decides victory. Some sources argued that since India had captured more territory than Pakistan, India had clearly won. However, others argued that India had taken significant losses considering the country's larger military and hence, the outcome of the war was inconclusive. Two years later, in 1967, there was a short border skirmish known as the Chola Incident between Chinese and Indian soldiers. In this incident 8 Chinese soldiers and 4 Indian soldiers were killed.

British journalist Neville Maxwell writes that the "hopelessly ill-prepared Indian Army that provoked China on orders emanating from Delhi, and paid the price for its misadventure in men, money and national humiliation". As a result of the war, the Indian government commissioned an investigation, resulting in the classified Henderson-Brooks-Bhagat Report on the causes of the war and the reasons for failure. India's performance in high-altitude combat in 1962 led to an overhaul of the Indian Army in terms of doctrine, training, organization and equipment. According to James Calvin, an analyst from U.S. Navy India gained many benefits from the 1962 conflict. This war united the country as never before. India got 32,000 square miles of disputed territory even if she felt that NEFA was hers all along. The new Indian republic had avoided international alignments; by asking for during the war, India demonstrated her willingness to accept military aid from several sectors.

And, finally, India recognized the serious weaknesses in her Army. She would more than double her military manpower in the next two years; and she would work hard to resolve the military's training and logistic problems. India's efforts to improve her military posture significantly enhanced her army's capabilities and preparedness.

Series of Skirmishes

India also reported a series of skirmishes after the 1962 war, which were never confirmed by China. One report provided by India shows that in late 1967, there were two skirmishes between Indian and Chinese forces in Sikkim. The first one was dubbed the "Nathu La incident", and the other the "Chola incident". Prior to these incidents had been the Naxalbari uprising in India by the Communist Naxalites and Maoists.

Bilateral Peace

In 1993 and 1996, the two sides signed the Sino-Indian Bilateral Peace and Tranquility Accords, an agreement to maintain peace and tranquility along the Line of Actual Control (LoAC). Ten meetings of a Sino-Indian Joint Working Group (SIJWG) and five of an expert group have taken place to determine where the LoAC lies, but little progress has occurred. India is concerned about China's military modernisation.

On 20 November 2006 Indian politicians from Arunachal Pradesh appealed to parliament to take a harder stance on the PRC following a military buildup on the border similar to that in 1962. Additionally, China's military aid to Pakistan as well is a matter of concern to the Indian public, which fought another war with Pakistan in 1999. On 6 July 2006, the historic Silk Road passing through this territory was reopened. Both sides have agreed to resolve the issues by peaceful means.

HOW THE POWERS—THAT-BE BUNGLED '62 WAR

As Chinese troops continue their probing actions along the Sino-Indian boundary, the passive response of the government in New Delhi brings to mind the experience of the 1962 border conflict with China, when slogans of Hindi-Chini-bhai-bhai deluded the Indian leadership into allowing the Chinese to roll into the plains of Assam. Subsequently, the leadership in New Delhi did everything to cover the debacle, but if Naville Maxwell's (the author of India's China War) comments are anything to go by, then the responsibility for the desaster of 1962, lies with both the political leadership and the military commanders of 1962. These have been highlighted by the Henderson Brooks Report, which remains a strongly guarded document in the vaults of South Block.

But to dispel the common belief, that the report exposes the blunders of the political leadership, and therefore is a closely guarded secret, it must be made clear that it, in fact, looks only at what went wrong militarily. The government of the day clearly did not wish this inquiry to look into high-level policies and plans. In fact, Lieutenant General Henderson Brooks was clearly directed not to fix responsibility onto specific individuals but the investigation was to look at mundane tactical issues like training, equipment, physical fitness of troops and the role of military commanders! Even the functioning of Army Headquarters was beyong the purview of this investigation, that Brooks, a second-generation British army officer, domiciled in India, from the Maratha Light Infantry Regiment, was asked to undertake.

The report was an unforgiving analysis about the problems along the frontier, discovering along the way what Lieutenant General B.M. Kaul, regarded by many as a lackey of then defence minister Krishna Menon and the government of the day, would liked to have kept hidden. It lad the blame on Army Headquarters for its direct interference, by bypassing the established chains of command, with deployment of troops on the frontline against the Chinese. The example of the General Staff in Delhi giving orders to the Dhola Post on the Thagla Ridge in the NEFA and now Arunachal Pradesh, was seen as incredible as the order for the charge of light brigade. But all in all, the report doesn't have any surprises and the publication of its 200 pages would only undo the myth that the 1962 conflict was a Chinese aggression. A series of studies have, over the years, clearly shown that Indian soldiers were in fact ordered to challenge the Chinese in a military confrontation which it could only lose. And the culprits were at Army headquarters who, time and again, ordered troops into a forward policy and gave them no hope for a fighting withdrawal, an operation of war—like Lieutanant General B.M. Kaul, then Chief of General Staff and Brigadier (late Major General) Monty Palit, VrC, then director of Military Operations. But the investigation, even if it wanted to, had no access to records of meetings in the ministry of defence, since then defence minister Krishna Menon had categorically disallowed any notes or minutes to be kept of his conferences, saying these were top secret in nature.

While the Indian Army has clearly learned its lessons from 1962 debacle, the muted response of India's politico-diplomatic establishments to China's brazen muscle flexing from Aksai Chin to Arunachal Pradesh, clearly leaves a lot to be desired. In 1963, Y.B. Chavan, who took over from Krishna Menon, made a statement in Parliament ascribing the reasons for the debacle to the leadership fallures in the Indian Army and the tactical mishandling of troops. He made no mention of the political flumbiling that led to India's humilitation.

Today, India's military commanders would do well to answer the question: are they prepared to take the blame for; yet another flasco if the Chinese walk across out frontline, not just to paint a few stones in Laddakh, but perhaps the walls of monastery in Tawang, which they have always claimed?

2 Chinese Threat on Border and Defence Preparedness by India

Notwithstanding the assertion made by S.M. Krishna, the Indian External Affairs Minister, that the India-China boundary happens to be one of the most peaceful of our borders, continued Chinese incursions along the Line of Actual Control and the series of strategic moves being undertaken by Beijing in regard to its relations with some smaller countries of the subcontinent, point to a sinister Chinese design of encircling India. It appears that Beijing still rues its decision of voluntarily withdrawing from the 90,000 sq km of Indian territory it had occupied in 1962 and has been harbouring a desire to make up the loss at an opportune moment.

China wears an inscrutable mask and India has so far been unable to see through it as it did in 1962. China is now India's largest trading partner and the amount of transaction between the two countries touched a whopping $ 52 billion last year. This has possibly given India a comforting idea that China would never choose to go for an all-out war in spite of the fact that the Chinese Army has been carrying on incursions into Indian territories not just in the western and central sectors but in Sikkim too where the border is now undisputed.

But the Government of India is trying to keep the people in the dark about some serious moves of the Chinese Army. Recently they penetrated deep inside Laddakh and painted the word China on rocks and boulders in an area which is not very far from the Pangong-Tso lake, a highly sensitive point near the international boundary. But long before there were reports that China had built a helipad in an area in the Arunachal Pradesh sector which, in fact, belongs to India. There is nothing new about the Chinese presence in Laddakh as the People's Liberation Army (PLA) has often been violating the boundary in the Pangong-Tso lake which is situated in the neighbourhood of the Chushul mountains acoross the Changla Pass in the northeast of Leh. Forty per cent of this lake belongs to India while the rest sixty per cent is Chinese domain. But China's patrol boats often penetrate deep into Indian waters and they sometimes willingly barge into Indian naval vessels. Intelligence reports, quoted by the national as well as regional media, have pointed out quite sometime back that China has built its own road network inside Laddakh.

The Government of India is well aware of the Chinese moves along the border and in recent past it has, on quite a few occasions, hurriedly moved Army units away from the Jammu and Kashmir border and posted them along the boundary with China. This happened sometime ago when Beijing had suddenly increased the strength of its Army near a mountain ridge which is very close to the trijunction of India, Bhutan and China. But the most inexplicable side of the whole story is the hush-hush atmosphere which India prefers to drape over the whole issue.

A.K. Antony, the Indian Defence Minister, was perfectly right when he had voiced his concerns sometime back about the unsatisfactory state of communication network on the Indian side of the border. He had reasons to do so as China has not only been strengthening its communication system in the area but trying to attract some smaller subcontinental countries in such a type of patron-client relationship which would go a long way towards putting India in a disadvantageous position.

This forms China's policy of 'encirclement', a diplomatic-military initiative Beijing has been practising for a long time. In line with this, China has been gradually pushing its outposts nearer to the Indian border, the most important example being Xigatse, the second most important city of Tibet which has been put on the Golmud-Lhasa extended railway line. Xigatse has now become a bustling centre of not only trade and commerce but Chinese espionage activity as well. So far as Nepal is concerned, in addition to the Kodari highway, which was built with Chinese assistance in 1960, a second highway connecting Nepal and Tibet has come up. Although the Maoists are no more part of the Nepalese Government, yet there are valid reasons to believe that the bashing of Indian priests by the Maoists at the Pashupatinath temple may have had Chinese blessings.

China is now one of the most important patrons of Pakistan in international politics and in return Pakistan has allowed Beijing to open at least four link roads from the Karakoram Highway one of which will connect the Gwadar deep-sea port which China has built for Pakistan. In the world energy market Beijing is now in brisk business of securing energy supplies most of which pass through the Persian Gulf. By using the Gwadar port China gets an automatic access to the Persian Gulf where it has substantially increased its naval strength in recent times. For Myanmar, it has developed the Irrawady corridor thereby creating a network of roads, rails and waterways. This corridor is extremely important for China as it would give its landlocked areas an access to the Bay of Bengal where Beijing is rapidly increasing its naval strength. In competition India has also agreed to invest $ 100 million for upgrading the Sittwe port and developing the Kaladan river system of Myanmar.

However, in matters of respective bilateral relations China has left India way behind. Beijing's relations with the Myanmar military junta are extremely cozy and it has always stood up for Yangon to block sanctions against the junta in international organisations. China has already secured rights for free use of Myanmar's river systems. Due to this facility it has been able to build up surveillance stations on the Coco Island near the Andamans. That India has recognised the probable Chinese threat from the sea becomes clear from New Delhi's decision to upgrade its naval station in the Andamans.

The military threat from China is real. The numerical strength of its Army is 2.5 million, more than double that of India, while the range of its missiles is more than its Indian counterparts. Quite a good number of Chinese missiles in Tibet carry nuclear warheads. This year China's defence expenditure has increased by 14.9 per cent. This would push up Beijing's defence budget to $ 70.2 billion, an increase of $ 9.1 billion from the previous year. While India lags far behind in this respect, China now stands very near to Japan, Russia and the UK in respect of military spending. Chinese experts are always at pains to point out that their country spends only about 1.5 per cent of its Gross Domestic Product (GDP) for defence. But China's GDP has been growing by more than 10 per cent annually. It has no staggering inflation and its currency is stable.

This has enabled China to build its war industry. China now not only produces arms and ammunitions for its own use but supplies them to a good number of other countries also. They include, apart from Pakistan, Sudan, Egypt, Tanzania, Albania, Iran, Iraq and Sri Lanka. In 2007 China successfully carried out its anti-satellite test. It has acquired technology for construction of aircraft carriers, for carrying out air-to-air refuelling and for developing anti-tank missiles. While its MiG-33 is much superior to the accident prone MiG-21 which the Indian Air Force uses, it has also developed a multi-role fighter aircraft christened CAC-J7 which is widely used not only by Pakistan but Myanmar and Bangladesh as well. Another very important arsenal rolling out of China is the basic jet trainer-cum-light attack aircraft, a product of the Hongdu Aviation Industry. Its export variety is called K-8 in Pakistan which uses it extensively and has a 45 per cent share in its joint production with China. China's participation in the production of the Jalalat class missile fast attack naval craft in the Pakistan Navy Dockyard at Karachi is too well known. Nowadays Pakistan, Sri Lanka, Myanmar and Bangladesh use large numbers of patrol boats, fast attack crafts and vessels for amphibious operations either designed or built by China. India's presence in this field is minimal, the only noteworthy example being the Hindustan Shipyard-built 1890 tonne patrol vessel "Shaurya" which is used by the Sri Lankan Navy.

China now considers itself a great power and a clash of interests with India is inevitable. It looks upon the Asia-Pacific region as its hegemony. As a consequence its likely to come into conflict with India's "look East" policy. So there are enough grounds, strewn all over, for escalation of tension between India and China, the most important of them being the unresolved border question with Beijing not accepting the Line of Actual Control and the McMahon Line. New Delhi recognises the danger and therefore it has recently decided on a series of steps like stationing of Sukhoi-30 aircraft at Tejpur, revival of abandoned airfields in Laddakh, posting of two Army divisions for the defence of Tawang and building of all-weather roads upto the farthest Army post in the border. Defence experts, however, opine that due to the Pakistan-centric defence policy pursued so long, not an illogical thing either, India's defence preparedness has to be improved considerably to meet the Chinese might in the extreme heights of the Himalayas.

Unfortunately the biggest impediment before such an important task is the attitude and self-deception of the Indian ruling class. Although George Fernandes, the Defence Minister during the NDA regime, always voiced concern about Chinese intentions, he did not get sufficient support from other members of the Vajpaiyee Cabinet. Manmohan Singh, the present Prime Minister, is. also advising restraint with respect to the attitude towards China. Obviously he is trying to sweep every uncomfortable information beneath the carpet. Manmohan Singh has reasons to do so as he is in the best position to know how unprepared his government is to match China force by force.

Some honest confessions are also emerging. Sometime back Admiral Sureesh Mehta, the former Naval Chief, was honest enough to admit the inadequacies of the Indian Navy. The other day Air Chief Marshal P.V. Naik, the incumbent Chief of the Indian Air Force, has said that the IAF is only one-third the size of its Chinese counterpart. But the political tribe is desperate to hide its failure.

Indira Gandhi always tried to keep herself posted with latest indepth information about the security affairs of her country. The same should be expected from Manmohan Singh. If he is honest enough he should ask explanations from Pranab Mukherjee, the Defence Minister for a large part of the previous UPA Government, about infra-structural development along the LAC and inadequacies of the armed forces. What has now prompted A.K. Antony and the Naval as well as Air Chiefs to admit serious drawbacks about India's defence preparedness?

Let Manmohan Singh be reminded of a hilarious assumption by the people of Sikkim. The condition of the road from Gangtok to Nathu La is atrocious. But local drivers who ply their vehicles along this road proffer a different reason for this. In the event of a war in the Nathu La sector the Indian side will be vanquished and swept aside by the Chinese Army within a few days. The Indian Army and the Government of India know this. So they do not repair the road to Gangtok in the hope that bad roads might ultimately turn out to be the only defence against the might of Beijing, the drivers point out.

CHINA'S POLICY OF SUBDUING INDIA'S QUEST FOR POWER

Subduing India's quest for power is one of China's many goals in modernizing its armed forces. A US Congressional report which says, China is developing a capability to project air and naval forces beyond its coastal areas, has among its goal "subduing India's quest for power", securing unification of Taiwan, preventing Japan's rise as the strongest Asian power, ensuring Chinese influence over the Korean peninsula and supporting Beijing's claims in the east and south China seas. China's foreign and defence policy initiatives, military analysts say, are quite obviously designed to marginalise India in the long-term and reduce India to the status of a subregional power. For many decades now, despite Indian protestations to that country, China has been pursuing a carefully orchestrated plan for the strategic encirclement and containment of India and has been gradually enlarging its sphere of influence towards South East Asia and the Bay of Bengal. China's strategic manoeuvring and its intransigence in resolving the long-standing territorial and boundary dispute with India are a source of soft potential conflict.

China continues to be in occupation of approximately 30 thousand square kilometres of Indian territory in Aksai Chin since the 1962 war and lays claim to large areas of Indian territory in the eastern sector. Pakistan has also ceded a part of occupied

Kashmir to China through this China built the Karakoram highway that now provides a strategic land link between China and Pakistan.

Despite the Border Peace and Tranquillity Agreement (BPTA) of 1993, the Confidence Building Measures (CBMs) in the Military Field agreed in 1996 and over a dozen meetings of the Joint Working Group and the Experts Group, even the LAC is yet to be demarcated. Political observers say, perhaps the real reason that compels China to drag its feet in resolving its dispute with India is to enable Pakistan to continue to destabilize India through its proxy war without fear of major military retaliation due to the specter of a two front war. The only conclusion that can reasonably be drawn is that China is deliberately stalling further progress on these substantive issues as its suits China to put them on the back burner for the time being.

India is also watchful of China's increasing military involvement in Myanmar which has the potential to impinge on India's trade and maritime interests. China's wooing of Nepal and Bhutan, its sale of sophisticated military technology to Pakistan, Bangladesh and Myanmar, and the possibility it acquiring naval bases, and overland and air-routes to such bases in the countries around India, are areas of concern for India's security. Even through China's navy is still decades away from acquiring the long-range capability necessary to operate with some degree of assurance and freedom in the Indian Ocean, these aspects need to be constantly monitored and vectored into India's calculations.

Since the Gulf War of 1991, China has stepped up its efforts to modernize the People's Liberation Army (PLA). The PLA army has been engaged in raising a large number of rapid deployment divisions and in improving mobility and logistics support capability, while simultaneously upgrading its ability to undertake operations, improve air defence capability and institute state-of-the art command and control systems. In this context, Chinese aspirations to gradually upgrade the PLA navy, to acquire deep penetration strike and strategic lift transport aircraft for the PLA air force and to obtain mid-air refueling capability for long range operations, are also relevant. All these endeavours aim at creating a modern fighting force capable of undertaking swift offensive operations in area away from China's borders in keeping with China's strategy of fighting a limited war under high-tech conditions. It is noteworthy that the upgradation of the military logistics infrastructure in Tibet is continuing at a steady pace. China has been actively engaged in building new roads, supply lines and airfields close to the Indian frontier.

POLICY TO BOX RESURGENT INDIA

In establishing close political and military nexus with Pakistan directed against India, China is seeking to box India into the geographical confines of South Asia to stultify its stature as an emerging global power. As remarked by P.R. Chari, Director, Institute of Peace and Conflict Studies, New Delhi, since the United States too is interested in bolstering the entity of Pakistan, despite its drift into social chaos and financial bankruptcy, an axis of powers-Pakistan, China and the US, with palpable anti-India compulsions is visible. Undoubtedly, China has developed close military relationship with Pakistan since 1965 largely designed to restrain Soviet expansion into the Indian Ocean via Afghanistan, but Pakistan has used the weapons, nuclear and missile technology acquired from China to bolster its defences against India and to allow it to be used by China to erode India's stature as a regional military and economic power.

India, aspiring to become a global power, is increasingly perceived as a potential giant on the strength of an expanding economy and market especially by the major industrial nations. In the Asian context, India is undoubtedly a force to be reckoned with and its demonstrated nuclear capability has enhanced its military stature even if the G-7 countries had been condemnatory of its underground nuclear weapons tests in may, 1998. Over the two years, much to the chagrin of China which is insisting on India [and Pakistan] honouring the UN Security Council Resolution and sign CTBT, the international community is gradually reconciling itself to the reality, though there is an understandable concern that the embittered Indo-Pak relationship may end up in a nuclear holocaust. Japan, Australia, Germany, Russia and even the US after the visits by President Clinton and Mr. Vajpayee to each other's country, are inclined to lift sanctions imposed after the Pokhran II nuclear tests. The Clinton visit to India in March last year has, apart from generating warmth in Indo-American relations, aroused rethinking on the part of countries like Japan and Britain to reassess their bilateral ties with India. A global partnership and security dialogue between India and Japan is something which China will carefully evaluate for its strategic impact on Asian security. There is, therefore, no scope of the Russian blueprint of strategic partnership between Moscow, New Delhi and Beijing in matters of international security and the establishment of a multipolar world of peace, security and development. Such a strategic partnership is envisaged by Russian President Putin who has visited China and India and spoke out his mind on this idea to the leaderships there.

It is plainly evident that the strategic direction of India's missile and nuclear programme is against China, however strong the denials of such a fear expressed by Defence Minister George Fernandes after Chinese protestations in the past. China's current nuclear posture of "creeping proliferation" would eventually include China. India could also profitably re-evaluate its policy of dealing with Taiwan in the present gingerly fashion and deepen its relations with Vietnam as part of an extra-regional strategy.

INDIA'S CHINA POLICY: IMPORTANCE OF A STRATEGIC FRAMEWORK

For many political observers, the global political architecture is undergoing a transformation with power increasingly shifting from the West to the East. The two most populous nations on the earth China and India are on their way to becoming economic powerhouses and are shedding their reticence in asserting their global profiles. Japan is gradually flexing its military muscle and the Southeast Asian tigers are roaring again after the 1997 "Asian Flu". Whether it is such hopeful prospects or the challenges ahead in the Korean peninsula, Taiwan, and Kashmir, it is clear that this new century will, in all likelihood, be an Asian century.

The future of this Asian century will to large extent depend upon the relationship between the two regional giants, China and

India. According the United States National Intelligence Council Report on emerging global trends, by 2015, international community will have to confront the military, political and economic dimensions of the rise of China and India. The bilateral relationship between China and India will define the contours of the new international political architecture in Asia and the world at large. As of today, however, the trajectory of the Sino-Indian relationship remains as complex as ever to decipher despite some remarkable positive developments in the last few years.

This article attempts to explore this complex, multilayered relationship in all its dimensions, largely from the perspective of Indian foreign policy priorities. It mainly focuses on the recent developments in the Sino-Indian relationship. It reviews India's and China's view of each other and their policies. It examines the trends of convergence that have emerged in the past few years. Additionally, it looks at the points of divergence and possible areas of concern in the relationship between Asia's giants.

Sino-Indian Convergence: Bilateral and Global

Bilateral relations between India and the People's Republic of China (PRC) have indeed come a long way after they touched their nadir in the immediate aftermath of India 's nuclear tests in May 1998. China had been singled out as the "number one" security threat for India by India's Defence Minister just before the nuclear tests. After the tests, the Indian Prime Minister wrote to the US President justifying Indian nuclear tests as a response to the threat posed by China. Unsurprisingly, China reacted strongly and diplomatic relations between the two countries plummeted to an all time low.

However, some six years later, the relations between the two countries seem to be on an upswing. The visit of the Indian External Affairs Minister to China in 1999 marked the resumption of high-level dialogue and the two sides declared that they were not threats to each other. A bilateral security dialogue was also initiated that has helped the two countries in openly expressing and sharing their security concerns with each other. India and China also decided to expedite the process of demarcation of the

Line of Actual Control (LAC) and the Joint Working Group (JWG) on the boundary question, set up in 1988, has been meeting regularly. As a first step in this direction, the two countries exchanged border maps on the least controversial middle sector of the LAC.

The Indian Prime Minster visited China in June 2003, the first such visit in a decade. The joint declaration signed during the visit stated that China was not a threat to India. The two states appointed special representatives in order to impart momentum to border negotiations that have lasted twenty two years, with the Prime Minister's principal secretary becoming India's political-level negotiator, replacing the India-China JWG. India and China also decided to hold their first joint naval exercise later in the year and discussions on joint air exercise continue. India also acknowledged China 's sovereignty over Tibet and pledged not to allow "anti-China" political activities in India. On its part, China has acknowledged India 's 1975 annexation of the former monarchy of Sikkim by agreeing to open a trading post along the border with the former kingdom and later rectified official maps to include Sikkim as part of India.

India and China have found substantial convergence of interests at the international level. Both share similar concerns about the growing international dominance of the US, the threat of terrorism disguised as religious and ethnic movements and the need to accord primacy to economic development. India and China have both expressed concern about the US ' use of military power around the world and publicly opposed the war in Iraq. This was merely a continuation of the desire of both states to oppose the US *hyperpuissance* ever since the end of the Cold War.

Like other major powers in the international system, India and China favour a multipolar world order where US unipolarity remains constrained by the other "poles" in the system. China and India zealously guard their national sovereignty and have been wary of US attempts to interfere in what they see as domestic affairs of other stares, be it Serbia, Kosovo or Iraq. Both took strong exception to the US air strikes on Iraq in 1998, the US-led air campaign against Yugoslavia in 1999, and more recently the

US campaign against Saddam Hussein arguing that these violated the national sovereignty and undermined the authority of the United Nations system.

Both nations also favour more democratic international economic regimes. They have strongly resisted efforts by the US and other developed nations to link global trade to labour and environmental standards, realizing clearly that this would put them at a huge disadvantage vis-à-vis the developed world, thereby hampering their drive towards economic development, a top priority. Both have committed themselves to crafting joint Sino-Indian positions in the World Trade Organization (WTO) and global trade negotiations in the hope that this might provide them greater negotiating leverage over the developed states. They would like to see further liberalization of agricultural trade in the developed countries, tightening of the rules on anti-dumping measures and ensuring that non-trade related issues such as labour and environment are not allowed to come to the WTO.

In recent years, India and China have attempted to build their bilateral relationship on the basis of their larger worldview of international politics. As they have found a distinct convergence of their interests on world stage, they have used it to strengthen their bilateral relations. They have established and maintained regular reciprocal high-level visits between political leaders. There has been a sincere attempt to improve trade relations and to compartmentalize intractable issues that make it difficult for their bilateral relationship to move forward.

India and China have strengthened their bilateral relationship in areas as distinct as cultural and educational exchanges, military exchanges, and science and technology cooperation. Bilateral trade has recorded rapid growth from a trade volume of US $265 million in 1991 to US $3596 million in 2001. In 2001, bilateral trade saw an increase of 23.4 percent over 2000. It is expected to rise to $10 billion this year. The two nations are even evaluating the possibility of signing a comprehensive economic cooperation agreement and a free trade agreement by the end of this year, thereby building on strong complementarities between the two.

Both states are also taking steps to upgrade their military-related cooperation, leading to greater understanding on the bilateral military front, something that would have been unthinkable just a few years ago.As a first step in this direction, the Chinese and Indian navies carried out joint search and rescue operations off the Shanghai coast in November 2003. Both states are also seeking to cooperate on the nuclear front with China planning to import heavy water from India to be utilized in the pressurized heavy water reactors near Shanghai.

Many observers have also pointed out a subtle shift in Beijing 's stance on Pakistan vis-à-vis India. China 's "neutral" position during the Kargil conflict and the intense Indo-Pak crisis following the terrorist attack on the India 's Parliament is seen by many as a reflection of China 's sincerity in its attempts to improve ties. In keeping with China's attempts to project itself as a responsible regional player, China is seen by some as supporting peace and anti-terrorist efforts in South Asia by cooperating with the US and India. China is also seen as playing a central role in encouraging Pakistan to negotiate with India by using its leverage over Pakistan.

After assuming office Prime Minister Manmohan Singh's government made it clear that it favoured closer ties with China and would continue to work towards improving bilateral relations with China. In his first address to the nation, the Prime Minister, Manmohan Singh, also emphasized the carrying forward of the process of further development and diversification of Sino-Indian relations. The late J.N. Dixit, National Security Advisor in the current government, wrote that "the Congress will continue the process of normalizing, strengthening and expanding India's relations with China, which is the most important factor affecting Asian security and stability". One of the first foreign visits of the new Indian foreign minister, Natwar Singh, was to China to attend the Asia Cooperation Dialogue in Qingdao, in East China's Shandong province and apparently had "substantive discussions" with his Chinese counterpart.

All this reflects on India continuing to build its relations with China on the convergence of interests that the two nations have achieved in recent years. Aside from the positive developments, one should not ignore the enormous obstacles that confront this bilateral relationship. There has been a dominant tendency in the Indian foreign policy establishment to focus on the strengths of its bilateral relations with China while pretending that problems confronting the relationship would somehow take care of themselves. The challenges in the Sino-Indian relationship are by no means insignificant nor will China take care of Indian interests. It is for India to recognize them for what they are and evolve a coherent strategy to tackle them.

Divergences and Challenges

The number one priority for China 's leadership today is economic growth and social stability. China soon underwent one of the most peaceful and orderly political transformations in its recent history, even though its exact ramifications remain far from clear. Hu Jintao became Communist Party chief in 2002 and President of China in 2003 replacing Jiang Zemin. He also finally ceded the effective control of the armed forces to Hu Jintao in September 2004. Hu Jintao is now formally in command of the vast party, government, and military bureaucracies that rule China. This shift, although important for the smooth working of the Chinese government, is unlikely to produce any radical change in China 's foreign policy. China 's focus is going to be on maintaining its high rate of economic growth in the coming years. It should be remembered that Hu Jintao is a product of the "evolutionary policies" of Deng Xiao Peng that emphasize economic growth and orderly governance. President Hu Jintao has made it amply clear that Western-style multiparty democracy is something that would not serve the Chinese people well, terming it a "blind alley" for China. Therefore, one can expect China to continue on its current economic trajectory and shaping its foreign policy accordingly.

China has enjoyed average annual rates of real income growth of around 10 percent in the last two decades of the twentieth century, something unprecedented historically. China accounts for about 5 percent of world trade and foreign direct investment (FDI) to China is predicted to reach an annual utilized rate of 100 billion in 2005. After its accession to the WTO, China 's already-high global economic profile is set to rise manifold. China will continue to focus on maintaining its high rates of economic growth in the coming years, even as some of the economic challenges China faces will become more acute. The burgeoning income disparities, restructuring of its states owned enterprises and the problem of non-performing loans in its banks are just a few of the economic problems China 's economy is likely to face in the coming years. So far China has managed remarkably even though the future remains uncertain.

Broadly speaking, Indians either view China 's economic growth as a façade or envy it. While India has achieved some remarkable growth rates in the last few years enjoying average annual rates of real income growth of six percent in the last two decades of the twentieth century, it still lags behind China. India accounts for less than one percent of world trade in goods and services. Currently, China outperforms India in terms of levels of growth, education, health, and living standards of its population, and global integration of its economy. China outpaces India, in sectors where the two compete for third country markets. Sino-Indian competition for these markets is bound to further intensify in the coming years.

Though some argue that the long term economic prospects of India are much better than China 's, China remains the undisputed economic powerhouse of the moment driving the Asian and global economy with India somewhere far behind. The fact of the matter is so long as India does not place its own economic house in order; it will remain a second-rate power even in Asia. And China will remain the Asian power that the world will look up to when trying to manage problems in Asia.

What should be equally, if not more, significant for India is the fact that it is China's economic transformation that has given it the capability to become a military power with China spending as much as $65 billion a year on its military. China's military may or may not be able to challenge US supremacy in the next few years but it will surely become the most dominant force in Asia. According to authoritative sources, China is set to overtake Japan in the next decade to become Asia 's major regional military power. The US involvement in the global war on terror has put the "containment" of China on the backburner and China has seized on this opportunity to strengthen its armed forces further.

China imbibed the lessons of US military undertakings such as the 1991 Gulf War, war in Afghanistan and the recent operation Iraqi Freedom. These have spurred China's pursuit of the latest Revolution in Military affairs (RMA) manifested in the buying, adopting of latest technologies and weapons systems (particularly from Russia) along with concomitant changes in doctrine and organizational structures. The People's Liberation Army (PLA) has been shedding its manpower since late 1990s to save funds so as to be able to focus on high tech. Despite a western embargo on China preventing transfer of military technologies, China has been able to deftly use US corporations to garner and apply dual-use technologies. China is simultaneously pursuing a qualitative and quantitative transformation of its nuclear infrastructure. China plans to deploy new road-mobile, solid-fuelled, long-range missiles over the next several years possibly to counter US ballistic missile defence.

Overtime, China 's enhanced military prowess will lead it to assert its interests more forcefully, thereby, adversely affecting Indian interests. As China becomes more reliant on imported oil for its rapidly growing industrial economy, China will develop and exercise military power projection capabilities to protect the shipping that transports oil from the Persian Gulf to China. The capability to project power would require access to advanced naval bases along the sea lines of communication and forces capable of gaining and sustaining naval and air superiority.

China 's assistance to Myanmar in constructing and improving port facilities on two islands in the Bay of Bengal and the Andaman Sea is the first step to securing military base privileges in the Indian Ocean. This can be used as a listening post to gather intelligence on Indian naval operations and a potential forward base for future Chinese naval operations in the Indian Ocean. India 's traditional geographic advantages in the Indian Ocean are also increasingly at risk with deepening Chinese involvement in Myanmar. China 's increasing naval presence in the Indian Ocean is of tremendous strategic consequence for India. There are also suggestions that the balance of air power in the China-India theatre has shifted in China 's favour with it acquiring an inventory of about 1500 modern combat aircraft for deployment in the theatre.

China remains the only major power in the world that refuses to discuss nuclear issues with India for fear that this might imply a de facto recognition of India 's status as a nuclear power. It continues to insist on the sanctity of the UN resolution 1172 which calls for India (and Pakistan) to give up its nuclear weapons program and join the Nuclear Non-Proliferation Treaty (NPT) as a non-nuclear weapon state. This was reflected in China 's lack of response to the Indian Foreign Minister's proposal of a common nuclear doctrine for China, India, and Pakistan. China would not like to get into any sort of nuclear dialogue with India that might give the impression of China recognizing India as a nuclear power. Moreover, while both India and China have a "no first use" nuclear doctrine, China 's doctrine is not applicable to India as it is not a party to the NPT.

China has done its best to maintain a rough balance of power in Indian Subcontinent by preventing India from gaining an upper hand over Pakistan. It has consistently assisted Pakistan 's nuclear weapons and ballistic missile programs to counterbalance India 's development of new weapons systems. India 's preoccupation with Pakistan reduces India to the level of a regional power while China can claim the status of an Asian and world power. China signed a charter to step up bilateral defence cooperation with Pakistan "to help maintain peace and stability in South Asia " even as it professes to improve its relations with India. Moreover, even as India and China share similar concerns regarding Islamic terrorism in Kashmir and Xinjiang respectively, China has been rather unwilling to make a common cause with India against Pakistan. China 's use of India 's neighbours to curtail Indian influence has not been restricted to Pakistan. China has actively sought to contain India all around its periphery by engaging Nepal, Bangladesh and Myanmar.

Despite resolving most of its border disputes with other countries, China is reluctant to move ahead with India on border issues. India 's discussion of border issues with China is seen as a concession. India remains satisfied with the "positive" and "satisfactory" Joint Working Group negotiations on the boundary issue. Despite the need for an expeditious demarcation of the Line of Actual Control, the talks seem to be continuing endlessly and the momentum of the talks itself seems to have flagged.

The momentum of the issue of Tibet seems to have been lost. Tibet has become a platform for the projection of Chinese military power. India 's tacit support to Dalai Lama's government-in-exile has failed to have much of an impact either on China or on the international community. Today even Dalai Lama seems ready to talk to the Chinese as he realizes that in a few years Tibet might get overwhelmed with the Han population and Tibetans themselves might become a minority. The proposed opening up of the Nathula trade route that connects Tibet and Sikkim has been much trumpeted by the Indian government as a major achievement of Indian diplomacy. However, this step is fraught with dangers as there is no certainty that internal security threat posed by Chinese infiltration would not get worse with the opening of Nathula. This has probably led to some rethinking in India on this issue.

There were disturbing reports during the Indian Prime Minister's visit to China, that Chinese troops had intruded into the Indian territory along a stretch of the unfenced border with Arunachal Pradesh. China refuses to recognize Arunachal Pradesh as part of the Indian territory, laying claim to 90, 000 sq. km. of its land. If recent reports are to be believed after a two-decade gap, China has resumed the supply of weapons to various insurgent groups fighting in northeastern India. China seems to be getting successful in hemming India in from both, the eastern and the western flanks.

China and India: Different Approaches, Different Outcomes

What the above discussion of the divergence and convergence between Sino-Indian interests reveals is the success of China in attaining its foreign policy objectives and the failure of India to preserve its vital interests vis-à-vis China. This cannot simply be attributed to China 's economic and military strength. While China is definitely the bigger player in the region and the world at large but its success vis-à-vis India owes as much to its power as to the way that power has been cultivated and used. While realizing fully well that it would take China decades to seriously compete with the US, it has focused strategic energy on Asia. Its foreign policy is aimed at enhancing its economic and military prowess to achieve hegemony in Asia. China 's recent emphasis on projecting itself as peaceful power is merely aimed at allaying the concerns of neighbours lest they try to counterbalance it. China's readiness to negotiate with other regional states and to be an economically "responsible" nation is also a signal to other states that there are greater benefits in bandwagoning to China's growing regional weight rather than opposing its rise in any manner.

However, while declaring that it will be focusing on internal socio-economic development for the next decade or so, China has actively pursued policies of preventing the rise of other regional powers. In case of India, this manifests itself in its cultivation of Pakistan as a close ally. From supplying it nuclear and missile technologies to building its military infrastructure, China has done all it can to build Pakistan as a counterweight to India. This policy has largely succeeded as India no longer enjoys its earlier conventional superiority vis-à-vis Pakistan possession of nuclear weapons by both nations ensures that any step that India takes to strengthen its nuclear weapons profile is viewed by the international community as highly destabilizing in the context of the "nuclear flashpoint" that South Asia has become for the world at large. China has thereby been successful in emerging as a "responsible" global player, despite its abysmal nuclear and missile proliferation record while the international community rails at India for making the world much more dangerous.

China's attempts to increase its influence in Nepal, Bangladesh, and Myanmar, its persistent refusal to recognize parts of India such as Arunachal Pradesh, its lack of support for India's membership to the United Nations Security Council and other regional and global organizations, all point towards China's attempts at preventing the rise of India as a regional and global player of major import. It is this strategy that China has consistently and successfully pursued without any apologies. In fact, this strategy has been so successful that today China no longer believes that India can be a serious rival for Asian hegemony and some have pointed out, India is off of China 's diplomatic radar.

In contrast to China 's well-laid out policy vis-à-vis India, India has from time to time oscillated from one extreme to another. George Tanham has famously pointed out that India has shown little ability to think strategically on national security. In the case of India 's China policy, it needs to be realized that there is nothing really sinister about China 's attempts to expand its own influence and curtail India 's. China is a rising power in Asia and the world and as such will do its utmost to prevent the rise of other power centres around its periphery like India that might in the future prevent it from taking its rightful place as a global player. This is not much different than the stated US policy of preventing the rise of other powers that might threaten its position as a global hegemon. Just as the US is working towards achieving its strategic objective, China is pursuing its own strategic agenda.

There is also nothing extraordinarily benign in China 's attempts to improve its bilateral relations with India in recent times. After working to curtail India 's influence in various ways, China would not like to see India coming close to the US in order to contain China. In this geopolitical chessboard, both the US and China are using India towards their own strategic ends. India must resist the tendency of reacting to the actions of other. India 's attempt to come up a coherent strategy towards China based on identified strategic objectives is of paramount importance. Prime Minister Manmohan Singh declared that it wants to have friendly relations with China, a reasonable foreign policy objective. However, without a clear articulation of India 's national security objectives, pursuit of friendly relations with China should not become an end in itself. It should be a means towards achieving India 's larger strategic objective of emerging as a major regional and global player.

India 's China policy is also symptomatic of a larger misunderstanding in the Indian and political establishment with regard to a nation's foreign policy. For the left-liberal strand in the Indian polity, foreign policy is merely an extension of domestic policy. As such since India is a secular, democratic, and peace-loving nation, India 's pursuit of its relations with other states should merely be a reflection of these virtues. This has given rise to much of the moral rhetoric in foreign affairs. On the other hand, the Indian right, because of its preoccupation with establishing a "Hindu" nation and minority bashing, have extended its narrow sectarian view to foreign policy. The consequence has been its obsession with Pakistan as evil incarnate in its foreign policy agenda and its inclination to view the world in black and white, friends and enemies, evil and noble. Shaped by these forces, Indian foreign policy has merely been one of responding to events around it rather than anticipating them and evolving long-term strategies to deal with them. India's China policy is a casualty of this reactionary approach.

India needs to develop its economic and military might without being apologetic. It needs to clearly articulate its national interests and engage China on a host of issues, from the border problem to the alleged dumping of cheap Chinese goods in the Indian market. India needs to recognize that appeasing China is neither desirable nor necessary even as a direct confrontation with China is not something India can afford, at least in the near future. It must also be recognized that while for India, managing its relations with China is at the top of its foreign policy agenda, China does not view India as a significant global player and is largely indifferent to India's growing profile.

India is a rising power in Asia and there is nothing wrong in demanding its rightful place in the interstate hierarchy. Simply put India and China are two major powers in Asia with global aspirations and some significant conflicting interests. As a result, some amount of friction in their bilateral relationship is inevitable. The geopolitical reality of Asia makes sure that it will be extremely difficult, if not impossible, for *Hindi-Chini* to be *bhai-bhai* (brothers) in the foreseeable future. This reality should be accepted by the Indian policy makers, rather than wished away. India should make a serious attempt to manage this friction by expanding the zone of cooperation with China even as it tries to steadfastly pursue its national interests. India should display the confidence to craft a foreign policy that best serves its national security interests without always looking over the shoulders to make sure that China is not displeased. Again, India can learn a lot by examining how China has managed its relationship with the US in the last few years.

While India certainly needs to engage China in an effort at reconciling security and political perspectives, it is naïve to assert, as many do, that India should first be sensitive to China's concerns, real or imaginary, before defining its foreign policy goals and strategic agenda. Does China consult India in its pursuit of its own strategic objectives? It does not and neither should India expect it to. In a similar vein, India should define its foreign policy agenda in view of its own national security imperatives.

But for this to happen, the government of India will have to formulate a clear China policy and, more importantly, a broader national security strategy. Ad-hocism just won't do. This should be the top foreign policy priority of the Indian government if it wants India to emerge as a global power of any reckoning. India should heed to Sun Tzu's advice and recognize that a merely tactical foreign policy approach without the backing of a sound strategy will only lead to nowhere.

INDIA'S CHINESE POLICY CHALLENGES UNDER CONGRESS GOVERNMENT

India's new government led by the Congress Party, has until now focused entirely on its relations with Pakistan. The reason for this could be that most of the foreign policy hands in the current policy establishment have been former High Commissioners in Pakistan and therefore at more professional ease to deal with it. However, India's most significant foreign policy challenge is China and not Pakistan. Pakistan despite its nuclear weapons arsenal is not our "strategic competitor"; it is only a, regional 'spoiler state'. But in India's aspirations to rise to an effective regional power status, China is a "strategic competitor" both in the South Asia context and also in the Asian security context.

India's policy making establishment and especially within the Congress Party, with its hangovers of 'Panch Sheel' and non-aligned mindsets, has short memories when it comes to China's policies of strategic destabilization of India. They are still under way. Similarly, the Indian media suffers from a total amnesia of China's perfidious policies in South Asia to the strategic detriment of India. China has adroitly exploited both these vulnerabilities of India. China in its approaches to South Asia in the last fifty-five years, with particular reference to India has relied heavily on "power politics", creation of 'spoiler states' on India's periphery and upsetting the natural balance of power in the Indian sub-continent. The new Indian Government policy establishment may like to consider the following observations when formulating its policy stances towards China:

* Only when countries have accepted the existence of conflict and sought to manage it through a balance of power have enduring periods of general peace resulted" -Former US President Nixon.
* "It can be a fundamental and analytically mischievous error to confuse peace with tranquillity, certainty or predictability." "To achieve peace, people do not necessarily have to become admirable or gentle." -Prof John Mueller.
* "Peace therefore cannot be aimed at directly; it is the expression of certain conditions and power relationships. It is to these relationships –not to peace-that diplomacy must address itself" -Former US Secretary of State, Henry Kissinger.

So while India must pursue peace and conflict-avoidance in its relationship with China, the new Indian Government should recognize that the route to peace lies through power relationships and power politics. But first, a look at the Congress Party's "China Baggage". The Congress Party Needs to Jettison its "China Baggage":

Contemporary Congress Party articulations give an impression that its perspectives remain time-frozen in the Nehruvian-era China politics. Current international strategic realities dictate that the following main planks of Congress Party's China perspectives are no longer relevant:

* Non-alignment is dead. The concept could operate in a bi-polar world only. Further, both the superpowers gave no credence to this concept. If India was given importance then, it was not because of Nehru and nor for its non-alignment policies. India was given importance for its intrinsic potential as a power in the making.
* 'Panch Sheel' (five principles of peaceful co-existence) enunciated by Chou-en-lai and Nehru stood negated when China sneakingly occupied Aksai-Chin in the 1950s and later the Sino-Indian War of 1962.
* "Panch Sheel" concept stood further negated in the following years when China in its policies of strategic de-stabilisation of India built-up Pakistan's nuclear weapons arsenal, attempted to make Myanmar a military client state and entered into a Mutual Defence Agreement with Bangladesh.
* Multipolar, world as espoused by China and currently being seconded by the Congress Party Government is an unworkable proposition in today's international strategic realities. Neither China nor France has been able to win concrete support for multi-polarity.

The Congress Government would be well advised to jettison its above baggage and formulate its approaches to China on the basis of power-politics and in consonance with existing global power relationships. Hans J Morgenthau, the most noted foreign affairs authority has remarked that: " A nation can only take a rational view of its national interests after it has parted company with the crusading spirit of a political creed." The Congress Party Government needs to jettison the crusading missions of the Nehruvian era. It only brought more conflict and contentiousness for India.

Power-Relationship Approaches of India to China

India's national security interests imperatives dictate that any long range formulation of its China policy should deliver the following end-aims:

- China's assistance to Pakistan in terms of WMD Proliferation is curtailed, if not ended.
- China's intrusive influence in the Indian sub-continent in the form of creation of regional 'spoiler states' acting as its proxies is curtailed.
- China's attempt to build a naval presence in the Indian Ocean through Pakistan, Bangladesh or Myanmar is impeded.
- China's unobtrusive influence in India's politics through the Communist Parties, a strategically unwise Indian media and India's pseudo-liberal establishment is rendered ineffective.
- China's strategic nexus with Pakistan and Bangladesh is neutralized.

A quick glance at the above would reveal that except for the last point, India on its own, cannot tackle these challenges. India would have to co-opt or be co-opted in existing global power relationships that are working to constrain China's power politics in their respective regions. To arrive at the answer, a brief look is required at the existing strategic realities and global power equations and these are:

- United States global predominance is estimated to continue well into the major portion of the 21st century.
- United States is the only superpower existent today with the strategic, political and economic might to enforce its will globally.
- Russia is unlikely under existing circumstances to emerge in a resurgent mode for another three to four decades. Its strategic power potential stands shrunk decisively.
- China's massive military modernization and expansion of her strategic assets are nowhere near to challenging US supremacy.
- China is a revisionist power. It challenges the status-quo and in the process generates strategic uneasiness in global strategic equations of its intentions and motives.
- China today stands strategically hemmed-in by the United States on its Western and Eastern flanks.

India therefore has no choice but to be co-opted in the United States scheme of things to protect her national security interests vis-à-vis China. The United States too is not engaged in 'Containment' of China; but only in 'Constrainment' so that its policies do not create strategic turbulence in contiguous areas.

In terms of South Asia alone, India's national security interests dictate that Pakistan needs to be cut to size and accept its asymmetric equation in the Indian sub-continent. India cannot hope that China will assist her in this direction. China is a major part of the problem of Pakistan's intransigence and military adventurism against India. Here again the United States enters into the picture in multiple ways: (1) To control Pakistan directly and coerce it into strategic compliance from desisting from military adventurism. (2) To neutralize China-Pakistan strategic nexus by building strategic counter-pressures against China. (3) United States global naval supremacy is unquestionable and in relation to India's Indian Ocean strategic interests, major convergence exists between India and USA.

Here again, in the South Asian context, the answer is clear, that in relation to China, the national security interests of India are best served by entering the power-relationships of the United States in terms of Asian security. Until India builds up her military and strategic power to levels commensurate with those of China, it has no options in her China policy but to get co-opted with the China policies of the United States.

Buildingup of her Strategic Assets by India as Part of its China Policy

In this connection two points need to be addressed, namely:

* China's attitudes towards India changed after the BJP Government's nuclear weapons tests in 1998. After the rabid Chinese reactions for a year or so, China realised that it had to adapt to the new strategic reality, that India had arrived to claim some strategic space in the "power-politics" scene. Hence the flurry of Chinese high level official visits thereafter and the stupendous growth of two way trade. An argument can therefore be made in terms

of China relations that India's power politics has stimulated trade exponentially.

* China's attitudes towards India changed as it dawned on Chinese leaders that India was getting drawn into an increasing strategic partnership with the United States and increasing military-to-military contacts also.

A major deduction from the above is that an essential component of India's policies towards China should also be the building up of her own independent strategies assets to add power to her diplomacy in the form of:

* SLBMs (Sea Launched Ballistic Missiles). The third leg of India's nuclear arsenal triad is overdue.
* ICBMs (Inter Continental Ballistic Missiles). At present Indian missiles do not have a reach upto Bijing.
* Cruise Missiles. With multimode launch capabilities.
* Nuclear Submarines. The project is over 15 years old. It needs to be resuscitated and put on priority.
* Strategic Bombers. These are an essential element of the nuclear triad.

China's missile arsenal is predominantly deployed in Tibet, Sichzuan and Yunnan— all targeted against India and with an inherent element of political coercion. Development of India's strategic assets as given above would make India's foreign policy approaches towards China more strategically equitable and in the process generating equitable responses from China.

The new Congress Government has come into power, seemingly obsessed with the conviction that the policies of the previous BJP Government must be changed at all costs. It needs to note that India's foreign and defence policies need to be bi-partisan in character and content. The previous Government adopted the "power politics" approach to China as evident from the nuclear weapons tests and also evolving a strategic partnership with the United States. Both these had an effect on China and its policies towards India and South Asia in general. One could also attribute the Chinese neutrality during the Kargil War 1999 to this approach

The Congress Governments in the past followed ill-conceived and ill-advised policies towards China based on mistaken beliefs. This led to India's national humiliation in 1962. The new Congress Government in power today should jettison its " China baggage" of the past and adhere to the "power politics" approach towards China. It is not to suggest that India enter into confrontationist stances with China; it is to suggest that while peace must be the quest in India-China relations it does not distract India from the parallel track of foreign policy i.e. To adopt power relationships and build strategic assets so necessary to maintain "real peace".

India's new policy establishment needs to be reminded what one Chinese author has observed on China's perspectives on international relations: " Power is the cornerstone of Chinese politics. Chinese politicians and diplomats are often recognized as masters of power politics having inherited a well-spring of experience of power play over the millennium".

CHINA LOOKING TO USE STAKE IN POK AS BARGAINING CHIP?

The Chinese foreign ministry did nothing to justify its decision to invest in the Neelam-Jhelum hydroelectric project in Pakistan Occupied Kashmir, which has drawn India's ire. The Chinese foreign ministry spokesman Ma Zhaoxu evaded a directly reply to questions on why China was investing in the disputed area. Indications are that China does not want the issue to come in the way of a smooth dialogue when the foreign ministers of the two countries meet in Bangalore on October 27, 2009.

"The Kashmir issue has been left over from history. Pakistan and India should properly handle it. We hope there will be peace and stability in South Asia," Ma said responding to a question about India's protest over the proposed Chinese investment. Ma was asked by another reporter how Chinese investment will help India and Pakistan to resolve the Kashmir problem. He repeated more or less the same words without trying to explain Beijing's decision.

The ministry spokesman's refusal to justify a decision taken during the recent meeting between Chinese president Hu Jintao and Pakistan prime minister Yousuf Raza Gilani may suggest that Beijing is taking a second look at its move to invest in POK.

India had earlier reacted to the move saying: "The Chinese side is fully aware of India's position and our concerns about Chinese activities in Pakistan-occupied Kashmiı We hope that the Chinese side will take a long term view of the India-China relations, and cease such activities in areas illegally occupied by Pakistan."

The issue is expected to come up when Indian foreign minister S.M.Krishna meets his Chinese counterpart Yang Jiechi on October 27, 2009. The Chinese foreign ministry confirmed that Yang will attend the trilateral meeting between the foreign ministers of India, Russia and China in Bangalore. Yang and Krishna will hold a separate meeting to exchange views on bilateral ties and regional and international issues of common concern, Ma said. China is also putting pressure on India to stop the proposed visit of the Dalai Lama to Arunachal Pradesh ahead of the forthcoming meeting between the Indian and Chinese foreign ministers.

China was firmly opposed to the Dalai Lama's visit to what he described as "the so-called Arunachal Pradesh". Beijing claims that Arunachal Pradesh is part of its own territory and describes it as "South Tibet". "We believe that this further exposes the Dalai Lama clique's anti-China and separatist nature," Ma said. China seems to suggest that Dalai Lama's visit to Arunachal Pradesh will further the cause of separatists seeking an independent Tibet.

He said India and China have agreed to further advance their strategic cooperative partnership by holding a series of commemorative activities, including a "country festival" to mark the 60th anniversary of establishing official diplomatic ties in 2010.

IS THE RED DRAGON SNARLING AGAIN?

The India-China theatre is a hotbed of activity. There are Chinese intrusions on the border and Indian protests, Chinese military build-up and India huffing and puffing to catch up. Separately, China is building strategic stakes in India's neighbourhood, while India appears to be watching helplessly. Globally, the global economic crisis is catapulting China to the high table faster than India can say 'George Bush'-see how China only has to say "boo" for Barack Obama to keep Dalai Lama out of the White House.

Meanwhile, the boundary dispute remains unresolved because China has been repeatedly intransigent. On the other hand, India and China are on the same page on global issues, and on trade they are dancing their way to the bank. Through all this, India maintains what appears to be a strange policy of appeasing the dragon. India allows the Dalai Lama to visit Arunachal in the teeth of Chinese howls, but pretends that intrusions by the Chinese have happened for years and the definition of "peace and tranquillity" is the absence of violence.

It all boils down to a failure to resolve the boundary dispute. While officials say they are moving "slowly but surely", strategists across the board in India say China's policy of low level intrusions serves to keep India off-guard, confused and groping and under pressure on the boundary. Its also a signal to India's other neighbours that India continues to fall short in being a "balancing power". Ultimately, it has to do with Tibet, Tawang and the Dalai Lama. Tawang was always sacred for Tibetans, but China has only recently upped its claims for the state as it works through the Tibetan question, particularly giving itself the power to appoint the next Dalai Lama. Earlier, China wanted to do a swap of Aksai Chin and Tawang, but that's off the table now.

But India is slowly learning to deal with a superior strategic competitor, its skills rusted by years of Pakistan-centric foreign policy. Speaking Punjabi works wonders in Pakistan, but knowing Mandarin doesn't always help in Beijing. Its the hard-nosed approach that does, and India is only now swallowing this unpalatable fact. For the first time, the Indian envoy in Beijing was chosen for his professional skills rather than his language proficiency. During the most recent round of border talks, India told China it would insist on Chinese commitment to the 2005 Guiding Principles where it agreed that while demarcating the boundary, interests of settled populations would be taken into account. Extrapolated, it meant that Arunachal Pradesh would stay with India. The Chinese subsequently went back on that commitment, and India let them. Until now.

In the Indian Ocean, India is putting strategic stakes in Maldives, and Mauritius to assert its maritime power, and reasonably hopeful of courting the Sri Lankans away from the Chinese. As former foreign secretary Shiv Shankar Menon said in a lecture, "the Chinese don't have any bases in the Indian Ocean." Its an important reality check in the middle of all this hype. There also appears to be some fresh thinking on developing the Andaman & Nicobar Islands as a strategic post, as indicated by Shyam Saran, PM's special envoy, which would, if done right, take care of the Chinese "threat" in Myanmar. India is learning much needed lessons from tiny Taiwan that dealing with China needs nerve and grit-never India's strong suit. On the Himalayan heights, however, the reality is very different, and frankly, India is largely responsible. While some of the "incursions" on the LAC are highly exaggerated by hyper-reporting, its undeniable that China's PLA has been guilty of intrusions and aggressive patrolling for at least a year now.

"Violations" by Chinese forces particularly in the western sector, resulted in 2285 instances in 2008, as compared to 778 instances in 2007. While Arunachal Pradesh has been repeatedly hit in the eastern sector, the Chinese have even opened up the resolved Sikkim border and the middle sector.

Militarily, China is streets ahead of India, with some 13 border defence regiments and many brigades along the border, so if, in these heated days, a conflict does indeed break out, India will be toast. China enjoys geographical advantage on the LAC and has built an advanced system of logistics. Indian troops have to go through much tougher terrain to get to their forward posts. China has built rail links between Beijing and Lhasa and onward to Xigaze and Yatung, near Nathu La.

Lhasa could then be a train ride away from Nyingchi, just north of Arunachal. In the western sector, China is widening the Karakoram Highway, which links China to Pakistan, from all-weather traffic.

China is certainly a challenge, but India has to learn to face it openly rather than ducking behind diplomatic platitudes. There needs to be a multi-hued China engagement policy-for instance, unlike Pakistan, more engagement is always better with China, because frankly, Indians don't "understand" the Chinese. Can India start a "peace process" with China?

CHINESE CAN'T 'SEE' MCMAHON LINE

Even as the Indian Army is caught in its own semantic jugglery whether to describe Chinese activities in the eastern theatre as 'incursion' or 'transgression' the fact is the People's Liberation Army (PLA) has crossed over into India no less than six times since January this year.

Worse, there might have been many more incursions because India's presence in forward areas remains woefully thin; it's possible other instances of PLA adventurism have gone unnoticed. Field posts of the Indian Army have reported six such cross-overs this year alone four times in Upper Subansiri district in the north and twice in Lohit district, east Arunachal Pradesh. These are termed "harmless transgressions" or accidental violations of LAC. Officially, PLA incursions are hard to record because no temporary or permanent structures have been built by the Chinese along the spottily demarcated boundaries.

The bone of contention the 890-km long McMahon Line extends from Bhutan in the west and climbs up to the northeast before taking a 90 degree turn southward for 260 km along the great bend of the Brahmaputra. It runs through treacherous Himalayan hilly terrains. This imaginary line is crescent shaped convex towards the Chinese side. "But the Chinese see the curve bending in the opposite direction and hence the difference in perception," a source said. The Army seeks to play down the violations along this line since there is a bilateral mechanism to sort these problems with the PLA at Border Personnel's Meetings (BPMs) held four times a year.

But the root of the problem in the eastern sector is that while India recognises McMahon Line as the border with China, the Chinese don't. They describe it as "so-called McMahon Line" which is the eastern part of the 4,057 km-long LAC extending from Laddakh in the west.

The line is named after Sir Henry McMahon, foreign secretary for British India and the chief British negotiator of the convention of 1914 in which the Simla Accord between British India and Tibet was signed. This agreement had effectively made the McMahon line the boundary between India and Tibet. Their fears have a basis. While the Chinese have built several airports close to the McMahon line, apart from super highways that run parallel to the border, the Indian side has little to show by way of investment. Former BJP MP Kiren Rijiju he is now with the Congress raised the issue of Chinese incursions in Parliament and expressed doubt about the preparedness of the Indian Army in the event of a conflict. For instance, there's just one motorable road to the forward areas along the border.

Rijiju says the Chinese are intruding in a well planned manner with the objective of closing in around Arunachal Pradesh. India's counter is by building a trans-Arunachal road. Recently, the IAF upgraded a MIG-21 pilot training base at Tezpur to a Su MK-III base. It also plans to bring in more frontline fighters into this area at a base to be developed at Chabua in Dibrugarh. Deployment of unmanned aerial vehicles (UAVs), too, is under consideration.

INFO

Arunachal Pradesh is the largest state in the Northeast almost as big as West Bengal but with the lowest population density (13/sq km) in the country. Even as the shadow of a hostile takeover by Chinese looms, the people here who speak more than 50 dialects are bound together by Hindi as the lingua franca. Fears of the 1962 conflict still haunt many particularly of the older generation. Not much has been done to remove these fears.

T G Rimpoche, firebrand Buddhist spiritual leader from Tawang, who is also an MLA, says, "No one is more Indian than an Arunachalee. Go to any remote part and everyone here knows Hindi. At the same time, they expect and want the Union government to recognise their sense of patriotism." Both Tara and Rimpoche say India should take a tougher line against China on

Arunachal. "The Indian attitude is too soft," Rimpoche said. Tara says the Indian Army's presence should increase manifold.

FOR LADDAKH, IT'S NO BIG DEAL

While the recent Chinese incursions into Laddakh followed by reports of military exercise by PLA have sent ripples throughout the country, the people of Laddakh appear unruffled. Chief executive councillor of Laddakh Autonomous Hill Development Council, Chering Dorjay, has told that the threat wasn't serious—adding chartly that the entry of Chinese helicopters (in Chunar, along LAC) in Leh was serious. He called the Chinese incursions in Pangong "unwitting".

Former MoS parliamentary affairs, P. Namgyal, who lives in Leh, said given the vastness of the border and absence of troops on either side, the border residents of both the countries can mistakenly enter into each other's territory. "The incursion of Chinese troops could also be a mistake," Namgyal added. The markets in the region are flooded with Chinese goods—an indicator of a porous border. "The exchange of goods between the two countries for more than a decade is owing to virtually open borders," Namgyal said. This has never caused any concern in defence circles, he added.

The Chinese have occupied 38,000 sq. km. of Aksai Chin area of Indian territory in the Himalayas. "What else can they take, given the presence of huge contingents of ITBP men along LAC?" asked Chering Dorjay. "China has even built roads in that area and we came to know about the occupation of 38,000 sq. km. much after the 1962 war," he added. However, threats by Chinese troops to shepherds is serious matter, he said.

Deputy commissioner of Leh A.K. Sahu, too, isn't disturbed by the Pangong breach. "The water body is shared by the armies of both the countries and, as such, there could not be any serious incursion there," Sahu said.

A senior police officer, speaking on the condition of anonymity, said "The vastness of the border makes it difficult for the Indian troops to man it. Hence, there are at times cases of border crossing by the people."

Disagrring with them was a Laddakh resident who did not wish to reveal his identity. "Indian troops have gone for massive upgradation of infrastructure and military capabilities along the border here," he said. "IAF choppers are constantly flying to detect any instance of border-crossing."

INDIA'S BOUNDARY DISPUTES WITH CHINA, NEPAL, AND PAKISTAN

The recent detonation of a series of nuclear devices by India and Pakistan has increased tension in South Asia and threatens to inflame long-standing boundary disputes that India has with China, Nepal, and Pakistan. The disputes with China and Pakistan have already triggered several wars. The new Hindu-nationalist government in New Delhi has reversed movement toward détente with Beijing and Islamabad. The areas in contention with China and Pakistan are among the largest land-boundary disputes in the world. The Indo-Nepali dispute over Kalapani is more recent and involves a small area.

India-China (Aksai Chin and Arunachal Pradesh)

In the 1962 Sino-Indian War, China seized a Switzerland-sized area, Aksai Chin (Aksayqin), and overran Arunachal Pradesh (an Indian state the size of Austria). There are also other, smaller pockets of disputed area. The PRC withdrew from virtually all of Arunachal Pradesh to the Line of Actual Control (LAC), which approximates the McMahon Line that is found in a 1914 agreement initialed by British, Tibetan, and Chinese representatives. Chinese and Indian forces clashed in the Sumdorong Chu valley of Arunachal Pradesh in 1986-87. Relations began to thaw in 1988.

On 7 September 1993, China and India signed an accord to reduce tensions along their border and to respect the LAC. During November 1996, China and India agreed to delimit the LAC and institute confidence-building measures (CBMs) along the frontier. The agreement pledged nonaggression, prior notification of large troop movements, a 10-km no-fly zone for combat aircraft, and exchange of maps to resolve disagreements about the precise location of the LAC. In August 1997 the sides ratified the CBM agreement. There seems to have been little substantive progress, except for a series of high-level visits. The most recent, on 27 April, was the first visit by a PRC Chief of Staff to India. However, two weeks before the visit the new Indian Defence Minister, George Fernandes, accused the PRC of repeated violations of Indian territory, including the construction of a helipad on "Indian" territory in the disputed zone, and of aiding Pakistan's nuclear and missile programs. On 3 May he publicly labelled China as India's number one threat and alleged that the PRC was stockpiling nuclear weapons in Tibet, expanding naval activity off the Burmese coast, and conducting surveillance against India from Burma's Coco Islands. After the visit of General Fu Quanyou and PRC protests, Fernandes said that his characterization of China as India's principal threat was a personal view, l ut he went on to pledge that the number of Indian troops along the frontier with China would not be reduced. Such a statement calls into question part of the agreed CBMs. (To view a map of this area click here.) China and India have yet to address their fundamental and very large land boundary disputes. Moreover, their bilateral relations are complicated by the issues of Tibet (Xizang), Sikkim, and Kashmir. India plays host to the Dalai Lama and a large number of Tibetan refugees. They present an implicit threat to Chinese control of Tibet, which it invaded in 1950. On its maps, the PRC continues to portray Sikkim, which was absorbed by India in 1974, as an independent country. In addition to the Aksai Chin, China and India dispute another section of Kashmir (the area west of Aksai Chin).

India-Pakistan-China (Kashmir)

When India and Pakistan became independent of Great Britain in 1947, the various princely states, including that of Jammu and Kashmir, could accede to either country. An armed revolt of Muslim peasantry against the Maharaja of Jammu and Kashmir prompted the Maharaja to accede to India in order to gain military aid. Pakistan objected and the countries went to war. The matter was taken up by the UN Security Council in 1948, which adopted a resolution calling for the restoration of order, the withdrawal of Pakistani forces and reduction of Indian forces, and a UN plebiscite. India and Pakistan objected to various of these provisions. They went to war over Kashmir again in 1965. In 1971 India intervened in Pakistan's civil war that led to the independence of Bangladesh. India and Pakistan came close to war over Kashmir in 1990. (To view a map of this area click here.)

UN observers monitor part of the Indo-Pakistani cease-fire line. The current line was established by the 1972 Simla accord and approximately follows the 1949 Cease-fire Line. The coordinates of the Simla line have not been published, and the line was never delimited in the forbidding Siachin Glacier, near the Chinese frontier, where India and Pakistan frequently trade artillery rounds. Firing incidents and allegations of infiltration are chronic along the entire cease-fire line.

The Indian-controlled part of Jammu and Kashmir became a state in 1974. The parts of Kashmir controlled by Pakistan, Azad Kashmir and the Northern Areas, have anomalous status as administered territories. In 1963 China and Pakistan delimited a boundary that India claims illegally gave part of Kashmir to China. In 1987 a Sino-Pakistani protocol formalized demarcation of their boundary. The termination of this boundary at the Karakoram Pass on the Chinese line of control suggests that Pakistan recognizes Chinese sovereignty over Aksai Chin, which is part of the former Princely State of Kashmir.

India and Pakistan have held sporadic talks. In June 1997, they agreed to eight issues for discussion, including the issue of Kashmir and their maritime boundary. Pakistan wants to set-up a separate task force on Kashmir; India has resisted the idea. Talks have made little progress due to changes in the respective governments. The recent efforts by US Ambassador Richardson to resolve the dispute seem to have been blown out of the water by Indian and Pakistani nuclear tests.

India-Nepal (Kalapani)

The dispute between India and Nepal involves about 75 sq km of area in Kalapani, where China, India, and Nepal meet. Indian forces occupied the area in 1962 after China and India fought their border war. Three villages are located in the disputed zone: Kuti [Kuthi, 30°19'N, 80°46'E], Gunji, and Knabe. India and Nepal disagree about how to interpret the 1816 Sugauli treaty between the British East India Company and Nepal, which delimited the boundary along the Maha Kali River (Sarda River in India). The dispute intensified in 1997 as the Nepali parliament considered a treaty on hydro-electric development of the river. India and Nepal differ as to which stream constitutes the source of the river. Nepal regards the Limpiyadhura as the source; India claims the Lipu Lekh. Nepal has reportedly tabled an 1856 map from the British India Office to support its position. The countries have held several meetings about the dispute and discussed jointly surveying to resolve the issue. Although the Indo-Nepali dispute appears to be minor, it was aggravated in 1962 by tensions between China and India. Because the disputed area lies near the Sino-Indian frontier, it gains strategic value.

Like most boundary dispute, those of India with its neighbours are symptomatic of wider bilateral relations. Boundaries are manifestations of national identity. They can be trip-wires of war. Recent developments in South Asia suggest that peaceful resolution of these disputes is receding from reach.

RESOLVING THE BOUNDARY DISPUTE: CHINA'S REASONS AND INDIA'S CHOICES

The final settlement of the Sino-Indian territorial and boundary dispute is not a question of 'if' but 'when'. Four pertinent reasons suggest that China can be ultimately trusted to settle the dispute. On its part, India can take certain steps to ensure that China's reasons do not alter and that 'compromise' is seen as mutually beneficial.

One, China has steadily resolved its territorial disputes with almost all of its 15 land neighbours. Negotiations with the Soviet Union and Vietnam began in 1964 and 1977 respectively. However, it was not until much later that the negotiation processes fructified; it was only in October 2004 that the eastern sector of the Sino-Russian border was finally resolved with the signing of the Supplementary Agreement. With Vietnam, China signed a land boundary agreement in 1999, although they continue to meet regularly at the governmental level to thrash out details pertaining to the Beibu Gulf and the placement of border markers. Therefore, boundary negotiations between China and its other neighbours have been long and arduous affairs. The slowness of the boundary negotiations between India and China needs to be seen in this context.

Two, China has settled 17 of its 23 territorial disputes since 1949, according to M. Taylor Fravel, Assistant Professor of Political Science at MIT. Fravel suggests that regime insecurity and legitimacy crises in peripheral border regions best explain why China not only made concessions but also favoured the peaceful resolution of its territorial disputes. Despite a significant rise in China's economic and military strength vis-a-vis weaker neighbours, China received less than 50 per cent of the contested land. China's 'peaceful development' and 'new security concept' are directly responsible for the gradual stabilization of its borders-both concepts demand peaceful and stable borders for sustained economic growth.

Three, the absence of territorial disputes on China's western flank is a consequence of its 'western development' strategy. Starting with Myanmar and Nepal in the 1960s, a flurry of diplomatic activity saw the resolution of China's borders with Tajikistan and Kazakhstan (in 2002), Kyrgyzstan (in September 2004), Russia (in October 2004), and Mongolia (in November 2005). The pacification of China's western border is driven by the need to build cross-border linkages for economic development as well as the suppression of the three evils-separatism, extremism and terrorism. China's two westernmost provinces that border India, Xinjiang and Tibet, are important to China not least due to the fear that an economic imbalance can potentially fuel secessionist sentiments amongst the Uighurs and Tibetans.

Four, China is likely to reserve the use of force to settle heartland disputes. The hard component of China's comprehensive national strength will continue to dictate an inflexible stance on Taiwan's reunification as well as territorial conflicts of strategic value. Therefore, China is unlikely to make concessions on approximately 30,000 square kilometres of Aksai Chin, not least due to the fact that the Karakoram highway that traverses it provides a strategic link between Pakistan, and China and a shorter route between Tibet and Xinjiang. However, even in the case of disputes over territory of great economic value, such as the South China Sea, China has emphasized the joint development and exploitation of resources, albeit without making any concessions.

As emerging powers, India and China will continue to be pitted against each other. The sheer size and altitude of the disputed area is likely to make demarcation a difficult and lengthy process. However, India can take certain steps to ensure it remains in China's interest to settle the dispute. India must do its utmost to convince China that it is not the target of the newly sealed Indo-US strategic relationship. India must clarify that the support for Tibetans in India is humanitarian and cultural and not a challenge to China's sovereign territoriality. China's friendship with Pakistan cannot be wished away; however, India can make itself important to China by promising trade and joint border development projects that make good business sense. India's inclusion into the Shanghai Cooperation Organisation as an observer in July 2005 was an important recognition of India's commitment to curbing cross-border terrorism.

Even though there are reasons to believe that China is not a revisionist state determined to use force to uphold its territorial claims, proactive steps to create lobbies with vested interests in resolving the dispute must be taken. The seventh round of Sino-Indian border talks in March 2006 helped provide a 'constructive and friendly' atmosphere. It is time for India and China to carry that forward and focus on opening Nathu La for trade, reviving the Stilwell Road for trade across India's northeast, building border free trade zones similar to the Sino-Kazakh one and establishing independent inter-linkages between border regions through transport linkages akin to the Kashgar (Xinjiang, China)-Gilgit (Northern Areas, Pakistan) bus service. Discussion on the Sino-Indian boundary talks must therefore go beyond the rhetoric on China's 'concirclement' of India; it must emphasize the domestic constraints and foreign policy concerns of the Chinese government and the resolution of territorial disputes that such a study reveals.

CHINA'S BORDER SPAT WITH INDIA

The recent meeting between India's National Security Adviser MK Narayanan and China's Vice-Foreign Minister Dai Banggio at Coonoor in Tamil Nadu was the continuation of a series of such meetings in the context of the border dispute between the two countries. While this is a good thing to go by, the main point is: what has been the actual progress in the matter? After every meeting, a standard joint communiqué is issued to the effect that the téte-a-téte was fruitful and the dialogue is being maintained in an atmosphere of friendship and mutual cooperation. Diplomatic jargon cannot be limitless; it must end somewhere.

Again, from time to time one hears of Chinese intrusion into Arunachal Pradesh, especially in the area of Sumdorong Chu Valley and the northern range of the Mishmi Hills. There is also the occasional media report that China claims this Northeastern state of ours on the grounds of a combination of history as well as geography.

India's drawback is that our foreign policy has always been linked to the vote bank. In fact it was a vote bank issue that created the border dispute with China in the first place way back in the late '50s and early '60s. The origin of this problem is worth discussing as this itself suggests the solution. Soon after China secured Tibet, Beijing sent a delegation to New Delhi under then Prime Minister Zhou en Lai with a proposal on Aksai Chin in northern Kashmir, adjacent to the Siachen Glacier. The delegation submitted to us that movement from Tibet to Sinkiang province was a huge problem because one had to traverse the inhospitable Kunlun Mountains en route. Hence it was suggested both countries could arrive at an understanding by which India could lease out Aksai Chin to China, as this would enable the latter to build an all-weather highway across this stretch of territory.

Thus movement from Tibet to Sinkiang would not then involve negotiating the Kunluns at all and India, too, could use this highway as a bonus. In any case, Aksai Chin was just an ice desert with an average height of 18,000-19,000 feet and nothing grew there, let alone having any human habitation. New Delhi reacted with its usual brash arrogance, thundering words to the effect that 'not an inch of our sacred motherland' would be given, et al. Zhou en Lai was shown the door gracelessly.

The Chinese delegation went back and decided to implement a tenet in Hindi conveying the meaning that if ghee cannot be taken out by a straight finger then a crooked finger would be used! China militarily attacked India and physically captured Aksai Chin by force in late 1962 and built the desired highway through it. China is still very much in occupation of this area, cocking a snook at India now and then! On our part we bemoaned our fate, blamed Beijing for gerrymandering into our territory and generally made a political nuisance of ourselves. Nothing helped, of course.

During its attack on India, China had also deeply transgressed into what was earlier known as the North East Frontier Agency that later became Arunachal Pradesh. However, after delivering a crushing military-cum-political defeat on India, China moved back to its own side of the border in this area. This apart, China disputes an area along the Uttarkhand-Tibet border named Barahoti.

China has a strong army garrison in this area at a place called Taklakot that keeps a watching brief over Barahoti. India, therefore, has been well and truly boxed in by China, courtesy New Delhi's folly of riding the high horse with Zhou en Lai's delegation of yore. Diplomacy has never been a strong point with us and the country has suffered badly as a consequence. The science and art of statecraft continue to be subservient to the omnipotent vote bank as far as our leaders are concerned.

New Delhi, for reasons best known to itself, brought out a Lok Sabha resolution in 1994 wherein it was categorically stated that we would retake Aksai Chin by force. Obviously this resolution was nothing but a vote bank gimmick that our näive citizens — including many members of our intelligentsia — swallowed all the way. While firmly occupying Aksai Chin, China periodically needles India over Arunachal Pradesh and Barahoti. Normally, Barahoti remains dormant but Arunachal Pradesh makes news, sometimes with alarm. This has been the state of affairs since 1962. No government at New Delhi since that year has tried to accept the reality and taken any pragmatic steps to reconcile the border situation with China, notwithstanding the fact that currently our relations with China are improving virtually by the day.

The question is, what needs to be done in order to resolve the ongoing impasse? There is only one solution: India must formally accept Zhou en Lai's suggestion of yesteryear but cede Aksai Chin to China. It is doubtful whether China will accept the lease aspect now. The Chinese are a very proud race and will never climb down. In any event, China holds the aces in this matter, never mind the McMahon Line's relevancy to us.

Truth to tell, this solution was hinted by China's previous regime under President Jiang Zemin through his then Foreign Minister Tang Jiaxuan during Prime Minister AB Vajpayee's tenure. While the Sikkim issue got reconciled, Aksai Chin could not be followed through due to the change of government in India in 2004.

China is not really interested in Barahoti and Arunachal Pradesh — Beijing uses these two as pressure points on New Delhi to see reason over the border dispute, a dispute that hinges purely on Aksai Chin. The sooner we come to terms with this, the better.

3 The Strategic Significance of Arunachal Pradesh for India

The past and contemporary rigidity of China on claiming the whole of the Indian State of Arunachal Pradesh as Chinese territory arises significantly from the strategic importance of this region in relation to China and its hold on Tibet. On the eve of Chinese President Hu Jin Tao's visit to India in 2006 the then Chinese Ambassador to India in a manner that was diplomatically abrasive, unwise and arrogant startled the Indian policy establishment by public assertions that the whole of Arunachal Pradesh was part of China.

"The Strategic Importance of Tawang" Some of the major reasons of the strategic importance of Arunachal Pradesh were highlighted and it was stressed that India could not afford any territorial compromises in this region. In the current season while China has once again focused on rigidly and persistently claiming the whole of this region, it is appropriate to refocus on the strategic importance of Arunachal Pradesh to India. The above referred Paper is reproduced below. Additionally, one would like to stress is that Arunachal Pradesh in India's hands strategically worries China most because it is from this region that India's missile ranges and coverage of Chinese heartland targets, offers the best locations.

Notwithstanding any peace rhetoric from China or efforts to lower temperatures in the India-China border standoff on the Tibet border, it would be realistic for Indian military contingency planning to expect a major Chinese military offensive against India centring on Arunachal Pradesh with Tawang as the initial prime target. That was the lesson of 1962 also.

China: The Strategic Reluctance On Boundary Settlement with India

China ever since its emergence as a monolithic Communist state in 1949 was involved in boundary disputes with virtually every nation on its peripheries. It led to border wars with the former Soviet Union, Vietnam and India. In the case of Vietnam and India, the border wars were perceived by China as punitive wars. China today has undertaken boundary settlements with virtually all countries with which it had disputes with the exception of India. Some in India hoped that with a generational change in leadership in China and with the economic, political and strategic rise of India, China may be prompted to move towards more accommodative stances on the China-India boundary dispute. China's President Hu Jintao would be visiting India from November 20, 2006 for four days. It has been already spelt out, that in terms of perspectives, China has given no indications that India could expect any significant breakthrough announcements by the Chinese president on the boundary dispute. The Chinese President's visit to India in November 2006 will be just one more item in the chronology of China-India relations. A politically correct visit at best.

Endless Round of Border Dispute Negotiations by China

Endless rounds of border dispute negotiations have taken place between China and India. These have taken place at two levels, namely:

Joint Working Group (JWG) discussions which commenced in 1988

Special Representatives talks at the level of India's National Security Advisers and Chinese Vice Minister level since June 2003. The JWG has already completed over fifteen rounds of discussions. The Special Representatives held Seventh Round of talks in March 2006. The standard responses after each round have been of the type that was stated in March 2006: "The two Special Representative continued their discussions for an agreed framework for the resolution of the boundary question in a constructive and friendly atmosphere".

Chinese leaders on visits to India come out with the oft-repeated statement that the boundary dispute should be left to future generations to resolve and meanwhile China-India relations in other fields should move forward. This is just an excuse to keep alive the border dispute as a strategic pressure point against India.

This leads to the question whether China is really serious about resolution of the China-India border dispute? The endless round of negotiations does not suggest so.

It is best exemplified by an Indian media news report that no meetings have been scheduled between Indian and Chinese Special Representatives for talks on the boundary dispute before the visit of Chinese President Hu Jintao on November 20 "as India doesn't expect any substantive progress on the border issue in the near future." Symbolically, China's reluctance can be read as dissatisfaction with growing US-India strategic relationship and keeping alive the border dispute as a strategic pressure point against India. Obviously China is actively involved in delays and prolonging the resolution of the boundary disputes for strategic reasons.

Strategic Reluctance on Boundary Settlement with India by China

Veiled references in the past were made by Indian official spokesmen that progress could not be made as China was constantly pressurizing India to accept a swap by India of Tawang in lieu of Aksai-Chin.

China has now come out in the open to demand and advocate this proposal. An Indian news-report covering the closed door meeting organized between Chinese distinguished experts and Indian academics by China's Institute of Asia-Pacific Studies, which is part of the giant official Chinese Academy of Social Sciences had this to report:

Chinese experts said that China would be magnanimous on the issue of Aksai Chin area if India agreed to give up Tawang. The high-level Chinese experts which included former Chinese Ambassador to India Chen Rui Sheng made it clear that the border dispute could be solved if India handed over Tawang to China.

The Strategic Significance of Tawang for India

At the outset it must be made clear that for the Chinese, Tawang is not just the Tawang Monastery region. For them Tawang implies the whole of India's Arunachal Pradesh. So as not to dilute their claim, they officially will not call it that Arunachal Pradesh should be returned to them. Coming to the strategic importance of Arunachal Pradesh or Tawang in Chinese parlance the following need to be recognized:

Arunachal Pradesh provides strategic depth to India's Brahmaputra Valley and India's other North Eastern states. Arunachal Pradesh provides security to Bhutan on it entire Eastern flank by geographical contiguity.

Bhutan would be then be in a pincer group of China on both it flanks if Tawang is given away. This would be detrimental to India's security. China's borders would then rest on the plains of Assam; India might as well write off its other North Eastern states. The Chinese obsession with the Tawang Region is totally strategic in its aims.

In any future conflict with China and if India singly or in coalition with some other power develops offensive capabilities against China, this region offers the shortest cut to China proper and to Tibet. India's communications infrastructure in this region developed in World War II for US military aid to China is existent and can be further improved.

Arunachal Pradesh offers all-wealthier lines of communication to India for military needs to the Tibet border as compared to Aksai-Chin. In terms of any air operations by China in this region, Arunachal Pradesh would provide multilayered air defence deployments on the ground as deterrence.

The region is rich in terms of mineral and natural resources prospects. There are many more reasons that one can state but the major ones should be enough. Arunachal Pradesh is of vital strategic importance for the territorial integrity and defence of India's North East states and should be non-negotiable.

China would be politically naive of it perceives that in the 21st Century, a powerfully rising India would accept the bait of a

Chinese strategic barter of Aksai-Chin in lieu of Tawang India would be more politically naive than China if it thinks that China would concede the area of Aksai-Chin through which passes its lifelines to keep Xinjiang under Chinese control. Both in Aksai Chin and in the Arunachal Pradesh area, the strategic interests of China and India clash in the most intense manner. It would be a magical wonder if China can turn around to be strategically accommodative of India's strategic sensitivities. China's strategic reluctances to solve the border dispute with India can therefore be expected to bedevil China-India relations for a long time to come.

ARUNACHAL PRADESH'S BORDER ROADS

The state of Arunachal Pradesh in India's northeastern frontier has been appearing quite regularly in the Indian national security and strategic imagination for some years now. Strident Chinese territorial claims, particularly over the Tawang hill tract, have managed to unsettle New Delhi and the Indian strategic community. Against this backdrop and given that Arunachal is the largest state in India's northeastern region in terms of territory, it becomes important to assess the border roads infrastructure and connectivity in this strategically-crucial frontier state.

The state was a theatre in the 1962 Sino-Indian war, in which India had faced major losses and had to fight in extremely unprepared conditions, with almost no road connectivity. While Indian forces did manage to resist strongly at several border points the fall of Tawang and Bomdi La towns were without resistance as there was no proper supply and road infrastructure to maintain Indian army positions. Air dropped supplies sometimes, fell into the hands of the Chinese who had occupied Tawang. This was 50 years ago but the road infrastructure and connectivity in Arunachal Pradesh still leaves a lot to be desired in terms of strategic preparedness for the Indian Army and for the general economic development of the state.

The need to construct proper roads in Arunachal Pradesh dawned on the Indian government only after it suffered in the war against the Chinese, and a skeletal network of roads was built subsequently in this difficult terrain mostly aimed at maintaining military posts and supplies in various strategic parts of the state. This was the first layer of work done on roads in the state, and only fed specific sectors such as Bhalukpung-Bomdi-La-Tawang, Itanagar-Ziro-Along-Mechuka, and the eastern sector which included a maze of roads with no inter-connectivity. The Assam government has four-laned the Stilwell Road in its territory but on the Arunachal side, the Road remains perennially under construction.

Internal connectivity within Arunachal Pradesh remains one of the pressing problems which need urgent attention-to travel to five different towns in Arunachal Pradesh, one has to cross back into Assam as many times. Air dropping of essential civil and military supplies in remote areas of Arunachal Pradesh is the prevailing norm and a number of AN-32 transport aircraft are used on a daily basis from the Guwahati, Jorhat and Dibrugarh supply bases in Assam. The road that leads to the central part of Arunachal Pradesh, particularly to its capital Itanagar, falls mostly in Assam and has been over the years ill-maintained and is prone to annual floods. The Border Roads Organisation which is in charge of maintaining these crucial roads have done a decent job, keeping in mind the difficult terrain, high rainfall and frequent landslides which sometimes sweep entire stretches of roads away, but overall, the effort is woefully inadequate..

The Trans-Arunachal Highway project which was announced by Prime Minister Manmohan Singh in 2008, has failed to pick up pace with preliminary feasibility studies still being conducted in many parts of the state. The Highway project comes very late, as the pressure on the existing road infrastructure has already increased manifold given the burden of civil supplies as also the massive convoys of army supplies and movement which has become necessary due to the current policy of trying to match Chinese army mobilization across the border. The need for a second network of border roads in Arunachal Pradesh is almost 10-15 years late, and will certainly take another 10-15 years, if not more, to come to fruition. It has been noted that in many parts of Northeast India, the second layer of road connectivity and infrastructure development has begun only when the pressure on the current infrastructure has become enormously high, often compounding implementation woes; the consistent and painful delays in project implementation, can be attributed to a clear policy planning failure on the part of both the central and state governments.

Similarly, the Bogibeel project for a bridge over the river Brahmaputra in Dibrugarh in Assam, was mooted more than a decade back, but saw work begin only just some years ago, and is now estimated to be completed only in the year 2030. This bridge has the potential to connect the middle and eastern parts of Arunachal Pradesh and save on traveling time, as these areas are now dependent on the Kaliabhoomoora Bridge across the Brahmaputra in Tezpur.

The central government still seems to be sleeping on major bottlenecks in terms of road infrastructure and connectivity as is evident in various parts of Northeast India. Major road expansion work is overdue in critical stretches such as Numaligarh-Kohima-Imphal and Guwahati-Shillong-Silchar-Aizawl, which has resulted in clogging the streets of major state capitals like Kohima, Shillong and Aizawl. The Trans-Asian Highway too, has made little progress. There needs to be greater urgency in policy implementation in order to serve the needs of not just Arunachal but the Northeast and the nation as a whole in terms of economic development and strategic military preparedness.

CHINA'S CLAIMS ON ARUNACHAL ABSURD: CHIEF MINISTER DORJEE KHANDU

The Chief Minister of Arunachal Pradesh Dorjee Khandu, termed China's claims to Arunachal Pradesh as its territory as "simply absurd". "I have been telling repeatedly that Arunachal Pradesh is an integral part of India and that Chinese claims are simply absurd.

"We are the only state in the northeast where Hindi is the link language among various tribes who speak different dialects," Khandu said after his swearing in. "Now, we are all set to welcome the Dalai Lama who is visiting the state from November 8."

He also said his government's topmost priority would be to work for the overall economic uplift of the state, especially focusing on developing infrastructure and boosting education and health sectors. "Now, after the people have given us a thumping victory in the elections, we need to work even harder to achieve accelerated pace of development and growth in the state," Khandu said.

"Social sectors, health, education, roads and infrastructure are the areas that we are going to give maximum thrust and focus to this time."

PM, WEN TALK PEACE, NOT DALAI

PM Manmohan Singh discussed the border issue with his Chinese counterpart Wen Jiabao in Thailand's resort town of Hua Hin, with both leaders stressing the need to narrow differences and preserve the peace. Both Prime Ministers refrained from specific discussion of the discord over Arunachal Pradesh and the Dalai Lama' visit to the state, both of which recently caused tension in ties. But they agreed it was imperative maintain peace along the disputed border area.

Officials accompanying the Prime Minister told the media that the two sides agreed to build further "trust and understanding". During the meeting, Wen insisted China wanted a "steady and healthy" relationship with India. New Delhi maintained that both leaders agreed not to allow differences to impede "functional cooperation".

Both leaders had a "productive meeting" that lasted nearly an hour on the sidelines of the ASEAN and East Asia summit. "We want to have a healthy and steady relationship with India. I hope we can use this opportunity to exchange our views on all related issues," said Wen. However, the contentious issue of the Dalai Lama's proposed visit to Arunachal Pradesh remains unaddressed, prompting analysts in India to predict the Wen-Singh meeting will not mean a softening of Beijing's tough stance toward New Delhi.

"In June, for example, no sooner than Hu Jintao and Manmohan Singh had appeared hand-in-hand at the first-ever

BRIC summit, hosted by Russia, than the Chinese state-controlled media ran fresh vituperative attacks against India," said strategic affairs analyst Brahma Chellaney. "India, in this decade, had hyped the outcome of every bilateral summit meeting with China to such an extent that today it is staring at the costs of such ritualized happy talk. In that light, a cautious appraisal of the Wen-Singh meeting is warranted," Chellaney added. Foreign ministry officials said Wen recalled the countries jointly establishing the Strategic and Cooperative Partnership for Peace and Prosperity in 2005.

DAY BEFORE PM-WEN MEET, RAO SAYS NO CURBS ON DALAI

A day before the crucial meeting between PM Manmohan Singh and his Chinese counterpart Wen Jiabao in Thailand, India said it shares a "complex relationship" with China marked by outstanding issues, all of which are likely to figure in the discussion between the two leaders on Saturday. Singh is expected to meet Wen on the sidelines of the ongoing East Asia and ASEAN summit. The meeting was hurriedly arranged after Wen expressed his intention to meet Singh last week.

"It is a relationship which has developed in many areas. It is also a complex relationship and there are outstanding issues between the two. The meeting provides an opportunity to address all such issues," said foreign secretary Nirupama Rao. Tibetan leader Dalai Lama's scheduled visit to Arunachal Pradesh has led to angry exchanges between the two countries, but Rao on Friday again reiterated that Dalai Lama was free to visit any part of the country. "We are against any political activity by Tibetans in our country. We regard Dalai Lama as a respected, spiritual figure and, as we have said earlier, he is free to visit any place in the country," said Rao. She admitted that Dalai Lama had expressed an interest in visiting the state which China claims as its own even though she added that she wasn't aware of it anymore.

Despite Rao's earlier statement to that effect, the Chinese foreign ministry on Tuesday had again issued a statement saying that it was firmly opposed to the Tibetan leader's visit to "so-called Arunachal Pradesh". The two sides, however, will have another opportunity to calm things down when their foreign ministers, S M Krishna and Yang Jiechi, meet next week in Bangalore during the ninth trilateral meeting of foreign ministers from India, China and Russia. Meanwhile, Singh said before his departure to Thailand that he would discuss with ASEAN leaders new initiatives to accelerate the process of engagement in areas such as greater economic integration, people-to-people contacts, agriculture, human resource development, education, science and technology and information and communications technology.

PM SNUBS CHINA, SAYS DALAI LAMA WILL VISIT ARUNACHAL PRADESH

Despite China's strong objections, India has not shown any inclination to block the proposed visit of Dalai Lama to Tawang in Arunachal Pradesh. The Prime Minister, Dr Manmohan Singh, on Sunday also described the border dispute between the two countries as "complex."

Dr Singh, during the gala dinner on Saturday night, reiterated the country's position that the exiled spiritual leader, "Dalai Lama is an honoured guest of India and a religious leader." Though Dr Singh and his Chinese counterpart, Mr ven Jiabao, apparently did not discuss the Dalai Lama's travel plans, sources disclosed that it was clearly indicated that the New Delhi adhered to the stand that the Tibetan leader was free to travel wherever he wished to. Despite the simmering differences, both the Prime Ministers agreed to strengthen efforts to build "political trust and understanding."

Asked whether Mr Wen sought to know specifically about the Dalai Lama's plans, the Prime Minister said that he reminded that the Dalai Lama was an honoured guest and "we do not allow him to indulge in political activities." The Prime Minister also reminded his Chinese counterpart that at the time of the Beijing Olympics last year, India took "resolute action against the Tibetan refugees, when there were reports that some of them disrupt the process."

Asked whether the Dalai Lama was visiting Tawang on November 8, the Prime Minister replied: "I am not aware of the Dalai Lama's plan. But I have explained our position." Much to the chagrin of China, the Dalai Lama plans to make a week-long visit to Arunachal Pradesh in the first week of November.

If the bilateral meet between the two premiers veered around soft words and congratulations, it was at the last night's dinner, the contentious issues became part of their menu. Territorial disputes, Chinese incursions, trans-border river disputes and other differences, which" cannot be wished away" were all discussed across the table. "We had a frank exchange of views during the gala dinner. We discussed all the issues and agreed that a mechanism for bilateral cooperation should be resolved amicably in the spirit of strategic and cooperative partnership." On a significant note, the Prime Minister observed, "we both agreed that there is the complex boundary question, which cannot be wished away."

Reiterating that boundary question "is a complex question, " the Prime Minister said that "pending the resolution of the boundary question, we both have an obligation to maintain peace and tranquillity along the border." Both India and China agreed that views on all the relevant issues would be exchanged during the Chinese foreign minister's visit to India on October 27. The other contentious issue of Beijing building a dam on the Brahmaputra was also raised, as the two premiers sat side by side. "I did raise this issue with Premier Wen Jiabao yesterday," the Prime Minister said. "I conveyed to him that cooperation in the area of trans-border rivers is of mutual benefit." Dr Singh then informed that Premier Wen said that "keeping in view the overall friendly relations and humanitarian aspects, the Chinese side has been providing hydrological data during the flood season." The Chinese premier also said that relevant "discussions on transborder river issues could be held through the expert level mechanism that we have constituted."

CHINESE ENVOY MEETS MEA OFFICIALS AS BEIJING VOICES CONCERN OVER PM'S ARUNACHAL VISIT

China's Ambassador to India Zhang Yang met officials of the Ministry of External Affairs (MEA) shortly after his government expressed "strong" dissatisfaction over Prime Minister Manmohan Singh's visit to Arunachal Pradesh during electioneering. There was no word about what Yang had discussed with the MEA officials. Earlier, Chinese Foreign Ministry spokesman Ma Zhaoxu had said: "We demand the Indian side address China's serious concerns and not trigger disturbance in the disputed region so as to facilitate the healthy development of China-India relations."

"China is strongly dissatisfied with the visit to the disputed region by the Indian leader disregarding China's serious concerns," Mas added in a statement posted on the ministry's website. He noted that China and India had "never officially settled" demarcation of their border, and China's stance on the eastern section of the China-India border was "consistent and clear-cut". The Indian Government has all along indicated that Arunachal Pradesh is an integral part of India and that the people of that state have a democratic right to elect a government of their choice.

Singh had toured and addressed an election rally in Arunachal Pradesh on October 3. Recently, China had blocked a part of a loan to India from the Asian Development Bank (ADB) for developmental projects in Arunachal Pradesh. China also protested a visit to the state last month by exiled Tibetan leader the Dalai Lama. India says China is illegally occupying 43,180 sq kms of Jammu and Kashmir. On the other hand, China accuses India of possessing some 90,000 sq km of Chinese territory, mostly in Arunachal Pradesh.

Singh had earlier visited Arunachal Pradesh on January 31 and February 1 and had then referred to it as "Our land of the rising sun" at a public rally, which was objected to by China. China apparently saw it as India's assertion of its claim on Arunachal, which it claims is a "disputed territory".

INDIA REJECTS CHINA'S PROTEST AGAINST PM'S ARUNACHAL VISIT

India rejected China's protest against Prime Minister Manmohan Singh's visit to Arunachal Pradesh, whose ownership is disputed by Beijing, with Finance Minister Pranab Mukherjee describing it as "nothing new" and the government expressing "disappointment". "It is nothing new. China had objected earlier to my visit to Tawang when I was the foreign minister," Mukherjee told reporters on the sidelines of an India-Bangladesh dialogue in New Delhi.

Earlier in the day, external affairs ministry spokesman Vishnu Prakash said: "We express our disappointment and concern over the statement made by the Chinese ministry of foreign affairs since this does not help the process of ongoing negotiations on the boundary question." He said Arunachal Pradesh, which borders Tibet, was an "integral and inalienable part of India" and its people are "proud participants in the mainstream of India's vibrant democracy".

He said China was "well aware of this position" of the Indian government. External Affairs Minister S M Krishna added: "I have said it in parliament that Arunachal Pradesh is an integral part of India. We rest it at that."

Their comments followed a Chinese foreign ministry statement that Beijing "is strongly dissatisfied with the visit to the disputed region by the Indian leader disregarding China's serious concerns". "We demand the Indian side address China's serious concerns and not trigger disturbance in the disputed region so as to facilitate the healthy development of China-India relations," spokesman Ma Zhaoxu said in Beijing.

Ma said China and India had never officially settled the demarcation of their border, and China's stance on the eastern section of the China-India border was consistent and clear-cut. Beijing in 2003 gave up its territorial claim over India's Sikkim state but maintains that nearly all of Arunachal Pradesh belongs to it. The mountainous state of Arunachal shares a 1,030 km unfenced border with China.

Also Tuesday, China's ambassador to India, Zhang Yan, called on the Indian foreign ministry to convey his government's stand on the prime minister's visit to Arunachal Pradesh. The Chinese statement, however, made no reference by name to Manmohan Singh, who visited Arunachal Pradesh October 3 to campaign for the Congress in assembly elections that took place in the state Tuesday.

At the same time, Prakash said that India was "committed to resolving outstanding differences with China in a fair, reasonable and mutually acceptable manner, while ensuring that such differences are not allowed to affect the positive development of bilateral relations". "We hope that the Chinese side will similarly abide by this understanding." An Indian lawmaker also slammed Beijing for criticizing Manmohan Singh's visit to Arunachal Pradesh.

"It is simply blasphemous on the part of China to oppose or express dissatisfaction over the visit of our prime minister to Arunachal Pradesh," Takam Sanjay, a ruling Congress MP in the Lok Sabha from Arunachal Pradesh said.

CHINA 'STRONGLY' PROTESTS PM'S VISIT TO ARUNACHAL!

Ten days after the event, China expressed "strong" dissatisfaction over Prime Minister Manmohan Singh's visit to Arunachal Pradesh during electioneering. "We demand the Indian side address China's serious concerns and not trigger disturbance in the disputed region so as to facilitate the healthy development of China-India relations," Chinese Foreign Ministry spokesman Ma Zhaoxu said.

"China is strongly dissatisfied with the visit to the disputed region by the Indian leader disregarding China's serious concerns," Mas said in a statement posted on the ministry's website. He noted that China and India had "never officially settled" demarcation of their border, and China's stance on the eastern section of the China-India border was "consistent and clear-cut".

Singh had toured and addressed an election rally in Arunachal Pradesh on October 3. Recently, China had blocked part of a loan to India from the Asian Development Bank (ADB) for developmental projects in Arunachal Pradesh. China also protested a visit to the state last month by exiled Tibetan leader the Dalai Lama.

India says China is illegally occupying 43,180 sq kms of Jammu and Kashmir. On the other hand, China accuses India of possessing some 90,000 sq km of Chinese territory, mostly in Arunachal Pradesh. "Arunachal Pradesh is an integral part of India. We rest at that. Regardless of what others have to say, it is Government of India's position that Arunachal Pradesh is an integral part of India. Period," Krishna said. The External Affairs Ministry also issued a statement expressing disappointment and concern over Chinese objection to Manmohan Singh's visit to Arunachal Pradesh.

BEIJING QUEERS PITCH AHEAD OF SINGH-JIABAO MEET

India's attempts to discern its way through the complexities of China's apparent carrot-and-stick diplomacy is not bearing fruit. While on one hand, as official sources revealed, the two sides worked together to arrange a meeting between PM Manmohan Singh and his Chinese counterpart Wen Jiabao during the upcoming East Asia Summit in Bangkok, Beijing queered the pitch for such a meeting by stating again that it was "firmly opposed" to Tibetan leader Dalai Lama's visit to Arunachal Pradesh.

Wen Jiabao had himself expressed a desire to meet Singh during the East Asia Summit starting later this week when he recently met petroleum minister Murli Deora during an SCO meet in China. Immediately after this, India worked hard to schedule a meeting between the two leaders along the sidelines of the summit and, as things stand now, the meeting seems a certainty. Wen Jiabao offered to meet Singh immediately after Beijing lodged a protest against Singh's visit to Arunachal. Perhaps under the impression that he made the offer in a genuinely damage-control mode, the Indian side worked overtime with the Chinese to ensure the meeting did take place.

However, China's seemingly recalcitrant stand on "so-called Arunachal Pradesh" continues to mar any attempt to build more confidence between the two nations. "China's position on so-called Arunachal Pradesh is consistent and clear and we firmly oppose the Dalai Lama's visit to the region. We believe that this further exposes the Dalai Lama clique's anti-China and separatist nature," Chinese foreign ministry spokesman Ma Zhaoxu said, adding that China's stance on Arunachal Pradesh was consistent. For India, the remark is a real dampner also because it shows scant regard for the fact that foreign secretary Nirupama Rao had categorically stated that India looked upon Dalai Lama as a religious leader and that he was free to go anywhere in the country. MEA sources reacted on Tuesday by stating that the latest Chinese outburst on Arunachal was totally uncalled for as India has already made its position clear. "India has made its position amply clear. The only restriction from our side is that no Tibetan should carry out any anti-China activity from Indian soil. As far as Dalai Lama is concerned, there is no restriction on him visiting any part of the country".

CHINA ACCUSES INDIA OF PROVOCATION, ITS MEDIA ALLEGES DEMOGRAPHIC CHANGES IN ARUNACHAL PRADESH

As the time approaches for the proposed visit of His Holiness the Dalai Lama to Tawang in Arunachal Pradesh next month to declare open a hospital built with contributions from the Tibetan exile community, China has stepped up its rhetoric against India. The recent visit of Prime Minister Manmohan Singh to Arunachal Pradesh to canvass for the candidates of his party in the just concluded elections to the State Assembly of Arunachal Pradesh on October 12 has been used as a pretext for the renewed criticism of the Indian policy on Arunachal Pradesh. Dr. Manmohan Singh's visit to Arunachal Pradesh has been projected as his visit to the so-called Southern Tibet.

China never fails to bring on record its protests and concerns over the visits of Indian leaders to Arunachal Pradesh for whatever purpose. The fact that it has done so after the recent electoral visit of Dr. Manmohan Singh should not, therefore, have been a matter of surprise and undue concern. What is disturbing is the kind of language used by a spokesperson of the Chinese Foreign Office in commenting on the visit and the even stronger language used by the "Global Times", in an editorial on the subject on October

14, 2009. The "Global Times" is a sister publication of the Party-controlled "People's Daily".

The fresh campaign against India on the subject was triggered off by the comments of a spokesperson of the Chinese Foreign Ministry. Ma Zhaoxu, the spokesperson, was quoted by the "Global Times" as saying on October 13 that China was "seriously dissatisfied" by the visit of the Indian Prime Minister, who was accused of "ignoring China's concerns by visiting southern Tibet". The "Global Times" quoted the spokesperson as saying further as follows: "China and India have not reached any formal agreement on the border issue. We demand that the Indian side pay attention to the serious and just concerns of the Chinese side and not provoke incidents in the disputed region, in order to facilitate the healthy development of China-Indian relations."

There has been a difference in the translation into English of the spokesperson's remarks by the BBC and the "Global Times". While the BBC quoted the spokesperson as telling India "not to trigger disturbances in the disputed region", the "Global Times" spoke of the spokesperson telling India "not to not provoke incidents in the disputed region."

The editorial of the "Global Times" titled "Indian PM's visit a provocative move" described the Indian Prime Minister's visit as a "provocative and dangerous move" and alleged that the visit was designed to put the area under India's de facto administration. It accuses India of encouraging the "immigration of more than one million Indians to the region" and warns: "India, however, will make a fatal error if it mistakes China's approach for weakness. The Chinese government and public regard territorial integrity as a core national interest, one that must be defended with every means......The disputed border area is of strategic importance, and hence, India's recent moves – including Singh's trip and approving past visits to the region by the Dalai Lama – send the wrong signal. That could have dangerous consequences."

The text of the editorial is annexed. The conventional wisdom is that since any military confrontation could affect China's economic development and its aspirations of rising as a major power on par with the US, Beijing will restrict itself to angry rhetoric and will not indulge in any ground action in the Arunachal Pradesh area. This wisdom has some validity, but overlooks the fact that China is feeling increasingly insecure in its peripheral areas because of the recent violent uprisings by the Tibetans last year and the Uighurs this year. Its increasing nervousness and feelings of insecurity in its border areas could lead to irrational and unpredictable reflexes vis-a-vis the Arunachal Pradesh issue.

We should avoid countering China's renewed rhetoric with our own rhetoric. While maintaining our cool, we should press ahead with the construction of the infrastructure in the Arunachal Pradesh area and strengthening our defensive capabilities there without talking about them from the roof-top. We should not advise His Holiness not to visit Tawang. When he visits Tawang, we should pay close attention to his personal security. The period before and after the visit of His Holiness to Tawang should call for extra vigilance from our side. China may not indulge in any ground action till the visit of President Barack Obama to China next month is over. What it might do after Obama's visit is a matter which needs close monitoring.

4 Visit of Dalai Lama Arunachal and Objection by China

Inspite of a "strong concern" expressed by China, India has made it clear that no restrictions would be put on the Dalai Lama's travel in Nov'09 to India's border state of Arunachal Pradesh, reported the *Press Trust of India* Sep 11. "We firmly oppose Dalai visiting the so-called 'Arunachal Pradesh'," it quoted Jiang Yu, the spokeswoman for China's foreign ministry, as saying. "China expresses strong concern about this information. The visit further reveals the Dalai clique's anti-China and separatist essence," Reuters Sep 11, likewise, quoted Jiang as saying in a faxed statement when asked to comment on the planned visit by the Dalai Lama. But India appears to be in no mood to succumb to the Chinese pressure this time. "There are no restrictions on travel of the Dalai Lama in India," the report quoted official sources as saying when asked to comment on Chinese opposition to the visit.

China had earlier raised objections even when Prime Minister Manmohan Singh undertook a visit to the state three years back and President Pratibha Patil did so earlier this year. Some see India's apparent rejection of the Chinese objection as an assertion of its sovereignty over the state of Arunachal Pradesh. "From India's point of view the Dalai Lama's visit will restate Arunachal Pradesh as Indian territory," the *Reuters* report quoted Bhaskar Roy, a New Delhi-based China expert, as saying.

DALAI LAMA VISIT IGNITES SINO-INDIAN BORDER DISPUTE

In early November, the Dalai Lama is going to visit the majestic Tawang Monastery, perched atop a ridge in the Indian province of Arunachal Pradesh. Surrounded by thick clouds and perennial mist, the monastery sometimes seems almost to be suspended from heaven. It is also at the very centre of thousands of square kilometres of terrain claimed by both China and India, although India currently possesses it. It now risks becoming a proxy battleground on which both India and China seek to proclaim their sovereignty. The religious leader's visit can be seen as a card played by both India and the Tibetan exile community to keep pressure on China.

Home to one of the most sacred Buddhist monasteries, Tawang is the birthplace of the sixth Dalai Lama, Tsayang Gyatso, in the 17th century. The current Dalai Lama passed through this region when he fled into exile in 1959. Chhime Chhoekyapa, the exiled Tibetan spiritual leader's aide, told the media that the Dalai Lama is "going there for teaching. This has nothing to do with politics, there is nothing political about it." In Chinese eyes, however, and perhaps Indian eyes as well, everything the Dalai Lama does has something to do with politics. And this is a region that Beijing calls "Southern Tibet."

When asked about the Dalai Lama's upcoming visit, Beijing officials have fumed. "China expresses strong concern about this information," said Jiang Yu, the spokeswoman for China's Foreign Ministry. "The visit further reveals the Dalai clique's anti-China and separatist essence. China's stance on the so-called Arunachal Pradesh is consistent. We firmly oppose Dalai visiting the so-called Arunachal Pradesh.". Tension has slowly been ratcheting up between the two Asian giants, with media commentators fanning the flames. "Is China itching to wage war on India?" asked Professor Brahma Chellaney in the September issue of the Far Eastern Economic Review. Reports have appeared in Chinese state media alleging that India was moving troops and fighter aircraft to the northeast, specifically into Sikkim and Arunachal Pradesh.

India, however, is acutely aware of its shortcomings in the territory it controls. The Chinese, with their extensive roads and railways, can actually come up to the Line of Actual Control, take a stroll and walk back. Two years ago, Chinese soldiers demolished a Buddhist statue that Indians had erected at Bumla, the main border pass above Tawang, according to a member of the Indian Parliament, Nabam Rebia. It takes several days for India's troops to get to the border. But slowly India is finding its voice as it struggles to speed up its own preparedness.

China claims around 90,000 square kilometres of territory, roughly the size of Arunachal Pradesh, regarding the area as "disputed." China lays claim to Tawang on behalf of the Tibetans. But in the exile community in Dharamsala, where the Dalai Lama and thousands of Tibetan refugees live, the community is not impressed. They do not claim Tawang as Tibetan, let alone Chinese territory. The Dalai Lama's travel plans were announced a week after his recent visit to Taiwan to visit victims of tropical storm Morakot. China denounced the Taiwan trip, although its complaints were remarkably muted. The visit to Arunachal Pradesh has now drawn further attention to China's treatment of Tibetan activists and the Dalai Lama's calls for cultural and religious freedom and autonomy.

Tawang became part of modern India when Tibetan leaders signed a treaty with British officials in 1914 that established the McMahon Line between Tibet and British-run India. Tawang fell south of the line. The treaty, the Simla Convention, is not recognized by China. "We recognize it because we agreed to it," said Samdhong Rinpoche, prime minister of the Tibetan government-in-exile. "If China agreed to it now, it would be a recognition of the power of the Tibetan government at that time."

Tawang's native population is almost entirely Buddhist. Its origin is obscure. It was a part of the kingdom of Tibet in medieval times although local tribal rulers have governed it from time to time. The British declared the area off-limits in 1873. India's independence from Britain severed it from Tibet. In 1962 Chinese troops conquered Tawang during the invasion of Tibet and for six months it was controlled by the Chinese. After their retreat, Tawang again came under Indian control.

India denied the Dalai Lama permission to visit Tawang the last time he requested to do so. This time it is playing the Dalai Lama card to the full. Officials in India's Ministry of External

Affairs insist that "things are changing" and that India is getting more assertive. On Sept. 16, India's foreign minister, S.M. Krishna, rejected China's opposition to the visit.

In an interview on IBN7, the sister channel of India's CNN-IBN, Krishna said China's objections had no merit. While the government has not explicitly said the visit will be permitted, Krishna said: "Arunachal Pradesh is a part of India and the Dalai Lama is free to go anywhere in India. The only question is that he is not expected to comment on political developments." Analysts say the Tibetan leader's visit will reassert Arunachal's status as an Indian territory. "The timing of his trip [to Arunachal Pradesh] is significant. It comes while the debate over his visit to Taiwan is still hot," said Bhaskar Roy, a New Delhi-based China analyst. "Tibetans are as good at playing these games as the Chinese. They know such a visit will keep up the pressure on China."

In Dharamsala, Samdhong Rinpoche, Tibet's prime minister in exile, called Beijing's objections to the visit "absurd," adding that "Arunachal Pradesh and the Tawang region are an integral part of India. If the Dalai Lama, who has stayed in India for the last 50 years, is visiting any part of the country why does this bother China? If the Dalai Lama goes to Chinese territories it can raise objections but in this case has no business to interfere." The Arunachal Pradesh government is urging New Delhi to ignore the Chinese opposition. "Chinese claims over Arunachal Pradesh are simply baseless and not correct. Arunachal Pradesh is an integral part of India and would continue to be so," said Chief Minister Dorjee Khandu. "They [the Chinese] are opposed to everything that His Holiness does," said a spokesman for the Dalai Lama's private office in Dharamsala.

Tawang's strategic importance cannot be ruled out. The place provides the shortest route from Tibet into India. The Dalai Lama himself took this route to escape into India in 1959. Indian defence officials have already raised alarms declaring China and not Pakistan to be India's biggest threat. They believe that control over Sikkim and Arunachal Pradesh would enable Chinese forces to overrun the entire northeast border region. Chinese troops repeatedly have attempted to gain control of Sikkim's evocatively named Finger Area, a tiny but key strategic location where Beijing does not dispute the frontier.

In June this year, General J J Singh, governor of Arunachal Pradesh and former chief of army staff, announced the deployment of two army divisions of around 25,000 to 30,000 soldiers each along the Arunachal Pradesh border with China. The strength of India's Sukhoi fighter jet fleet in the Northeast is being increased. It remains to be seen if the Dalai Lama's visit will be the trigger that causes them to be used.

DALAI LAMA AN HONOURED GUEST OF INDIA, AND FREE TO TRAVEL ANYWHERE

A day after holding discussions with Chinese Premier Wen Jiabao on the sidelines of 15th ASEAN Summit, Prime Minister Manmohan Singh described Tibetans' spiritual guru Dalai Lama as "an honoured guest of India, adding that he is free to travel anywhere he wishes to (in India)." Replying to a query on the issue of the proposed visit of Dalai Lama to Arunachal Pradesh, Dr. Singh said although he was not aware of Dalai Lama's proposed visit to Arunachal Pradesh but he reconfirmed that "Dalai Lama is an esteemed person for India." China had raised strong objections to the Dalai Llama's proposed visit to the monastery town of Tawang in Arunachal Pradesh earlier. China had also objected to the Prime Minister's visit to Arunachal Pradesh during campaigning for the recently held Assembly elections in the State.

CHINA SHUTS TIBET TO FOREIGNERS BEFORE ANNIVERSARY

China has closed Tibet to foreign tourists and deployed soldiers armed with machine guns in the streets of Beijing — part of a raft of stringent security measures ahead of the 60th anniversary of communist rule. Even kite-flying has been banned in the capital. Although the Oct. 1 commemorations, including a massive military review and speech by President Hu Jintao, are centered on Beijing, the clampdown extends to the farthest reaches of the sprawling nation.

Online, blocks on sensitive political content and social

networking sites such as Twitter and Facebook have been expanded, and there has been a spike in e-mail spam containing spyware sent to foreign journalists. Communist officials across the country have been told to prevent travel to Beijing by petitioners seeking redress from central authorities and to try to resolve their complaints locally.

Security in the capital is as tight and in some ways even tighter than during last year's Beijing Olympic Games, with submachine gun-toting SWAT units mixing among the crowds in a city centre festooned with national flags and colourful dioramas. Residents have been barred from flying kites as a precaution against aerial hazards, and those who live in the diplomatic apartments that line the parade route have been told not open their windows or go out on their balconies to watch. Knife sales have been restricted, and notices in apartment lobbies urge residents to report anything suspicious.

The National Day celebration follows the most violent and sustained unrest against Chinese rule in decades in its far western regions of Xinjiang and Tibet. Ethnic rioting in Xinjiang's capital of Urumqi killed nearly 200 people in July and the Turkic Muslim region remains on edge over a recent string of mysterious needle attacks in public places.

As in the wake of rioting in March 2008, foreign tourists have been banned from Tibet, according to local officials and people working in the travel industry. The March 14, 2008, riot in Lhasa target Chinese shops and migrants who have moved to the Himalayan region in increasing numbers since communist troops entered in 1950.

Su Tingrui, a salesman with Tibet China Travel Service, said that the company's general manager was called to a meeting Sunday night by authorities in Tibet's capital of Lhasa — 2,500 miles (4,023 kilometres) from Beijing. He said the ban was not issued in writing but conveyed during the meeting and will extend to Oct. 8. Other agents in Beijing and Lhasa said that the government had stopped giving out special permits needed to visit the region to foreigners. "For October, business will be noticeably affected," said a receptionist surnamed Wang with the

Four Points by Sheraton hotel in Lhasa. The suspension of permits "is probably part of the extra security arrangements. You are beginning to see a larger number of police and military troops in the streets this month, and police and military at intersections where there used to be nobody guarding."

Security in Tibet was intensified in the weeks leading up to the Beijing Olympics last year and then again this past February and March around sensitive political anniversaries. Those in the industry said Tibetan tourism took a further knock after the Xinjiang rioting, which has also left Urumqi hotels virtually empty. "To tourists there's no difference whether the July rioting was in Xinjiang or Tibet. They think it's dangerous to come down here," said Zhang, a staffer at the Tibet Hongshan International Travel Agency, based in Lhasa.

Tan Lin, an official with the business administration office at the Tourism Bureau of Tibet, said foreign tourists would be banned from Tuesday onwards, but those who have already arrived would be allowed to stay.

Hu Shisheng, head of the South Asia office at China Institutes of Contemporary International Relations, said the ban was motivated by government fears that overseas pro-Tibet groups could use sympathetic students or tourists to stage protests — as occurred in Beijing during the Olympics. China says the violence in Tibet and Xinjiang was masterminded by such groups, although authorities have provided little evidence.

The security measures in Beijing and elsewhere may seem like overkill to some, Joseph Cheng, a professor at the City University of Hong Kong, said. But Chinese officials believe they are worth it to prevent even the smallest incidents while presenting an impression of a strong, stable nation.

"In the last one or two years in the preparation for the Olympics there has been a tremendous emphasis on showing the best face of China," Cheng said. He added that local government and public security officials are told: "We want no incidents, so if anything happens, you are in trouble." Associated Press researcher Zhao Liang in Beijing contributed to this report.

CHINA TO INDIA: JUDGE DALAI LAMA BY DEEDS, NOT WORDS

As the Dalai Lama arrives in the national capital, China has attacked "the Dalai clique" for allegedly masterminding violence in Lhasa a week ago and urged India to see through the "lies" of the Tibetan spiritual leader and judge him by his deeds rather than merely words. The Dalai Lama, who has been living in exile in Dharamsala, Himachal Pradesh, since 1959, will meet Vice-President Hamid Ansari, External Affairs Minister Pranab Mukherjee while stressing that India has always recognized the Tibetan Autonomous Region as part of China. "India's one China policy remains unchanged. There is no review of that," Mukherjee said.

However, China's ambassador to India Zhang Yan, asked for his view on the Dalai Lama as a religious leader and an icon of non-violence, said: "That's his (Dalai Lama's) claim. He is a political figure. He used non-violence to cheat the international community and win their support." "I hope our Indian friends can see through the nature of his intentions and are not misled by him. We urge them to take a correct stand on the incident in Tibet and judge the Dalai Lama by his deeds rather than words," the Chinese envoy told reporters. "We attach importance to deeds and not words," the Chinese envoy stressed.

Zhang Yan also expressed Beijing's opposition to the meeting between US Speaker of the House of Representatives Nancy Pelosi and the Dalai Lama in Dharamsala-the seat of the Tibetan government-in-exile. "China's position is firm and clear. We oppose any country, any organization or any person from interfering in Chinese internal affairs," he said. "Tibet is an internal affair of China. We don't allow any country to meddle in China's internal affairs. Any attempt to do so is doomed to failure," he said. He attacked the Dalai Lama and his followers for allegedly masterminding and engineering the violence that engulfed Lhasa last week, resulting in the death of at least 16 people. "A week after the violence in Lhasa, the Chinese embassy faces a serious threat from the followers of the Dalai Lama. Still, we need heavy protection from the law-enforcement authorities. The Dalai Lama is the head of the government-in-exile. He can control them," he said.

Claiming that the Tibetan activists went on a rioting spree in Lhasa March 14 that killed innocent civilians and policemen, Zhang Yan underlined that the motive of "premeditated rioting incited by the Dalai clique" was to "sabotage" efforts of the Chinese government to organize "successful Olympics" in August. "The Dalai Lama tried to deny the connection. We have enough evidence to prove that these are hypocritical lies," Zhang said. Urging the Indian media to take a correct stand on what he called the "incident" in Tibet last week, the Chinese envoy screened a documentary aired by the Chinese Central TV that showed vivid images of Tibetan activists looting and burning shops and houses in Lhasa.

"I have kept the Indian government informed of all developments in Lhasa, Tibet, and in my embassy. The government is very well informed and can take a correct stand in keeping with the policy of India," he said. In the wake of the unrest in Lhasa, India reacted cautiously, calling on all parties to pursue a non-violent solution of the Tibetan issue. "The Indian government has taken appreciable measures in this regard. We express thanks for the support and understanding of the Indian government," the Chinese envoy said while profusely thanking the Indian authorities for ensuring the security of the Chinese embassy, consulates and staff. India has crucial stakes in Tibet, which borders its territory, as it is in some sense crucial to the ongoing attempts at resolving its border dispute with China. Beijing claims the Tawang monastery, situated in Arunachal Pradesh, to be part of Tibet, and, therefore, part of its territory. India has recognized the Tibetan Autonomous Region to be part of China, but has rejected China's claim on the northeastern state Arunachal Pradesh. The two countries are engaged in talks to resolve the long-standing border issue.

CHINA'S POLICY ON TIBET SHORT-SIGHTED: DALAI LAMA

The Dalai Lama accused China of having a short-sighted and

narrow-minded policy on Tibet, stemming from political insecurity and racial and cultural arrogance. In a statement released in New Delhi on the eve of the 41st anniversary of the Tibetan national uprising day, the spiritual leader appealed to the world to persuade Beijing to change its stance on Tibet.

The Dalai Lama, citing examples of prominent lamas who have fled China recently, said, "China's treatment of Tibet continues to evade the realities in Tibet. This approach is short-sighted and counterproductive. These policies are narrow-minded and reveal the ugly face of political insecurity." Ugyen Thinley Dorjee, the 17th Karmapa and head of Kagyu Sect of Tibetan Buddhism, and Agya Rinpoche, head of the Kumbum Monastery in Tibet, both fled China recently. Accusing China of cultural genocide in Tibet, the Dalai Lama said there is a lack of political will and courage to address the issue of Tibet sensibly and pragmatically through dialogue.

Regretting China's attitude to himself, the Dalai Lama reiterated in his statement that he is not seeking separation, but "genuine autonomy" for the Tibetans, which will not only ensure the preservation of their culture and environment but also lead to stability and unity in China. While reiterating his commitment to a dialogue with China, the Dalai Lama appealed to the world for support for a peaceful resolution of the Tibetan problem. India, which recognizes Tibet as an autonomous region of China, has been the home of the Dalai Lama since he fled Tibet in 1959 after a failed uprising against Chinese authorities. India is also home to thousands of Tibetan refugees and the seat of a Tibetan government-in-exile.

CHINA VS. THE DALAI LAMA

On the 50th anniversary of his escape to India, the exiled 14th Dalai Lama stands as a bigger challenge than ever for China, as underscored by Beijing's stepped-up vilification campaign against him and its admission that it is now locked in a "life and death struggle" over Tibet. Traveling incognito, the Dalai Lama, then 24, crossed over into India on March 30, 1959, after a harrowing, 13-day trek through the Tibetan highlands with a small band of aides and family members. His arrival became public only the following day. Since then, he has come to symbolize one of the longest and most-powerful resistance movements in modern world history. Chinese rule over Tibet has created, as he put it recently, "hell on Earth."

Little surprise Beijing now treats the iconic Dalai Lama as its Enemy No. 1, with its public references to him matching the crudeness and callousness of its policies in Tibet, where it has tried everything — from Tibet's cartographic dismemberment and rewriting history, to ethnically drowning Tibetans through large-scale Han migration and systematically undermining Tibetan institutions. Unnerved that the Dalai Lama's soft power has stood up to its untrammeled power, China today has taken to haranguing propaganda while enforcing a security lockdown across an increasingly restive Tibetan region, half of which it has hived off from Tibet and merged with Qinghai, Gansu, Sichuan and Yunnan provinces.

With the Dalai Lama having parlayed his international moral standing into an indomitable influence over global public opinion, a desperate Beijing has had to fall back more and more on Cultural Revolution language. Consider one of China's recent outbursts against its nemesis: "A jackal in Buddhist monk's robes, an evil spirit with a human face and the heart of a beast. We are engaged in a fierce battle of blood and fire with the Dalai clique." The Dalai Lama gave up his demand for Tibet's independence more than two decades ago, yet the Chinese propaganda machine still brands him a "splittist" and Premier Wen Jiabao demands he renounce separatist activities, as if China holds a historically and legally incontestable entitlement to Tibet.

The more Beijing has sought to isolate the Dalai Lama internationally, the deeper a thorn he has become in its side. Recently, China bullied its largest African trading partner, South Africa, into barring the Dalai Lama from attending a peace conference in Johannesburg. Yet it faced major embarrassment when the European Parliament and the U.S. House of Representatives passed separate resolutions on Tibet, with the former calling for "real autonomy for Tibet" and the latter demanding Beijing "lift immediately the harsh policies imposed on Tibetans." Both legislatures backed the Dalai Lama's initiative for a durable political solution to the Tibet issue. The Dalai Lama was lucky he fled Tibet in the nick of time before China made him a prisoner. In 1956, when he had traveled to India to participate in the celebrations on the 2,500th anniversary of the Buddha's Enlightenment, the Sinophile Indian prime minister, Jawaharlal Nehru, convinced him to return to Lhasa, although the Dalai Lama's advisers feared for his safety. But after his return, conditions in Tibet began to deteriorate relentlessly.

Had he not escaped from the Chinese-guarded Norbulingka Palace in Lhasa on March 17, 1959, disguised as a Tibetan soldier, the Dalai Lama may have met the same fate as the 11th Panchen Lama, who disappeared in 1995 soon after he was anointed at the age of 6. The March 10, 1959, Tibetan mass uprising indeed was triggered by popular fears that the Dalai Lama would be kidnapped after he was asked to come to a Chinese army-camp event without bodyguards. The uprising was harshly suppressed in a yearlong bloodbath. And in the period since, more than more than a million Tibetans reportedly have lost their lives due to official Chinese policies.

In exile, the Dalai Lama has helped keep the Tibetan movement alive and preserved Tibetan language and culture by establishing a network of schools. The transition of the Tibetan government-in-exile to democratically elected executive and legislative branches ought to serve as an example for the autocrats in Beijing. Instead, having turned Tibetans into state serfs under its rule, the communist dictatorship observed a national holiday last Saturday for belatedly discovering that it "emancipated" Tibetans from serfdom through Tibet's conquest.

Had the Dalai Lama not managed to slip away in 1959, China would have installed an impostor Dalai Lama long ago, in the same way it has instated its own Panchen Lama in place of the official appointee it abducted. But now it has no choice but to wait for the exiled Dalai Lama to pass away before it can orchestrate any sham. To frustrate Beijing's plans, the present Dalai Lama needs to publicly lay down clear rules on succession.

In fact, it was the long, 17-year gap between the 1933 death of the 13th Dalai Lama and the November 1950 assumption of full temporal powers by the present incumbent at the age of 15, after the Chinese invasion already had started, that cost Tibet its freedom. The hurried installation of the Dalai Lama in political office could not stop China from completing its conquest of Tibet. A similar long gap in succession and grooming now could strike a devastating blow to the Tibetan cause to regain autonomy. That is why it has become imperative to clarify the rules to choose the 15th Dalai Lama, including whether he is to be discovered in the free world and not in Chinese-controlled Tibet, as the current incumbent had earlier suggested. Another issue that needs to be sorted out is whether the present Karmapa Lama, the third-ranking Tibetan spiritual leader who fled to India in late 1999, can fill in as an unofficial, transitional successor to the Dalai Lama.

For India, Tibet is the core issue with China, which became its neighbour owing not to geography but to guns – by gobbling up the traditional buffer. The recent congressional resolution recognized India for its "generosity" in playing host to the Dalai Lama and Tibetan refugees. But this is more than just munificence: The Dalai Lama is India's biggest strategic asset because without him, the country would be poorer by several military divisions against China. India thus has a major stake in the succession issue, including in overseeing the training and education of the heir.

TERROR AT DOORSTEP; PM TELLS FORCES TO STAY ALERT

Prime Minister Manmohan Singh has virtually sounded the Code Red in the ongoing anti-terror alert, asking the armed forces to be vigilant since the situation in the Afghanistan-Pakistan region was spiralling out of control.

"There are regular intelligence reports of imminent attacks in the country. This is a matter of deep concern, and there is no room for complacency," said the PM, addressing the top military brass at the annual combined commanders' conference.

"The terrorist attack on our embassy in Kabul on October 8, 2009 is yet another grim reminder of the forces we are pitted against. The overall situation in our immediate neighbourhood has worsened since I last spoke to you," he added. The fast-deteriorating situation in the Af-Pak region, which has become a revival ground for Taliban, in fact, came in for special mention during a conference.

This comes just a day after defence minister A K Antony held the situation was "very serious" in Pakistan, where extremists have unleashed a spate of attacks on governmental forces and targets, including one on the Army headquarters at Rawalpindi. Army chief General Deepak Kapoor, too, said the threat of a terror spill-over into India was a clear and present one. The Indian security forces, he added, were, however, geared towards giving "a befitting reply" to the Taliban if "they try to carry out destructive activities in our country".

This comes in the backdrop of Pakistan Taliban chief Hakimullah Mehsud threatening to dispatch terrorists to fight India once an Islamic state had been created in Pakistan. The PM, on his part, said the "horrific" 26/11 terror attacks on Mumbai had confirmed "our worst fears" about the lethal dimensions of terrorism and non-traditional threats to India's security.

"There are both State (read Pakistan) and non-State actors involved in the business of terrorism. India is a democracy and an open society and is, therefore, sometimes highly vulnerable," he added. India needs to improve its defensive mechanisms against all forms of terrorism, asymmetric warfare and aggravated militancy. "The armed forces must be fully-equipped to deal with all threat scenarios," he said. "Our troops should be trained to fight anywhere, anytime and under any conditions. Their ability to deal with non-traditional threats must receive greater attention," he added.

Talks of Vigilance Against China, but Remarks 'Censored'

On a day when China once again needled India, PMO apparently decided discretion was the better part of valour. PM Manmohan Singh did dwell on the need for greater vigilance vis-a-vis China during his address to the top military brass, but all references to the country were censored out in the "extracts" of his speech later released to the media.This indicator of the continuing ultra-defensive mindset vis-a-vis China came even though PM himself, as one senior military officer put if, did not say "anything earth shattering".

All that PM stated was that India needed to remain vigilant and take necessary steps to bolster developmental work along the Sino-Indian border, in a reference to China's massive build-up of military infrastructure along LAC. "PM also talked about the 'complex relationship' India had with China. He said there was an ongoing process to resolve border issues with China but that it would take sometime."

DALAI LAMA'S VISIT ON OR OFF? DHARAMSALA WON'T COMMENT

Caught in a storm between India and China, the Dalai Lama's office in Dharamsala appeared unsure about his proposed visit to Arunachal Pradesh in November. The organisers did not give out a schedule of his visit and said they wouldn't comment on it either.

Soon after Beijing expressed its "firm opposition" to the Dalai Lama's trip to Arunachal Pradesh, the Tibetan leader's secretary, Chimme Choekyappa, told from Dharamsala: "There are reports in newspapers about his visit. Please read them. And please do not force me to speak on it." A top MEA source told in Delhi, "India has made its position amply clear.

The only restriction from our side is that no Tibetan should carry out any anti-China activity from Indian soil. As far as Dalai Lama is concerned, he is free to visit any part of the country."

AFTER TOUGH LINE ON PM'S VISIT, CAUTION MAY RULE IN DALAI CASE

The intensity of Chinese statements on Arunachal Pradesh has led to a feeling in a section of the government that it might have been a bad idea to break from recent practice to clear Tibetan spiritual leader Dalai Lama's visit to Tawang monastery in 2009. Though the government has stuck to its position that the Dalai

Lama was free to travel to any part of India and this included Tawang, the bite in Beijing's pronouncements indicates testing diplomacy closer to when the leader visits Tawang in Nov. 2009. Another welter of statements can be expected unless some damage control works.

Those privy to official thinking agree that the harsh manner in which Prime Minister Manmohan Singh's visit to Arunachal Pradesh was criticised did take India by surprise. Though the Chinese have "objected" to the PM or other senior leaders visiting Arunachal Pradesh earlier as well, the unambiguous criticism of India for "overreaching" itself was noted.

The "advice" in write ups that India could not expect to become a power without resolving issues with both China and Pakistan has led to an assessment that a more cautious approach could have been warranted. All the more so as stirs in Xinjian and Tibet have heightened China's sensitivities. "In a closed state, there is a sense of paranoia as well," a source said. It was still not clear how far the Chinese were prepared to bump up the boundary dispute with India. There might be descalation, but this was far from clear as yet. The war of words has only showed up how badly India lags in border infrastructure in Arunachal Pradesh and underlines what some feel was an error in provoking China. "We need to at least match 50% of what China is doing before we up the ante," an official felt.

Not allowing Dalai Lama to proceed to Tawang — a major seat of Tibetan Buddhism with its abbots being appointed by Lhasa till 1950 — would have been problematic. It could have been a factor in the Arunachal elections and on a larger scale attracted the charge of bowing to Chinese pressure. But it would have been not very different from last year when a similar decision was taken. And it would not end up highlighting the asymetry at the Line of Actual Control. As government sources admit, India's efforts to build roads and improve mobility are likely to take time. There was no point in stepping on Chinese toes at a time when the dragon state's responses due to its recent internal troubles were not wholly predictable. And though current tensions with China could subside, a likely meeting between Singh and his

Chinese counterpart Wen Jiabao at the sidelines of the ASEAN meet next month might need skilful negotiating.

There has been criticism that not enough attention was being paid to foreign policy making as moves were not being "thought through". This was painfully evident in the case of the Sharm el-Sheikh joint statement with Pakistan and it has showed up in dealings with China. To now ask the Dalai Lama to defer his visit would be embarrassing and invite domestic scorn. But short of that efforts were needed to assuage the Chinese. It now seems clear that statements by senior government figures downplaying Chinese intrusions as media creations were a defensive response as there was concern that Beijing's belligerence would not be easy to match. The irony lay in government being largely correct that there was actually no increase in intrusions. But as things turned out, the disclaimers did not pacify China.

5 China : Demonstration of Strength at 60

CHINA'S 60-YEAR RISE IN WORLD STAGE

Military and civilian marchers accompanied by floats turned Tian'anmen Square into a scene of joyous celebration here as China celebrated the 60th birthday of the People's Republic. Leading the mass pageant was the formation presenting the national flag and national emblem; 1,949 young men held up and escorted the flag, the largest-yet displayed during China's national day parades in Tian'anmen. The flag weighs about 150 kilograms and covers nearly 600 square metres, bigger than a basketball court.

In succession, four giant portraits of late Chinese leader Chairman Mao Zedong, chief architect of China's economic reform Deng Xiaoping, former President Jiang Zemin and incumbent Hu Jintao, were carried through the square escorted by some 36,000 marchers. The leaders' voices recorded at significant historical moments, from Mao's proclamation of the founding of the central government to Hu's calling for the building of a comprehensive well-off society, were replayed during the procession.

The portraits were accompanied by floats featuring different themes, including "self-reliance" for the Mao period, "reform and opening-up" for Deng's era, Jiang's "three represents" and Hu's "scientific development". China's early leaders, especially Mao, are still well remembered by the public. A new portrait of Mao replaced an old one hanging over the gate of the Tian'anmen rostrum before National Day.

Opposite the square was a newly erected portrait of Dr. Sun Yat-sen, a forerunner of the Chinese democratic revolution. The two great men fixed their eyes upon the joyous crowds and the once-in-a-decade celebration. Deng was most renowned for masterminding the reform and opening-up drive, which saved China from an economic breakdown after the chaotic 10-year Cultural Revolution (1966-1976) and ushered an amazing economic development that earned respect from the world.

In Jiang's period, he proposed the important thought of "three represents", requiring the Communist Party of China to always represent the development requirements of China's advanced social productive forces, the progressive course of China's advanced culture and the fundamental interests of the overwhelming majority of the Chinese people. While the portrait of Hu Jintao filed past the centre of the square, Hu's remark — "work hard to achieve new victories in building a moderately prosperous society in all respects and write a new chapter of a happy life for the people" — was broadcast. The remark was delivered at the Communist Party of China's (CPC) 17th National Congress on Oct 15, 2007, which endorsed the doctrine of Scientific Outlook on Development in the CPC's constitution and unveiled the party's determination to promote more coordinated development on the basis of social harmony, environmental protection and energy conservation in addition to economic expansion. Following the portrait phalanxes, or the first chapter of the civilian pageant, were 43,000 people from all walks of life and 19 floats, featuring China's achievements ranging from agriculture, industry to democracy, space programme, education, science and sports.

Earth-shaking changes have taken place in China since the government implemented the reform and opening-up drive. The agriculture formation reflected China's highly improved grain production capacity that feeds the 1.3 billion population. China has become the world's top producer of various kinds of farm products, with grain output hitting 528 million tonnes and poultry production topping 72.80 million tonnes in 2008.

The industry formation reminded people of how the moribund industrial sector survived the disastrous Cultural Revolution era and transformed into a powerful production force, that finally turned China into the world's workshop. The county, which had to import even a box of matches 60 years ago, is exporting goods from lighters to satellites all over the world. Formations featuring China's pursuit of clean energy and increasing efforts in environmental protection followed. Floats carrying sculptures of trains, airplanes and automobiles revealed the country's expanding traffic infrastructure and increasing demand for renewable energy to prevent severe environmental degradation.

Marchers in dark blue uniforms along with a float carrying a domestically-built rocket and a huge terrestrial globe illustrated China's ambitious space programme. China's first space walker Zhai Zhigang showed up on a float along with four colleagues who have entered space aboard the Shenzhou series of spaceships. Students from various universities, sports stars including famous hurdler Liu Xiang, legendary gymnast Li Ning and gold medallists of the 2008 Beijing Olympics were in other formations, showcasing achievements in education and sports.

The procession also recalled people's sadness about the devastating floods in 1998 and the 8-magnitude earthquake that mainly hit Sichuan Province last year, but also highlighted Chinese people's indomitable spirit in overcoming difficulties. A total of 8,500 marchers and 34 floats then filed along Chang'an Avenue, featuring the accomplishments and unique character of 31 mainland regions and Hong Kong, Macao and Taiwan.

The Taiwan float, carrying some sculptures of landmark constructions and two miniature airplanes flying from each side of a rainbow, highlighted the improved cross-Strait relations between the Chinese mainland and the island, which began direct air and sea transport links and postal services at the end of last year. In the final part of the civilian pageant, the Chapter of the Future, thousands of children and Young Pioneers and a simulated boat passed the Tian'anmen rostrum. With 60,000 doves of peace and numerous coloured balloons released into the sky, the child marchers surged toward the Golden Water Bridge at the north of Tian'anmen Square, bringing the parade to a climax.

State leaders standing on the Tian'anmen rostrum waved to the cheering audience and performers in the square. The mass military and civilian pageant lasted two and a half hours.

DEMONSTRATION OF MILITARY CAPABILITY

China's National Day military parade held no big surprises but there were tantalising clues for experts assessing the modernisation of the world's biggest fighting force. Many focused on the Dongfeng 21C missile, which could force U.S. aircraft carriers to keep a greater distance if it is successfully developed into an anti-ship ballistic missile (ASBM). That would make it harder for the United States to come to Taiwan's aid in the event of a conflict.

"The parade is a clear signal to Taiwan. The variety and quality of new arms on display has to be intimidating to Taiwan military officials," Wendell Minnick, Asia bureau chief for Defence News, said from Taipei. "China is basically saying to Taiwan independence advocates, 'forget it, you're going to lose'."

China views self-ruled Taiwan as a breakaway republic, to be retaken by force if necessary, although currently warming ties make an armed conflict less likely. "This missile is not completely developed yet but what we saw in the parade gives us a pretty good indication that they are reaching that capability," said Matthew Durnin, a Beijing-based researcher with the World Security Institute, adding that China still faces challenges in developing the integrated systems and satellites needed to properly guide an ASBM.

Beijing is modernising the military to rely more on advanced technology and less on the sheer manpower of its 2.3 million soldiers. But its increased defence spending has raised fears, especially in Washington and Tokyo, about a lack of transparency. "From the standpoint of a mutually beneficial strategic (relationship) and greater transparency in military spending... China should have a system so that ties can be friendly and peaceful," Japanese Chief Cabinet Secretary Hirofumi Hirano told a news conference in Tokyo.

Fighters, bombers and helicopters flew over central Beijing during the parade to the delight of citizens and also the national leaders on the podium. "China's aerospace industry, especially the fighters and bombers, has progressed slowly but still continues to be a bit of a weak point for China," Durnin said. "While parts of (the newest fighters) may have been developed in China they are still very dependent on Russian technology."

Washington may instead see a threat in the Dongfeng 31 intercontinental ballistic missile, or ICBM, which can be trucked around and is harder to target than silo-based missiles. "It's definitely a demonstration of strength for the Americans and Taiwanese," Minnick said of the parade.

But there were also clues in what wasn't shown. Some strategists had expected that China might display a submarine-launched, nuclear-capable ballistic missile, or a new, highest-range land-based ICBM known as the Dongfeng 41. "So I think that probably says we know these programmes are in development, we know they are close to fruition, they just probably weren't quite to the stage that China was comfortable or motivated to show them in the parade," Durnin said.

CHINA'S MILITARY MODERNIZATION: ITS IMPLICATION

The People's Liberation Army (PLA) is on course to become the most significant military force in East Asia after the United States within the next decade, by modernizing to create a military capable of defeating regional forces and credible enough to deter intervention by outside forces. As China expands its area of operations, U.S. and PLA forces will come into contact with increasing frequency, which makes continued U.S.-China strategic consultation critical to avoid accidental confrontations. Larry Wortzel of the U.S.-China Economic and Security Review Commission and David Finkelstien, Director of the Chinese Studies Centre at the CNA Corporation, offered their assessments of China's military modernization and the threat it poses to the United States and Asia in the third of Carnegie's China policy debates. Carnegie senior associate Michael Swaine moderated the event.

Contingencies and Capabilities

The first Gulf War "shocked the PLA into confronting the

stark reality that it was incapable of fighting twentieth-century warfare," according to Finkelstein. In 1993 the PLA embarked on a holistic modernization program designed to develop the capabilities necessary for the small, high-technology conflicts typical of the latest generation of warfare.

The PLA also designed its modernization program to prepare for several contingencies. Open-source data indicate that China is preparing for possible conflict with the United States, potentially over Taiwan, and is also focused on being able to defeat Taiwan.

Wortzel argued that China is close to achieving that goal and is capable of dominating the militaries of other Asian powers (excepting Japan). The fact that the United States treats China as an enemy in its strategic planning is a driver of Chinese military planning, according to Wortzel.

Implications for the United States

The potential for miscalculation and misreading of intent are the biggest threats to the PLA and the U.S. armed forces, and as the PLA expands its area of control into parts of the Pacific to which the U.S. has traditionally had unfettered access the potential will increase. Confidence-building measures and regular defence consultations are the best way to reduce the threat posed by the PLA.

However, Wortzel and Finkelstein agreed that as long as China's decision-making process remains opaque the United States must maintain a sufficient deterrent. The U.S. should also ensure that allies are not selling sensitive military technology to the PLA. Both participants stressed that while the PLA is preparing for scenarios in which they could engage with the U.S. military, conflict is far from inevitable, given the deep economic and strengthening political ties between the two countries.

Continued military-to-military exchange is crucial to preventing an arms race and to reduce the likelihood of unintentionally igniting a security crisis. Each side should make clear what actions will lead to conflict.

CHINA TO PARADE ITS NEW AND IMPROVED ARSENAL

The government's 60th-anniversary event will showcase military technology, most of which was made in China. Beijing dislikes its army's image as a poorly equipped force of rural enlistees.

Military vehicles park near Tiananmen Square during a rehearsal for a parade marking the 60th anniversary of the People's Republic of China. (Nelson Ching / Bloomberg / September 18, 2009)

Reporting from Beijing-For the first time in a decade, Beijing on Thursday will showcase its latest armored vehicles, ballistic missiles and fighter jets in a demonstration of military ambition meant to befit the nation's economic rise. The display of hardware — part of the government's 60th anniversary celebrations — will no doubt stoke national pride. But it's also a chance for China to show an international audience that the world's third-largest economy is investing heavily in military technology, a strategic sector that Beijing believes will strengthen its regional security and global influence.

Expected to be on display is a new generation of missiles that could potentially strike American naval ships and pound

Taiwanese soil from the Chinese mainland. It is the product of two decades of enhanced military spending aimed at overhauling a woefully inefficient and technologically challenged fighting force. "They have been focusing on catching up in areas where the technological disparity has been the greatest, and cultivating pockets of excellence within" the People's Liberation Army, said David Yang, a political scientist at Rand Corp. "That said, the PLA is a massive, even ponderous, organization, and its professionalization and modernization will remain an arduous process for years."

With 2.3 million members, the Chinese army is the largest standing army in the world. Beijing has spent years trying to overcome the army's long-held image as a poorly equipped force consisting mostly of rural enlistees. The army lacks combat experience, having last engaged in a major conflict in 1979 with Vietnam. Earlier this year, officials announced heavy recruitment of college graduates. More important, Beijing has increased military spending each year by double-digit percentages. China's official military budget was $70.3 billion this year, up sharply from $14.6 billion in 2000, according to Washington-based GlobalSecurity.org.

Chinese state media have trumpeted the fact that almost all the new weaponry to be unveiled at the parade was domestically produced, a major leap from the days when China was almost totally reliant upon the Soviet Union for sophisticated armaments. China's fighting capabilities were not nearly as advanced 10 years ago, the last time the country celebrated its national anniversary with a military parade. "This year's display should signal a more balanced relationship between military might and economic development with the showing off of a range of new equipment that is at least one to two generations more advanced," said Tai Ming Cheung, a Chinese military expert at UC San Diego.

Regional powers including Japan, South Korea and India are undoubtedly paying attention. China's military policy traditionally has been focused on preventing Taiwan from achieving formal independence. But China has become an active weapons exporter, and watchdogs including Amnesty International have criticized it for supplying arms to countries with poor human rights records such as Sudan and Myanmar. With its expansion onto the global stage, China feels more empowered to secure its borders and defend its shipping routes carrying oil supplies, analysts said. Beijing has also bristled at American surveillance activity off its coast, resulting in standoffs this year.

"A threat is really two parts: capability and intentions," said Mark Stokes, executive director of the Project 2049 Institute, which promotes international security. "We're learning about China's capability. Intentions are not clear at this point." Chinese military officials have sought to downplay suggestions that the country is engaging in saber rattling by parading its military arsenal. "A country's military ability is not a threat to anyone. What is important is its military policy," Gen. Gao Jianguo said.

Part of that growing ability to be showcased will be the Dong Hai 10 cruise missile, a land attack weapon; the Dong Feng 31, an intercontinental ballistic missile capable of hitting Washington with a nuclear warhead; and the Dong Feng 21, designed in part to be able to knock out U.S. ships defending Taiwan. In total, 108 missiles are scheduled to roll past the rostrum at Tiananmen Square during the 66-minute parade. They will be complemented by 5,000 soldiers and 150 aircraft, including an "early warning and control" aircraft to detect enemy planes, as well as China's latest-generation J-10 fighter jets.

The technology has proved to be a moneymaker, leading some observers to believe the showcase involves an element of marketing. China sold $264 million worth of its military aircraft last year to allies such as Pakistan, according to the Stockholm International Peace Research Institute. China was the world's ninth-largest arms exporter last year, with $468 million in sales, according to the institute. That pales in comparison with the $6.1 billion sold by the U.S. in 2008. China's sales could be higher, however, because of unreported sales of arms and military technology.

Over the summer, residents of Beijing were given a preview of this week's parade. Streets were periodically shut down and some pockets of airspace temporarily closed to commercial aircraft to allow tanks, planes and helicopters to rehearse. On a recent weekday, Zhuang Yu, a 21-year-old tourist from Shaanxi province, was watching video of past military parades at a Chinese Communist Party memorabilia store located at the entrance of a public toilet at the southwest end of Tiananmen Square. "The news of this year's parade makes you feel like the country is becoming stronger," she said. "Maybe foreigners get nervous when they see so many soldiers and tanks. But I think it makes most Chinese feel safer."

CHINA MILITARY POWER IS STILL HIDDEN

President Hu Jintao called for even stronger armed forces as China flexed its muscles in a National Day parade, but experts said the PLA's marching skills might exceed actual fighting ability. Illustrating the importance China attaches to its growing military strength, the People's Liberation Army kicked off a dazzling celebration in Beijing of the nation's 60th birthday by showing off a range of home-grown weaponry.

China has boasted that the nuclear-capable missiles, fighter jets, aerial drones and other advanced arms on display mark a "quantum leap" made possible thanks to a long-running campaign to upgrade the once-backward PLA. Hu hailed this push in a speech to a packed Tiananmen Square, ahead of the massive military parade. "The PLA... must carry forward their glorious tradition, build up military strength and perform their duties earnestly," he said.

Official media gushed after the parade about the "cutting-edge" arms that have caused concern overseas about Beijing's military intentions, but analysts noted China had far to go before it could truly project military power abroad. "We can make absolutely no conclusions about the actual tactical abilities of the troops or the capabilities of the equipment from what we have seen," Dennis J. Blasko, a former US military attache to China, told AFP. "The fact that nothing broke down en route and all marchers completed the parade is admirable, but does not speak to tactical capabilities," he said.

Blasko noted one apparent advancement — the intercontinental ballistic missiles which state-run Xinhua news agency described as a military "trump card" were now on mobile launchers. "The key is its mobility, thus improving its survivability and insuring a true second-strike capability," he said. But aside from hardware such as the Jian-10 fighter jet, much of what was seen on Thursday represented upgrades or variations on weapons seen in the 50th anniversary parade in 1999, he said.

However, the array of home-grown systems showed China was making clear progress in moving away from its long-term reliance on Russian arms purchases, experts said. And the mix of ground, naval and air force components showed the PLA – which encompasses all those branches – was growing more diverse.

"The era of a 'heavy' PLA is over. A lighter, more diversified and capable military able to complete various missions was on display," a Western diplomat well-versed in military issues, who spoke on condition of anonymity, told AFP.

Chinese Defence Minister Liang Guanglie boasted last month that much of his nation's weaponry now rivals that included in Western arsenals, but analysts said China has much to do before it comes close to challenging American power. "Despite rapid strides in military modernisation, China still has a lot of catching up to do," said Minxin Pei, a China scholar at the Washington-based Carnegie Endowment for International Peace. "Most of its neighbours, including Japan, India, South Korea, and Taiwan, have more advanced and better-trained air forces and navies than it does," he said in a research note.

China also is believed to possess too few of some systems, such as major missiles, for them to be significant in strategic terms in the near term. "This was a demonstration of what China knows how to do but this is just a show – the entire military is not equipped with what we saw this morning," said the Western diplomat.

AS CONCEPT OF DETERRENCE

The difference between amateur and professional PLA watchers became very clear; while it was called the April 23rd

PLAN Naval Review to mark the 60th anniversary of the founding of China's People's Liberation Army (PLA) Navy as a "dog and pony" show, Lt Col (Ret) Dennis Blasko used this opportunity to clearly the Chinese concept of deterrence and to address some of the misconceptions out there.

The following is a bio of Col Blasko. Mr. Dennis J. Blasko served 23 years in the U.S. Army as a Military Intelligence Officer and Foreign Area Officer specializing in China. Mr. Blasko was an army attaché in Beijing from 1992-1995 and in Hong Kong from 1995-1996. He served in infantry units in Germany, Italy, and Korea and in Washington at the Defence Intelligence Agency, Headquarters Department of the Army (Office of Special Operations), and the National Defence University War Gaming and Simulation Centre. Mr. Blasko is a graduate of the United States Military Academy and the Naval Postgraduate School and has written numerous articles and chapters on the Chinese military and defence industries. He is the author of The Chinese Army Today: Tradition and Transformation for the 21st Century.

PURPOSE OF POWER DEMONSTRATION

Martin McCauley writes: The Chinese Navy was on parade in the waters off Qingdao on Wednesday. It was held to commemorate the 60 anniversary of the founding of the country's Navy. It was also the first in a series of military parades in honour of the 60 anniversary of the founding of the People's Republic that would be celebrated on October 1. On that day Chinese ground and air forces would take part in a spectacular show of strength. The naval parade was intended to demonstrate to the world the might of the Chinese navy. The most advanced ships and naval aircraft were on display. Two state of the art destroyers that had participated in the international operation against pirates off the coast of Somalia were there a well. Naval units from foreign countries also contributed to the celebrations. The intention is to impress foreign observers and that was certainly achieved.

Military parades are part of China's strategy to demonstrate its ability to defend itself. The aim is to reveal to potential aggressors that if attacked China would rebuff and defeat them. Deterring wars is just as important as fighting them. Military might is not the only element which makes up successful deterrence. The size of the territory, population, economic weight and political and social stability are important parts of what is called 'comprehensive national power'.

Deterrence can either be offensive or defensive. The former forces the opponent to accede to Chinese demands without going to war. The latter is to convince opponents that if they attack they will fail and the costs of such actions will be too high. Present policies being pursued to maintain the integrity of the territory and to prevent Taiwan, for instance, from becoming independent are clearly elements of offensive deterrence. The precepts of deterrence were laid down in 1936 by Mao Zedong, who maintained that only offensive deterrence was acceptable to the Chinese. It consists of various strands. One is to possess the requisite military forces; another is to have the willpower to use them; and it must be made clear to those being deterred that China has the military power and is willing to use it.

The naval parade off Qingdao and the fortcoming military parades in Beijing on October 1 are supposed to demonstrate to the world how rapidly the Chinese armed forces have modernised. One drawback, however, is that the impressive display of military hardware reveals very little about the ability of the armed forces to use the new weapons. In this respect the US military are at a great advantage. Fighting wars in Iraq and Afghanistan reveal the technical competence or otherwise of the men and equipment. It also allows the US to develop and test more modern weapons and tactics. Critical to success is intelligence gathering and the use of information technology in combat.

Washington is near the stage where it does not need to use nuclear weapons to achieve its objectives. It is developing devastatingly destructive conventional arms to do the job. All the Chinese military can do is to gather as much intelligence as possible about these new weapons. Then it has to develop similar weapons to deter the US from attacking China. The parades are also held to boost national pride in the eyes of the general public. They are as well a warning to separatists and those who seek to weaken the Chinese state that they are fighting a losing battle. An important objective is to weaken the desire of the people of Taiwan for independence. The aim is so to impress them with China's might that they will request unification with the Middle Kingdom. A tall order but nonetheless an important goal for Beijing. The next stage is to develop deterrence in space. China is only just embarking on his demanding task. One Chinese specialist has even written that the technological gap between China and the United States may be unbridgeable. What China needs are space weapons which will deter a potential aggressor. Winning a space war is quite a different matter. Hence the spate of military parades has two main objectives: to reveal how powerful China is and to intimidate all potential aggressors. China has to be careful not to revel too much in martial glory. It might lead its neighbours to perceive China as a growing threat to their own security. So Beijing has to tread a fine line and attempt to convince everyone that its armed might will not be used abroad. They are only for domestic defence. Will everyone believe this?

MILITARY PARADES DEMONSTRATE CHINESE CONCEPT OF DETERRENCE

Chinese warship in Qingdao

On April 23rd the People's Liberation Army (PLA) Navy had conducted a "naval parade" in the waters off of Qingdao. This naval review was celebrated the 60th anniversary of the establishment of the PLA Navy and honor in advance the 60th anniversary of the founding of the People's Republic of China, which itself was feted in Beijing on October 1st by another military parade primarily composed of ground and air units. For those impressed by military hardware, April 23rd should be a memorable day.

Like the Beijing parade, the event in Qingdao aims to promote Chinese national pride in its armed forces. It was intended to display the progress made by the PLA Navy in its on-going modernization. Surely the most advanced ships and aircraft in the Chinese Navy participated in front of an audience comprised of both Chinese and foreign observers. The two destroyers that took part in the PLA Navy's first long-distance, extended operational deployment to combat piracy off the Somali coast may be part of the review. Naval units from other countries, as well as senior foreign officers, have been invited to attend and participate.

Unspoken by Beijing during the build up to this event, however, is the parade's contribution to China's military strategy. The role of military reviews and foreign visits is openly identified in PLA doctrine as an important component of China's strategic deterrence posture. Contrary to the notion that China's strategic intentions are not transparent, the PLA's multi-level deterrence strategy has been enumerated in numerous military newspaper or journal articles, official publications such as White Papers, and, in particular, in the PLA Academy of Military Science's textbook, The Science of Military Strategy, first published in Chinese in 2001 and then translated into English in 2005.

China's Concept of Deterrence: What is it?

The most recent foreign analysis that mentions China's deterrence posture focuses on its nuclear deterrence policy (China Brief, March 4). In fact, while nuclear deterrence is an important element of China's deterrence strategy, the PLA's concept of deterrence is much more expansive. The Science of Military Strategy defines deterrence as "the military conduct of a state or political group in (1) displaying force or showing the determination to use force (2) to compel the enemy to submit to one's volition and (3) to refrain from taking hostile actions or escalating the hostility". Strategic deterrence also "is a major means for attaining the objective of military strategy". By its nature, deterrence seeks to change "the pattern of the opponent's psychology".

According to The Science of Military Strategy, "Warfighting and deterrence are two major functions of the armed forces". Therefore, the mission of the Chinese armed forces is not only to be prepared to fight wars, but also to deter or prevent their outbreak. Specifically, the role of China's strategic deterrence is "to deter foreign invasion, defend the sovereignty, rights and interests, and to deter the conspiracies of internal and external rivals for separating and subverting China, so as to protect the stability of national political situation, defend territorial integrity and national unification".

In addition to the military component, non-military factors such as territory size, population, economic strength, political and diplomatic efforts, all of which make up "comprehensive national power," contribute to strategic deterrence strength. These concepts have also been explained in Beijing's series of White Papers on National Defence. For example, the 2008 edition of the White Paper states: "[China's military strategic guideline of active defence] lays stress on deterring crises and wars. It works for close coordination between military struggle and political, diplomatic, economic, cultural and legal endeavors, strives to foster a favourable security environment, and takes the initiative to prevent and defuse crises, and deter conflicts and wars. It strictly adheres to a position of self-defence, exercises prudence in the use of force, seeks to effectively control war situations, and strives to reduce the risks and costs of war. It calls for the building of a lean and effective deterrent force and the flexible use of different means of deterrence".

Deterrence can be adopted by those in a strategically offensive posture or those on the strategic defensive. The former pursue deterrence for the purpose of compelling the opponent to submit to their demands without going to war, while the latter seek to make the "opponent feel his attack may fail or lead to the loss outweighing the gain". China officially adopts a strategic defensive posture in the international arena; concurrently, it is arguable that the Chinese government pursues a strategically offensive form of deterrence toward perceived threats to domestic stability or national unification.

While China's strategic posture is defensive in nature and seeks to deter conflict, The Science of Military Strategy acknowledges the objective of strategic deterrence "is attained by non-fighting means or fighting a small war" to prevent a larger one. China's military doctrine is not passive at the tactical and operational levels of war and the PLA fully understands the decisive nature of the offensive. Even in a strategically defensive posture, "[t]he strategy to gain mastery by striking only after the enemy has struck does not mean waiting for enemy's strike passively... [Striking only after the enemy has struck] doesn't mean to give up the 'advantageous chances' in campaign [operational] or tactical operations, for 'the first shot' on the plane of politics and strategy must be differentiated from 'the first shot' on the plane of tactics ... if any country or organization violates the other country's sovereignty and territorial integrity, the other side will have the right to 'fire the first shot' on the plane of tactics".

These precepts, which are part of the PLA's strategic guidelines, are consistent with the "active defence" principles described by Mao Zedong in 1936: "the only real defence is active defence, defence [sic] for the purpose of counter-attacking and taking the offensive. As far as I know, there is no military manual of value nor any sensible military expert, ancient or modern, Chinese or foreign, that does not oppose passive defence, whether in strategy or tactics".

DETERRENCE: ITS ELEMENTS

The Science of Military Strategy describes three components necessary for deterrence:

- Possession of "an adequate deterrent force," a force that is both capable and credible;
- The determination to use that force;
- Communication "between the deterrer and the deterred" to assure that the opponent perceives and believes in the credibility of that force and the will to use it.

A capable force is the foundation of deterrence. The PLA's modernization program, particularly the developments over the past 10 years, has resulted in a much more capable force than its predecessor of previous decades. Today, the PLA sees its "core military capability" to be "winning local wars in conditions of informationization" with the secondary goal of conducting military operations other than war. As stated in The Science of Military Strategy, "Strategic deterrence is based on warfighting ... The more powerful the warfighting capability, the more effective the deterrence ... those making purely bluffing threats and intimidations hardly can afford deterrence ...". New equipment is a major part of the PLA's modernization, but even more important is the quality of its personnel, organization and force structure, training, and logistics. While many improvements in capabilities have been achieved, the PLA recognizes numerous challenges as it continues its modernization process.

The willingness to use military capabilities must be communicated and the opponent must comprehend China's capabilities and determination. The deterring side seeks to build "momentum" to convince others of its seriousness: "Demonstrating momentum by showing the disposition of the strength to the enemy is to display clearly one's deterrent force for bringing about psychological pressure on and fear to the opponent and thus force him to submit. Such deterrent forms as large-scale military review, joint military exercise, and military visit, etc., are usually adopted".

The naval review in Qingdao and the military parade in Beijing can be seen as demonstrations of momentum attained from military modernization and thus a contribution to China's deterrence strategy. While potentially impressive from a hardware point of view, these activities reveal little about the degree of competence the force has attained to actually employ these weapons according to the PLA's new warfighting doctrine or to sustain them in austere locations far from their home bases.

China's "Integrated Strategic Deterrence" Posture

The conventional military weapons and strategic nuclear

delivery systems on display off Qingdao and in Beijing in part are directed toward foreign audiences to assert China's ability to defend its borders and protect its sovereignty (including territories in dispute with others). They also are aimed at China's own population to illustrate the fruits of Beijing's investment in the military and at the same time remind "terrorist, separatist and extremist forces" that the Chinese Communist Party and China's armed forces seek to maintain stability and protect the population from chaos.

The Science of Military Strategy states, "China currently has a limited but effective nuclear deterrence and a relatively powerful capability of conventional deterrence and a massive capacity of deterrence of People's War". While its nuclear force seeks to deter nuclear attacks (or blackmail) against China, conventional capabilities are designed to deter, and if necessary defeat, threats to China's "national sovereignty, security, territorial integrity" and safeguard "the interests of national development". These missions include defence from aggression against the mainland and increasingly are concerned with missions beyond China's borders to protect a wide range of China's development interests.

Article 1 of China's Anti-secession Law extends the deterrence strategy to "the question of Taiwan" by "opposing and checking [i.e. deterrence of] Taiwan's secession from China by secessionists in the name of "Taiwan independence," promoting peaceful national reunification, maintaining peace and stability in the Taiwan Straits, preserving China's sovereignty and territorial integrity, and safeguarding the fundamental interests of the Chinese nation." Beijing consistently opposes any form of "outside interference" in regard to its objective of peaceful reunification and specifically disputes arms sales or military alliances with the island. Numerous warfighting capabilities developed over the past decade are aimed at deterring foreign (i.e. United States) intervention by air or at sea in the vicinity of Taiwan—some of which may be on display in Qingdao and Beijing.

At the same time, the People's Armed Police (a component of the Chinese armed forces, but not part of the PLA) is tasked "to deter and deal with emergencies which endanger public security". According to the National Defence Law of 1997, both the PLA and militia "may assist in maintaining public order in accordance with the law". The People's Armed Police routinely works with the civilian Ministry of Public Security police force as the first line of defence in domestic stability.

Finally, The Science of Military Strategy predicts "the day of employing deterrence of space force is not far off ...". Bao Shixiu, a senior fellow at the Academy of Military Science, wrote in 2007 after the Chinese anti-satellite test: "Currently, China does not have a clear space deterrence theory ... China's nuclear deterrence theory and its perspective on the use of nuclear weapons offer important and relevant guidelines .... The basic necessity to preserve stability through the development of deterrent forces as propounded by Mao and Deng remain valid in the context of space". Bao acknowledges the "technical gap, especially in the military area vis-à-vis the United States, is difficult if not impossible to fill" and concludes "if China owns space weapons, their number and quality will be limited in their capacity to act as an effective defence mechanism and will not be a threat to other countries".

Chinese military writings present both a professional and realistic evaluation of their strategic intentions, strategy and general capabilities. A multi-level deterrence posture is an integral element of PLA doctrine. It is likely much of the PLA's new equipment entering the force will be on display in the coming months for both Chinese and foreign eyes to see. What will be less visible is the degree to which the Chinese armed forces have been trained to operate and maintain its new weapons in accordance with a new joint doctrine that it has never executed against a hostile enemy.

Near the end of The Science of Military Strategy caution is recommended: "Therefore, imprudent decision to use force is never permitted.... The reason for the existence of the army is to prevent and win a war.... We may not launch a war in a hundred years but we can never be unprepared for war for even one day". The weapons featured in the parades in Beijing and off of Qingdao need to be assessed in the context of the PLA's modernization process, its strategy and doctrine, and threat environment.

6 China's Plan for Developing Defence Technologies by 2020

The Chinese government plans to enhance its capability to innovate, develop and rapidly supply new-generation weaponry over the next 15 years under a new national development program.

The outline of the development program of science and technology for national defence for 2006 to 2020 was passed by the Commission of Science, Technology and Industry for National Defence at a meeting on Thursday in Qingdao, east China's Shandong Province.

The outline states that national defence industry will focus on development of:

- new and high-tech weaponry;
- high-tech industries for both military and civilian purposes;
- manufacturing technologies for military industries;
- basic and frontier technologies for national defence;
- and guaranteeing technological innovation for national defence.

The outline stresses that the country will develope high and new tech weaponry to reinforce a mechanized and informaiton-based army. The coming 15 years will also see improvements in new technologies and their industrialization for both military and civilian use. The program will include new and high-technologies for the space industry, aviation, ship and marine engineering, nuclear energy and fuel, and information technology for both military and civilian purposes.

The outline says that China will upgrade its defence industry with digital technology. Special projects to be carried out include large aircraft, pressurized water reactor and high-temperature gas-cooled reactor nuclear power stations, manned space missions and lunar probe programs. According to the outline, the program will form a team of world-class experts in the research of key basic and frontier technologies, and a guaranteeing system will be created to support the work.

DEFENCE TECHNOLOGY

China is accelerating reform and innovation in its defence-related science, technology and industry, promoting strategic and specialization-oriented restructuring of defence industry enterprises, enhancing the capabilities of independent innovation in the R&D of weaponry and equipment, and striving to establish a new system of defence-related science, technology and industry which caters to both military and civilian needs, and channels military potential to civilian use.

Promoting Innovation in Structures and Mechanisms

To meet the needs of weaponry and equipment development, as well as development of the socialist market economy, China is constantly reforming its management system of defence-related science, technology and industry. According to the Plan for Restructuring the State Council passed by the First Session of the Eleventh National People's Congress in 2008, the Science, Technology and Industry Commission for National Defence of the People's Republic of China has been superseded by the State Administration of Science, Technology and Industry for National Defence.

In 2007, the State Council approved Some Opinions on Deepening the Reform of the Investment System of Science, Technology and Industry for National Defence, which explicitly proposes a new investment system featuring effective government regulation and control, participation of social capital, standardized intermediary services, vigorous supervision and management, and positive military-civilian interaction. As a result, an open development pattern for defence-related science, technology and industry is taking shape. The investment field has been further broadened, and investment structure further optimized. Ways of investment have been diversified to include not only direct investment, but also injection of capital and investment subsidies.

China is speeding up the transformation of the structures and mechanisms of the defence industry enterprises, and is in the initial stage of establishing a new system of defence-related science, technology and industry that features a small core, extensive cooperation and a large military potential reserve among civilians. Structural contradictions in defence-related science, technology and industry have been gradually and fundamentally solved through strategic restructuring and the streamlining of the main body of the defence industry. China is steadily promoting the transformation of defence industry enterprises into joint-stock enterprises, actively exploring approaches to diversifying the structure of property rights, giving priority on helping qualified competitive enterprises to be reorganized and listed on the stock market, and encouraging specialization-oriented restructuring and the integration of the efforts of enterprises, universities and research institutes. Relevant laws and regulations have been improved to standardize and supervise the process of reorganizing the defence industry enterprises and getting them listed on the stock market.

Improving the Weaponry and Equipment Research and Production System

Establishing a sound licensing system for weaponry and equipment research and production. In accordance with the Implementation Measures for Weaponry and Equipment Research and Production Licensing promulgated in May 2005, the defence-related science, technology and industry has adopted a licensing system for weaponry and equipment research and production featuring management of categorization. While maintaining state control over weaponry and equipment research and production, the document allows the non-public sector to enter this field and compete for research and production projects. In March 2008 the State Council and the CMC issued the Regulations on the Licensing Administration of Weaponry and Equipment Research and Production, further improving the system.

Enhancing the basic capabilities of weaponry and equipment research and production. Defence-related science, technology and industry are striving to enhance the informationization of weaponry and equipment design and development, and to render product design more digitalized, modularized, standardized and reliable. It has built digital simulation and hardware-in-the-loop(HIL) simulation facilities and a number of important advanced experimentation and demonstration facilities, which has resulted in a higher design capability and R&D success rate.

This sector has also increased final assembly and integration capabilities, and a number of key enterprises have realized systems integration of assembly, experimentation and testing. This has substantially raised core manufacturing capabilities by giving priority to resolving processing and technical issues in complex parts processing, precision manufacturing and special welding.

In addition, a number of large-scale basic experimentation facilities serving the entire industry have been constructed, as well as specialized testing and experimentation centres for reliability testing and burn-in screening of components and parts, and improved measures, standards and other basic support conditions for defence industries have been put in place. With the improvement of basic capabilities, a leapfrogging development in the ability to provide weaponry and equipment has been achieved.

Building a dynamic innovation system for defence-related science, technology and industry. The government has taken the lead to create a favourable environment for innovation and guide innovation activities through policies and investments.

With the research institutes and enterprises of the defence industry as the backbone and with institutes for basic research and institutions of higher learning as a vital new force, China is giving full play to the advantages of integrating enterprises, universities and research institutes, and making efforts to increase its capability for independent innovation in defence-related science, technology and industry.

To consolidate the foundation of human resources for the innovative development of defence-related science, technology and industry, both the national major projects of science and technology and important projects for defence scientific research and weaponry and equipment R&D have been taken as platforms to identify, cultivate, employ and attract talented people.

Enhancing Cooperation with Other Countries

Following the principles of mutual benefit and common development, China is conducting cooperation with foreign countries in defence-related science, technology and industry. It emphasizes exchanges and cooperation with developed countries in defence industry technology to draw on their experience in technological development and management.

It enhances mutually beneficial cooperation with developing countries, and engages in joint R&D and production in major cooperative projects, in accordance with the national conditions and specific requirements of the partners. On the export of military items, it adheres to the following principles: It should only serve the purpose of helping the recipient state enhance its capability for legitimate self-defence; it must not impair peace, security and stability of the relevant region or the world as a whole; and it must not be used to interfere in the recipient state's internal affairs.

China's defence-related science, technology and industry actively conduct cooperation with other countries in the field of hi-tech industries, combining military and civilian needs, and makes great efforts to develop hi-tech civilian products with high added value. Major breakthroughs have been made in developing the international market for space products.

China has exported its first satellite; and the earth resources satellite project with Brazil has played an important role in both countries' economic development. China has significantly enhanced its cooperation with other countries in aviation products and technologies, and made new headway in developing the international market for civil aircraft.

China's shipbuilding industry has exported products for civil use in series and batches, further increasing its share in the international market for such products.

ISSUE OF WHITE PAPER ON CHINA'S DEFENCE TECHNOLOGY

China is striving to establish a new system of defence-related science, technology and industry which caters to both military and civilian needs, according to a white paper issued. The white paper on China's National Defence in 2008, issued by the Information Office of the State Council, says China is accelerating reform and innovation in its defence-related science, technology and industry, promoting strategic and specialization-oriented restructuring of defence industry enterprises, enhancing the capabilities of independent innovation in the R&D of weaponry and equipment.

The paper says China will establish a licensing system for weaponry and equipment research and production. In accordance with the Implementation Measures for Weaponry and Equipment Research and Production Licensing promulgated in May 2005, the defence-related science, technology and industry has adopted a licensing system for weaponry and equipment research and production featuring management of categorization.

"While maintaining state control over weaponry and equipment research and production, the document allows the non-public sector to enter this field and compete for research and production projects," says the paper. In March 2008 the State Council and the CMC issued the Regulations on the Licensing Administration of Weaponry and Equipment Research and Production, further improving the system, says the paper.

The paper noted that China will enhance the basic capabilities of weaponry and equipment research and production. "Defence-related science, technology and industry are striving to enhance the informationization of weaponry and equipment design and development, and to render product design more digitalized, modularized, standardized and reliable," it says.

According to the paper, China is cooperating with foreign countries on defence-related technology following the principles of mutual benefit and common development. On the export of military items, it adheres to the following principles: It should only serve the purpose of helping the recipient state enhance its capability for legitimate self-defence; it must not impair peace, security and stability of the relevant region or the world as a whole; and it must not be used to interfere in the recipient state's internal affairs.

The paper says China's defence-related science, technology and industry conduct cooperation with other countries in the field of hi-tech industries and develop hi-tech civilian products with high added value. Major breakthroughs have been made in developing the international market for space products, it says. China has exported its first satellite; and the earth resources satellite project with Brazil has played an important role in both countries' economic development, according to the paper. The white paper, the sixth of its kind Chinese government issued since 1998, gives an overall picture of China's national defence ranging from the security environment, national defence policy, to defence expenditure and arms control.

MANNED SPACEFLIGHT PROJECT

Chinese astronaut Zhai Zhigang on EVA mission seen in the video grab taken on Sept. 27 carries a Chinese national flag to the space. (PLA Daily/Qiao Tianfu)

Manned spaceflight is the centralized embodiment of the technological capabilities and comprehensive power of a state. From the "Shenzhou I" space ship blasting off in 1999 to the extravehicular activity conducted by the astronaut of the "Shenzhou VII" space ship in 2008, China's manned spaceflight has realized 7 material breakthroughs in a short period of just 9 years. At 16:41 on September 27, 2008, Zhai Zhigang, astronaut of the "Shenzhou VII", successfully made the first space walk.

HIGH-TECH WEAPONS ADD WINGS TO THE CHINESE TROOPS

Weaponry and equipment are the important material and technological foundation on which the military strength of a country is built. There's no way to import truly key technologies and if a country wants to own them, it can only depend on its own innovations.

In mid-September,2009, in cooperation with brother naval aviation units and submarine troops, a support base of the South China Sea Fleet of the PLA Navy conducted an actual-troop and actual-equipment exercise under complex conditions.

The weapons and equipment with the new-type armed helicopter, the new-type main combat tank, the big-caliber self-propelled artillery, the heavy anti-tank missile, the new-type aerial defence missile and the self-propelled anti-aircraft artillery as the mainstay have formed the armament system of the PLA Army featured with the capabilities of rapid maneuver and three-dimensional attack.

The PLA Navy has realized the upgrading of the ship-based

and aircraft-based precision-attack weapons and the coordinated development of the armaments for submarines, surface ships and naval aviation.

In the air, the PLA Air Force has the third generation of light and heavy fighters, the second generation of modified fighters, the tactical transport aircraft, new-type fighter-bomber, refueling aircraft, airborne combat equipment and new generation of near-distance, medium-distance and long-distance ground-to-air missiles. The PLA Second Artillery Force (SAF) has basically formed a ground-to-ground missile system which includes both nuclear and conventional missiles, both solid-fueled and liquid-fueled missiles of near, medium and long ranges with complete types of warheads. In addition, a number of new-type equipment for command and control, information acquisition, early warning and detection and information countermeasure have become the "amplifier" of the battle effectiveness of the troops.

CHINA DISPLAYS ADVANCED DEFENCE TECHNOLOGY

China displayed its military might by exhibiting a series of brand new precision assault weapons during the on-going Zhuhai airshow, which opened on Monday in South China's Guangdong Province. The weapons on show included precision-guided bombs and long-range striking systems hailed by military experts as symbols that the People's Liberation Army has entered an era of precision attack. In a rare collective appearance, the airshow also brought together a number of new air, naval and surface-to-surface missiles, reports said.

For example, the LT-2 500-kilogram laser-guided bomb and the LS-6 glide-guided bomb, developed by the China Aviation Industry Corporation I, both made debuts at the show. Both types of bombs were designed on the basis of traditional bombs, reports said. The China Aerospace Science and Technology Corporation displayed two types of precision-guided bombs FT-1 and FT-3, which enjoy a high percentage of hits and can be widely used for short-distance air raids and blockage as well as disrupting an enemy's air defence and crippling naval ships, reports said.

The China Aerospace Science and Industry Corporation (CASIC), another State-owned weapons manufacturer, exhibited around 20 types of missiles at the sixth China International Aviation and Aerospace Exhibition, Xinhua News Agency reported. The P12 strategic missile system developed by CASIC, was regarded as the most intriguing and eye-catching item on display. CASIC said the missile defence system demonstrates China's capability to defend the country's airspace and territory.

Yin Xingliang, CASIC general manager, said China's missile systems had reached the technical level of developed countries in the late 1990s. Yin also said CASIC had worked for the peaceful utilization of technologies in the military industry and aerospace technologies in the civil aviation industry. After about 50 years of development, China is catching up with the worlds most advanced technology in the design of air-to-air missiles, said Jin Xianzhong, a senior missile designer, in an Internet interview with the Xinhuanet.com yesterday.

CHINA ADDS PRECISION STRIKE TO CAPABILITIES

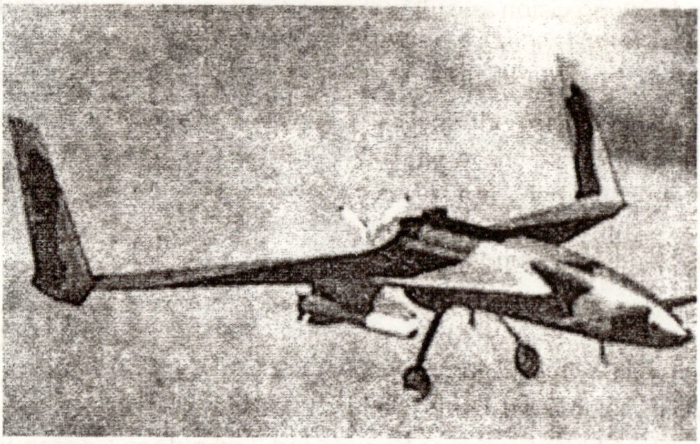

China has been developing and purchasing weapons for precision-strike warfare. This is the hard edge of the People's Liberation Army's (PLA) doctrinal drive toward using increasingly sophisticated information technologies such as C4ISR (command, control, communications, computers, intelligence, surveillance and reconnaissance) to improve the capabilities of weapon systems (DTI March, p. 39). The PLA's near-term goals appear to be greater asymmetric capabilities to target U.S. naval assets in the western Pacific and in space as part of an anti-access strategy. Long-term, however, greater precision will be a feature of most new weapon systems.

China's growing C4ISR capabilities were demonstrated in March by its coordinated two-fleet operation to intercept two U.S. Navy ocean survey vessels. Chinese ships found and harassed the USNS Victorious, operating in the Yellow Sea, and USNS Impeccable, which was about 75 mi. south of Hainan Island. The fallout was diplomatic, as Washington and Beijing clashed over interpretations of the Law of the Sea Treaty, which Beijing contends gives it rights to deny access to military survey missions. This incident, though, was reminiscent in timing and scope to the April 2001 clash that saw China "capture" a U.S. Navy EP-3 electronic intelligence aircraft off Hainan. China's aggressive challenge of Japanese claims in the East China Sea, plus Washington's refusal to cease its survey missions could be flashpoints. In February, a provincial Communist Party newspaper contained a threat to sink U.S. survey ships. In this second of three articles on China's growing regional power, DTI examines the country's efforts to improve its ability to target and destroy threats.

Since the early 1990s, Chinese military scholars have been warning of the need for China to prepare to defend against, and if necessary, conduct military operations in space. In late 2006 reports emerged of China's use of high-power ground-based lasers to "dazzle" U.S. surveillance satellites. On Feb. 11, 2007, China launched the first successful intercept by its SC-19 direct-ascent antisatellite (ASAT) system, derived from its KT-1 solid-fuel space-launch vehicle, with an interceptor stage whose development was likely aided by China's micro-satellite programs. A target FY-2 weather satellite was probably illuminated by large phased-array radar developed for tracking Shenzhou manned space capsules. A far less-noted potential co-orbital ASAT demonstration occurred on Sept. 27, 2008, when the Shenzhou-7 manned spacecraft, which had just launched a BX-1 nanosatellite, passed within 45 km. (28 mi.) of the International Space Station. Following the U.S. Navy's shootdown of an errant satellite on Feb. 21, 2008, and a Mar. 5, 2008, announcement that Russia would resume ASAT development, it is likely that China will continue ASAT testing.

China's direct-ascent ASAT also proves that it is capable of developing a long-range antiballistic missile (ABM) system, a U.S. pursuit that China has opposed. China had an ABM program from 1963-80 that produced a short-range interceptor prototype and long-range radar.

Chinese sources told DTI at the recent IDEX expo in Abu Dhabi that they have tested the new FD-2000 surface-to-air missile (SAM) in an antitactical ballistic missile (ATBM) mode. Developed with help from Russia's Almaz-Antey Co., the FD-2000 also draws from the earlier passive-guided FT-2000 SAM, which reportedly benefited from U.S. Patriot SAM technology.

These indigenous SAMs are entering PLA service, and will complement about 1,000 Almaz-Antey S-300/PMU-1/PMU-2 SAMs purchased since the early 1990s, giving the PLA air force the most formidable air-defence network in Asia. The PLA has also developed short-range SAM systems—including man-portable air-defence systems—for tracked vehicles and trucks. Among these is the TY-90 Yitian for trucks and armored personnel carriers that was disclosed in 2005, but displayed for the first time at IDEX this year.

Increasing precision is also the hallmark of new PLA surface-to-surface missiles and air-launched weapons. New Chinese nuclear ballistic missile warheads feature smaller sharp-tip warheads, signifying higher precision. One warhead configuration for the 12,000-km.-range DF-31A ICBM places at least one warhead on a delivery bus that is apparently capable of radical maneuvering to evade ABM defenses.

Medium-and short-range ballistic missiles (SRBMs) are also being upgraded for greater precision. The U.S. and Japanese navies have long been concerned with the PLA program to create an antiship ballistic missile, by placing a maneuverable terminally guided warhead on the 2,400-km.-range DF-21, and likely, on the

600-km. DF-15. Asian military sources are also concerned that a new 3,000-km. version of the DF-21 may have multiple terminally guided warheads.

An early 2009 Taiwanese estimate places the DF 15, DF-11 Mod2 and new land-attack cruise missiles (LACMs) of the second artillery missile force targeting Taiwan at more than 1,500, with newer versions having navigation satellite (navsat) guidance. In 2007 a Chinese source told DTI that the PLA will also be using two new shorter-range SRBMs, the truck-mounted 250-km. B-611M and 150-km. air-transportable P-12. Both are maneuverable, navsat-guided weapons with modular warheads. The PLA is also developing longer-range artillery rocket-based SRBMs, like the 200-km. navsat-guided WS-3. Some Chinese sources indicate that an antiradar or passive-guided 300-km. version of the WS series is possible.

Asian sources say the PLA has developed two families of strategic-range LACMs: the DH-10, which equips new units of the Second Artillery, and YJ-62/C-602, which equips PLA navy destroyers and land-based antiship missile units, and is to be developed into an air-launched version for the PLA air force. The air force is expected to equip a new version of the 1950s-era Soviet Tupolev Tu-16 Badger bomber, the Xian H-6K, with the weapon. The H-6Ks modified with more powerful engines, now have a potential 3,000-km. radius—enough to reach Guam. Rumors have long surrounded a potential long-range bomber program at Xian Aircraft Co., and a new stealthy version of Xian's JH-7A fighter bomber is also in development.

Tactical combat aircraft in the PLA air force and navy are receiving new Russian and indigenously designed air-to-air and ground-attack weapons. The air force's first Sukhoi Su-27SK fighters had the helmet-sighted Vympel R-73 missile a decade before the Raytheon AIM-9X entered U.S. service. The BVR self-guided Vympel R-77 followed the Su-30MKK into PLA service early this decade. But new Chengdu Aircraft Corp. J-10 and Shenyang Aircraft Corp. J-11B multirole fighters will carry air-to-air missiles designed by Luoyang Opto-Electric Co. (LOEC), which include the self-guided PL-12, thought to have a range approaching

100 km. in lofted delivery. Chinese sources also indicate LOEC is developing a high off-boresight air-to-air missile (AAM) similar to the South African Denel A-Darter, and a long-range ramjet-powered AAM.

Russian Su-30s in PLA service have been equipped with several guided munitions, including the Zvezda Kh-31 antiradar and antiship ramjet missile, Zvezda Kh-59 interdiction missile and optical image-correlation-guided KAB series bombs. At the 2005 Moscow air show, a Russian source disclosed that Russia had assisted China's development of electro-optical targeting pods, which have been photographed on J-10, JH-7A and some Hongdu Q-5 fighter-bombers. These will help guide two new families of laser-and navsat-guided bombs developed by LOEC and China Aerospace Science and Technology Corp. (CASC). The latter's FT family includes the 500-kg. (1,100-lb.) FT-1 navsat-guided bomb, the FT-2, which adds range-extending wings, the 250-kg. FT-3 and the 100-kg. FT-5, which is reportedly comparable with Boeing's Small Diameter Bomb. At last November's Zhuhai air show, LOEC revealed a dual-optical navsat-guided bomb. CASC's bombs can be expected to follow suit.

Precision is being packed into smaller munitions like the new 45-kg. AR-1, a laser-guided missile designed for the CH-3 unmanned combat air vehicle (UCAV), similar in capability to the U.S. Predator-1. Guizhou Aircraft Co. has likely developed a larger turbofan UCAV comparable to the MQ-9 Predator-B/Reaper.

Most of China's new precision-strike systems are for sale. Pakistan and Iran have benefited from China's ballistic and cruise missile technology, and from sales of conventional systems. Many more countries are likely to consider the $22-million Chengdu FC-1 and $41-million J-10 fighters, especially when equipped with precision-guided munitions like the PL-12 and FT-1. This form of power projection will soon be joined by the PLA's increasing power-projection capabilities, the subject of the final installment. Richard D. Fisher, Jr., is a senior fellow with the International Assessment and Strategy Centre of Arlington, Va., and author of China's Military Modernization: Building for Regional and Global Reach (Praeger, 2008).

7 India–China Conflict by 2012: A Great Possibility

As over the years Southeast Asia has been lifted by a resurgent China so have feelings of distrust towards the country, and nowhere more so than India which is still smarting from a border war it fought with China less than a decade after it found it had a new "neighbour." The 1962 border clashes with China were a direct consequence of the Tibetan problem which had seen the Dalai Lama flee to India. Suddenly, instead of a benign Buddhist nation on along its northern territory, India had communist China, and the Tibetan buffer state was no more. Disputes that had previously been a diplomatic matter between two friendly nations became frayed as China's take on Tibet's historic relationship with India took on a darkened tone to that which had preceded it under the Buddhist-led regime. China's rise to prominence on the international stage since then has not always been smooth, and its diplomacy has often been seen as regional bullying.

China's recent use of its veto power at the ADB to deny India development funds for its northern state of Arunachal Pradesh coupled with Rio Tinto executives being detained for spying closely following a denial by Australia of China's desire to acquire some of the countries mineral assets looks more aggressive than peaceful. Indeed, such is the forceful nature of China's statements these days that the country is in danger of losing the goodwill it built up during the hosting of last year's Olympics.

Recent past events in Tibet and Xinjiang are now starting to spark regional concerns. In an interview with Bharat Verma, editor of the Indian Defence Review, claims that China will attack India by 2012 to divert the attention of its own people from "unprecedented" internal dissent, growing unemployment and financial problems that are threatening the hold of Communists in that country. "China will launch an attack on India before 2012. There are multiple reasons for a desperate Beijing to teach India the final lesson, thereby ensuring Chinese supremacy in Asia in this century." says Verma. Noting that one of the joys of reading India's free media – no censorship here – is the inevitable crackpots it throws up. However, China needs to be wary of signals, intentional or otherwise, of the diplomatic, and public relations image that it often portrays. Still wanting to be appreciated, if not loved internationally, China continually throws spanners into its own works with a far too heavy handed diplomatic and militaristic approach. India's military spending, as a percentage of GDP, is 2.5 percent. Is it really necessary for China to be spending 4.3 percent of its GDP – which again is considerably larger than India's – on its military?

Verma's points – a covert operation by Beijing giving North Korea nuclear technology and missiles – are the sort of nonsense one can fairly easily debunk. However, when mixed in with his views on Pakistan, as he points out, long China's western ally against India, and a Pakistan/US alliance diminishing Pakistan's reliance upon China, a "nervous" Beijing, able to strike at India becomes just a little more rational. With China apparently hell bent on upsetting other countries via using diplomatic means gained to reward it for its development in a manner that seems more akin to punishing nations it has commercial disputes with, the concerns are writ large on the wall. Government interference in Chinese commerce is steadily growing, and China will take commercial action at a governmental and diplomatic level to get its way. Whether that leads to the apocalyptic scenario that it attacks India seems rather off beam. But Verma, in his article, has drawn a line of concern in the sand.

VANISHING OF CHINA'S MILITARY ADVANTAGE OVER INDIA

The difference between China's official words and actual deeds could lead to another conflict with India similar to the one in 1962. First, China does not like India's emerging status as a global power. Second, it is paranoid that if India completes its planned military purchases in the next five years, conquering and humiliating it would remain a distant dream. Third, China wants to grab the town of Tawang, birthplace of the current Dalai Lama, on the Indian side of the Tibet border. This is a symbolic Chinese ploy to let the Tibetans know who their real masters are.

In mid-August China began a massive military exercise called "Stride 2009," deploying 50,000 troops in areas far from their home bases for live-fire drills. According to analysts, the exercise shows China's readiness to respond quickly to unrest in any part of the country. It also demonstrates the effectiveness of China's infrastructure, which allows the quick deployment of troops hundreds of miles away. The program culminates on Oct. 1, China's 60th anniversary. China maintains 30-40 divisions of reserve forces in its central provinces. But Tibet and the Indian border are outside this area of quick deployment, linked by a single rail line built on permafrost. While the exercise sheds lights on China's reserve force, it is not India-specific yet. Still India, lately busy on the Pakistan border, may need to alter its defence posture.

China's former leader Deng Xiaoping put the border dispute with India on the back burner in 1978. But he made an agreement with India that both countries would maintain a standstill in the Himalayas and avoid military build-up. The promise held until 1998, when China began improving its military infrastructure in the Himalayas and building multiple missile bases. But it did not increase its ground forces, which stood at 200,000 soldiers.

India also kept its bargain and did not add a single soldier to its 30,000 in the east and 20,000 in the west. India even held off building new roads and improving infrastructure in its border areas. In hindsight that was a mistake. Recently, China's building of an intercontinental missile base at Delingha, north of Tibet, has set alarm bells ringing. Most of Russia and India are within its missile range, and being far from Taiwan keeps it sheltered from the U.S. gaze.

In the past 30 years India has held 13 high-level talks with China on the demarcation of the border, the last one in July this year. Each proved fruitless. China wants the Tawang tract and will not talk about vacating the Akash Chin plateau in Kashmir. To make its point it has begun building more roads, missile bases and airfields in addition to its existing military infrastructure. It is also encouraging Nepal to enter into a free trade treaty, giving the Chinese an excuse to add more roads and possibly a rail link to bring them closer to India.

Tibet has become more restive in the past ten years. Last year's pre-Olympic riots blew the lid off China's tight security when its 200,000 force had to be split between law and order and border guard duties. While China marginally increased the force during the riots, India augmented its force only slightly. Now its military strength in Tibet is insufficient to conquer India or the Tawang tract, although border skirmishes remain a possibility. India has its own evaluation of the China threat. A decision to engage China through diplomatic channels between 2001 and 2005 produced no results, so India decided to go for a military build-up. Eight mountain divisions trained to fight in the Himalayas will be augmented by two more, and an additional 60,000 ground troops will be sent to the east closer to Tawang and to the state of Sikkim. Also, some 20,000 additional troops will be added to the current strength in the west in Laddakh.

Three airfields lying derelict in the east and three in the west have been activated. A major airbase only 200 miles from the Tibetan border will be upgraded to serve India's premier Sukhoi fighter. This airfield is a major threat to China's rail link. India has also initiated other road-building activities. One will connect Laddakh with the rest of India via Manali-Rohtang. Another will connect Itanagar, capital of Arunachal Pradesh state, with neighboring Assam.

These developments could effectively neutralize China's current advantage. Besides, Indian troops are much more capable in jungle and mountain warfare than they were in 1962. India's conflict with Kashmir in Kargil in 1999 has presumably shown China that Indians cannot be beaten on the ground as easily as they were in 1962. China won the 1962 battle with India by indulging in classic Chinese warfare tactics – confusing the enemy with conciliatory signals. On the ground, India had incompetent generals leading a brave bunch of soldiers. Additionally, Chinese soldiers had an advantage with their Soviet copies of German-designed submachine guns called "burp guns." The rapid-fire submachine guns overwhelmed the Indians, who were carrying World War II Lee Enfield rifles.

Things have now changed; India's current assault rifle is comparable to China's and India's generals have learned the art of war. India will receive new military hardware in the next five years. Its newly commissioned nuclear submarine will be fully operational by 2012 or 2013, and the Russian aircraft carrier on order is expected to join the Indian navy. Indian-made light combat aircraft and imported medium combat aircraft will be operational in squadron strength.

All this hardware, plus ultra-light artillery fit for action in the Himalayas, will soon become operational. By 2014 India will have twice its current firepower and ten times that of 1962. So China is planning a new strategy that includes cruise-missile attacks on the Indian heartland and confrontation on the high seas. The biggest threats to India are missiles launched from Tibet and China's naval armada in the Indian Ocean.

Chinese cruise missiles with a range of 1,500 miles launched from Tibet and intermediate-range ballistic missiles launched from Delingha are big threats. India's industrial heartland and military bases lie within their range, and new guidance systems make the missiles highly accurate. There is no known defence against a massed attack by some 200 cruise missiles. India's only hope is that they would miss their targets after traveling 600 miles over the Himalayas.

China is depending most on its naval armada in the Indian Ocean. It has a surveillance station off the Myanmar coast and a newly built naval port in Gawdar, Pakistan. Both are militarily significant. But India counters this advantage with its naval base at the western mouth of the Gulf of Malacca on Andaman Island. If an overconfident China decided to test Indian resolve by creating an incident, India could retaliate by capturing China's surveillance base off the Myanmar coast. This could escalate hostilities, but China would risk losing its oil supplies if it stepped up the conflict.

It is pointless for China to wage war with India. Instead, the two countries should engage in greater trade and business, which can bring more prosperity. An unsuccessful invasion of India would be a terrible loss for the Chinese.

CHINESE MILITARY STRANGLEHOLD TIGHTENS AROUND INDIA

Martin McCauley writes: The Chinese leadership regards India as a long term threat to its dominance of Asia. A third key player in Asia is Russia. Moscow regards itself as a great power and is seeking a strategic alliance with China. But Beijing will only grant Moscow a 'partnership' and distances itself from any tight military or economic alliances. This indicates that China believes it will dominate relations with Russia in the future.

India is quite a different story. There are .hose who surmise that India will beat China to world dominance sometime in the future. They point to the fact that India has a functioning democracy, albeit imperfect, an understanding of the importance of the rule of law, a growing middle class with technical expertise and, last but not least, command of the English language. India's population is now about 1.1 billion and may surpass that of China within the next 20 years. Its economic growth rates are not as impressive as those of China but it has a more dynamic domestic market which can soak up locally produced products.

China and India have never seen eye to eye since the founding of the People's Republic in 1949. They fought a war in 1962. The problem is the Siliguri corridor which is 200km long and 40 km wide. It is strategically of key importance because it links mainland India to its North East region. A part of it is in Arunachal Pradesh which is claimed by China. Were Beijing to acquire it, China would have a land frontier with India in the north. To the north of Arunachal Pradesh is Bhutan and to the south Bangladesh. Indian security specialists surmise that China and Bangladesh have a long term aim of cutting India off from its North East region by blocking the Siliguri corridor. If China could acquire part of Arunachal Pradesh it would have a land frontier with Bangladesh in the north.

Illegal migrants from Bangladesh and terrorist groups such as the United Liberation Front of Asom (ULFA), who have safe havens in Bangladesh, use the corridor to penetrate India. Some analysts speculate that the UFLA has already moved its base to China.

Bangladesh and China have enjoyed diplomatic relations since 1975. Beijing has always encouraged Dhaka to adopt an independent foreign policy and move away from India's orbit. Beijing may even have given Bangladesh assurances that it will come to its aid in the event of a military standoff with New Delhi. The two countries have signed many agreements on economic, cultural and military matters. Beijing has extended soft loans and military equipment comes at 'friendship prices'. However Dhaka has been careful not to enter into a strategic military partnership with Beijing. It wishes to reap the benefits of a flexible, loose, expanding relationship.

China is a major supplier of military hardware to Bangladesh. Artillery, missiles, armoured personnel carriers and personal weapons are among the equipment acquired. Naval contacts are even more important. Most Bangladeshi naval craft, including frigates, missile boats and gun boats, are of Chinese origin.

New Delhi fears that Dhaka may grant China the right to set up military bases in Bangladesh. These would permit China to monitor Indian army and air force movements and would seriously compromise India's ability to defend the Siliguri corridor in the event of hostilities. Even more worrying for India is the possibility that Bangladesh might grant China naval port facilities in Chittagong. The model here is Gwadar in Pakistan and Hambantota in Sri Lanka. Ostensibly these ports are being developed as commercial entities but, almost certainly, they will be used by China's navy.

China now acts as mediator in conflicts involving Bangladesh. In November 2008, Myanmar (Burma) and Bangladesh deployed their navies in the Bay of Bengal as a result of Myanmar granting licences to several oil companies to explore for oil in disputed waters. After the Chinese intervened, the two navies backed off and negotiations are under way to resolve the dispute.

Under the Bay of Bengal are huge reserves of oil and gas. Chinese companies are actively exploring and drilling in the Bay. The aim is to pipe the oil and gas to China. Bangladesh has proven reserves of over 15 trillion cubic feet of gas and Myanmar over 81 trillion cubic feet. Pipelines will take the hydrocarbons from offshore platforms through Myanmar to Kunming in southern China. The almost 3,000 km natural gas pipeline to Kunming is expected to be operational in 2012. A 1,000 km oil pipeline will have a throughput of about 400,000 barrels per day.

Bangladesh and China are building a 900 km highway which will link Chittagong with Kunming through Myanmar. This will lower transport costs by cutting out the long sea journey via Singapore. How will India counter China's increasing ability to monitor the activities of its naval, air and ground forces? We may soon see Chinese naval ships and submarines in the North Andaman Sea. One response would be to blockade Chittagong. China now has increasingly close military relations with Myanmar, Bangladesh, Sri Lanka and Pakistan. The noose is tightening around India's neck.

8 Nepal as New 'Strategic Partner' of China

In China's foreign policy towards Nepal since the Maoist ascendance to power. China had earlier adopted a policy of 'non-intervention' in the internal matters of Nepal and largely stayed out of Nepalese internal politics. However, the demise of the monarchy and the ascendance of political parties have forced China to reshape its Nepal policy. Moreover, frequent protests by Tibetans in recent months alerted the Chinese to the possibility of the China-Tibet border being misused. Consequently, China has sought to engage Nepalese political actors at all levels, primarily to secure the border with Nepal. With the Maoists in power, China also hopes to use its ideological commonalities to suppress the Tibetan movement in Nepal. When the Maoists emerged victorious in the April 2008 elections, China adopted a wait and watch policy because it was unsure of their intentions. After all, the Maoists were backed by India and were catapulted to the political centre stage only after a comprehensive peace agreement in which India had played a substantial behind the scenes role. However, media reports reveal that after several interactions with Maoists leaders.

China has begun to feel quite comfortable with the Maoist-led government. The Maoists' ideological linkages with China and their keenness to neutralize India's influence in the region have also made them an obvious choice for engagement. It has been reported that in interactions with Chinese the Maoist leaders gave the impression that the future of democracy in Nepal could be guided by the example of the Communist Party of China. Indeed, there are many in Nepal who argue that persistence with the Maoist tag in the party name despite joining competitive politics indicates that the party may work towards a single party system in the future, given that dictatorship of the proletariat has prime of place in the Maoist lexicon. In fact, some hardline leaders of the party have suggested a people's republic similar to that of China on a number of occasions even after Maoists joined the political mainstream.

These ideas might have encouraged China to attempt to consolidate its position in Nepal by continuously engaging the Maoists at the political, economic, military and social levels, and thus secure its strategic interests in the region. In fact, twelve high-level Chinese delegations, including two military teams, visited Nepal in the course of 2008-2009. During these visits, China has repeatedly assured economic, technological and military aid to Nepal. The Maoist-led government was also asked to adopt a 'One-China' policy, not to allow Nepalese land for anti-China activities, take strong action against Tibetan refugees and grant special facilities for Chinese investments in strategic sectors. Beijing has also initiated Track-II diplomacy with Nepal and invited Nepalese scholars to undertake visits to Chinese think tanks.

Some of the important visits from China to Nepal were:

- 25 February 2009: Assistant Chinese Foreign Minister Hu Zhengyue led a 14-member delegation.
- 19 February 2009: Liu Hongcai, Vice Minister of the International Department of the central committee of the CPC led a delegation to take part in the inaugural ceremony of the 8th convention of the UML in Butwal.
- 10 February 2009: A high level Peoples' Liberation Army (PLA) delegation, one of the largest delegations in two months, arrived in Nepal.
- 06 December 2008: Lieutenant General Ma Xiaotian, deputy chief of General Staff of the PLA headed a ten-member delegation. China agreed to provide US $2.61 million worth of security assistance to Nepal.
- 01 December 2008: China's Foreign Minister Yang Jiechi visited Nepal.
- 24 July 2008: Chinese Vice-Minister for Foreign Affairs, Wu Dawei, visited Nepal. He pledged a grant assistance of 100 million yuan as economic and technical cooperation.

- 04 March 2008: Assistant Minister for Foreign Affairs of China, He Yafei, undertook a three-day visit to Nepal.

Nepal's engagements with China have also increased manifold with the visit of delegations both at State and non-state levels. Apart from visits at the official levels, private visits by political leaders, journalists and academicians are also sponsored by China as part of public diplomacy. During these visits Chinese authorities have reportedly assured all kinds of support to the Maoist government in its efforts aimed at laying the foundation for a 'New Nepal'. For the Nepalese Maoists, growing Chinese engagement is a win-win situation in line with their 'policy of equidistance', which has been deliberately adopted to counter-balance India's influence in Nepal.

The increasing level of bilateral engagement also indicates that China is wooing Nepal as a new strategic partner. This has been confirmed by the statements made by various Chinese officials. For example, on 16 February 2009, Chinese Foreign Minister Yang Jiechi said in Beijing that China would prefer to work with Nepal on the basis of a strategic partnership. In fact, Vice Minister of International Department of the Central Committee of Communist Party of China, Liu Hongcai said in Kathmandu in February 2009 that "we oppose any move to interfere in the internal affairs of Nepal by any force." Similarly, on November 04, 2008, Liu Hong Chai, International Bureau Chief of the Chinese Communist Party, stated that "China will not tolerate any meddling from any other country in the internal affairs of Nepal-our traditional and ancient neighbour."

China has also submitted to Kathmandu a draft Sino-Nepal friendship treaty. The draft states that China will not attack Nepal and would respect Nepal's sovereignty and territorial integrity. Nepal would recognize 'One China' policy and not allow its territory to be used for "anti-China" activities. The draft treaty in fact looks more like a strategic one that is tilted highly in favour of Chinese security concerns. China needs this agreement because it does not have confidence in the democratic arrangements and future governments in Nepal, and wishes to consolidate its position while the Maoists are in power.

China has penetrated the Nepalese political system by gaining the confidence of hardline communist leaders both in the CPN-UML and the CPN-Maoist. China is also known to have played a major role in facilitating the alliance between the CPN-UML and the Maoists. Prior to Jhala Nath Khanal becoming UML Chief, a four-member Chinese delegation visited Kathmandu on May 10, 2008 and met Khanal and other Maoist leaders. A senior delegation from the Communist Party of China led by vice Minister Liu Hongcai was also in Kathmandu in February 2009 to attend the inaugural ceremony of the 8th national convention of the UML. The victory of Khanal as chairman of the UML, who is close to Prime Minister Prachanda, has been crucial for the survival of the Maoist-led coalition government. The nature of Chinese engagements in Nepal goes beyond the political domain. They might also be aimed at influencing the process of drafting of the new constitution to ensure that China's long-term interests are served, particularly in hydropower and other strategically important projects. China has also assured Nepal help in the modernization and integration of registered Maoist guerrillas into the Nepal Army.

Considering the strategic and economic interests Beijing has in Nepal, in terms of energy from hydro projects and as a transit country between China and India, China may expand its state level engagements by entering into long-term agreements at various levels. The proposed new friendship treaty marks the beginning of this process. Moreover, the treaty may enhance the bargaining power of the Maoist government vis-à-vis India to resolve some of the long standing disputes between the two countries.

Any foreign presence in Nepal is a concern for India. Given the centuries-old socio-cultural and economic ties between India and Nepal, recent Chinese insistence on closing the Indo-Nepal open border is a matter of concern for both countries. The Indo-Nepal relationship was acknowledged as "unassailable" during the official visit of Nepalese Prime Minister, Puspa Kamal Dahal to New Delhi in September 2008. But an 'equidistance policy' can only come at the expense of India-Nepal relations.-

'NEW FRONT' OF CHINA ON INDO-NEPAL BORDER

The Chinese clamour over Arunachal Pradesh has raised many eyebrows in India. Even as the meeting between Prime Minister Manmohan Singh and Chinese Premier Wen Jiabao in Thailand on Saturday was being looked at as an effort to cool down the tension between the neighbouring countries, the Dragon nation has opened another anti-India front. This time in Nepal. Silently but speedily China is spreading its wings in the erstwhile Hindu kingdom, mainly to unleash anti-India propaganda. Besides acquiring some major construction projects in Nepal, the Chinese are also making their presence felt by opening language centres in Nepali cities on the Indo-Nepal border. These centres are teaching Chinese language. But, what raises suspicions on Chinese intentions is the fact that these centres are open only for Nepali citizens.

The surge in Chinese activities in the neighbour country is a matter of concern for India which is already fighting terrorism being pushed into the country from Pakistan. It's a known fact that China often uses Nepal as a buffer state against India. After the Indo-China war of 1962, the Dragon country has made constant efforts to increase its influence in Nepal. Though it did not succeed much till Nepal was under the rule of monarchy, the fall of monarchy and growing Maoist grip over Nepal has given a fillip to Chinese plans.

A clear indicator of this is the construction of Sikta barrage in Agaiya village of Banke district (Nepal). Its construction was delayed for almost three decades owing to Indian protest. But, once Maoists held sway over the Nepali government, the construction was given a go-ahead in 2006. Moreover, the contract for the project was given to Chinese firm – Sinehydro. In fact, a team of 40 Chinese engineers is engaged in the construction of the Sikta barrage in Agaiya district of Nepal. The district touches the Indian district of Shravasti. The distance from Indian border to the barrage is barely 14 kilometres. The possibility of Chinese infiltration in important zones of war on Indian border areas due to the presence of Chinese engineers cannot be ruled out.

Also, after the completion of the barrage the flow of river Rapti towards India will be diverted towards Nepal which will create acute water shortage in Indian area. Efforts have also been started to divert the flow of rivers flowing towards Indian area from Parchu lake located in Chinese area adjoining the state which may lead to floods in the borders districts of India during monsoon. Not only this, if the and Sikta barrage ever breaks down due to technical reasons it will severely impact the security arrangements made on the India border. China, thus, seems to be working on these two projects under well-planned policy to tease India. Similarly, China has established the office of 'Maitri Sangh' in Nepal adjoining Indian border territory. Meanwhile, a 10-member team comprising five Chinese and five Tibetan national recently visited Nepalganj headquarters of Banke district (Nepal). The team toured the Indo-Nepal border and secretly clicked photographs of the Rupaidiha main gate located on Indo-Nepal border. The Indian intelligence agencies, however, learnt about this when the team had already left for Kathmandu. Assistant army Nayak Devendra of Shashtra Seema Bal (SSB), when contacted, told TOI that he will report the incident to his senior officers.

Nepal's Prime Minister Mr. Madhav Kumar Nepal and Chairman of the Nepalese Congress (NC) Party Girija Prasad Koirala have assured China that Nepali soil will not be allowed to be used against China under any circumstances. Talking with the Chinese delegation led by politburo member of the Chinese Communist Party, Mr. Zhang Gaoli, separately, September 1, 2009, the two veteran politicians of Nepal, according to the high placed sources, did try to convince China towards Nepal's firm stand on 'One China Policy'. However, Beijing is not that fool to believe such parroted/repetitive assurance of Nepali politician, say Kathmandu based analyst.

"The lame duck government has not even asked official clarifications from those lawmakers from the Madhesh parties who had assured the Tibetan community in exile in India that they will raise the issue of 'Free Tibet' in Nepal's Constituent Assembly (CA) during their last meet with Dalai Lama in

Dharmasala of Himanchal Pradesh, India", laments a Kathmandu based analyst who preferred anonymity. 'The recent meet of the Nepal law makers has raised suspicion in the minds of the Beijing authorities as regards the Nepalese structured stance that she remains firm on "One China Policy' of Nepal. And Beijing understands the Nepali intentions well. According to PM's political advisor Mr. Raghujee Panta, PM's upcoming visit to China, Constitution drafting process and ongoing peace process were also discussed during the meet.

CHINA-SOUTH ASIA POLITICAL RELATIONS: A VIEW FROM NEPAL

"Peaceful co-existence" is the main principle in China-South Asia relations. The fundamentals of this principles are i) mutual equality, ii) non-interference in each other's internal affairs, iii) mutual respect to territorial integrity, iv) cooperation against hegemonism and power politics, and v) mutual accommodation and benefit (Wang Hongwei, 2005). In view of the colonial and feudal background, the main principle and fundamentals of China-South Asia ties are progressive. If one closely examines the natural and spiritual realities that persist between China and South Asia, the main principle and fundamentals of their ties can not truly be more than egalitarian.

China and South Asia are linked by land and water, mountains and rivers. Unlike East Asia and South East Asia and China, Chinese and most of South Asian ties are contiguous, more natural and comprehensive. Mountains pass through and major rivers flow down to China and South Asia from the Tibet Autonomous Region (TAR) of China. Now, it is science and technology that is poised to harness snow and water for larger benefits of the people. In China and South Asia, it has yet remained a geo-political as well as ecological truism that link maintained by mountains and rivers are more stable than opportunistic alliances offered by nuclear power.

Another basic articulation of China-South Asia relations is Buddhism. Gautam Buddha, who was born and had acquired knowledge about the ultimate truth in South Asia, very much lives life-size every where in China. The civilization of China and South Asia thus holds common source of inspiration with a profound degree of continuity. As Buddhism does not stand as an anti-thesis for any other religion, it helps to create an internal capacity to absorb, acculturate and assimilate in both China and South Asia. In short, geo-politically charged neighborhood in an intense natural and spiritual sense is what stands out in China-South Asia relations.

China's politics till the recent past was concentrated on its east coast of the Taiwan Straits. Asia as a whole ranked relatively low in its security agenda since creation of the People's Republic of China. But the Cold War era did not leave China untouched. Tibet in particular conditioned China in formulation of its South Asia policy and to the stability in its frontier regions. The tenets of this policy were: Peace at the south-west border region of China. Efficient signing of border treaty with the neighboring countries was part of this policy to ensure peace along China's long border.

The Tibetan question. This question raised by the external forces had made China acutely sensitive of its national integration and domestic stability. Chinese policy recognized Tibetan separatism as having serious implications for the national integration and domestic stability. It also recognized that the forces supporting the Tibetan separatism were working by proxy, and many aspects of the separatist moves were utterly non-transparent. So trying its best to correctly understand the external as well as internal features of Tibetan question, and appreciating highly those neighboring countries and organizations who did not allow Tibetan separatists to engage in activities and also did not permit outside powers to support such activities on their soil, China's South Asia Policy tried proactively hard to work at the two inter-related fronts at the same time-discouraging the separatist elements and, praising and encouraging those countries and organizations who did not support and did not provide any ground to support the Tibetan separatism.

Independent relations with South Asian states. China was aware of the unequal interstate relations that do not allow development of cordial and trustily ties between them. Difference in size, power and interpretation of agreements had affected relations between states in South Asia. During the Cold War years, the dominating trend in the interstate relations was exploitation and gains at the cost of other, and a tendency to have "sphere of influence." Exchange and cooperation between China and a number of small South Asian states was not liked by India. But China continued to cultivate ties with small South Asian countries independently. It supported independence of these countries, and their independent decision making. After 1962 border war with India, the importance of independence of the countries in South Asia-particularly of those small and non-nuclear power countries-had increased for China. China realized that only unilaterally wishing for cooperation might not be wise and realistic.

Therefore in view of a Chinese analyst, "It is undeniable, ...after the 1962 border war, China's policy toward Nepal might have reflected, to some extent, a strategy in which China supported Nepal, along with other small countries in South Asia, to check India's influence" (Hua Han, 2005). Despite so, China provided unflinching support to late King Birendra's proposal to declare Nepal a "Zone of Peace" in mid 1970s. It was indicative of China's firmer conviction that the indigenous will and ability of neighboring small states in South Asia to independently conduct their foreign and defence affairs together with its independent foreign policy and self-defence strategy was more important and conducive for peace and stability of China's frontier regions than mere lonely Chinese efforts directed at the same. It was this sense of working together which had been the driving force for China to reciprocally commit to the independence of the small South Asian states. Whatever financial, material and military assistance China has provided to these countries were corollary of the said policy.

The United States of America (the US) has ever been at the centre stage whether it was the end of the bi-polar Cold War, 9/11 terrorist attacks and the subsequent US campaign against terrorism, and now the US campaign for democracy. It is the only power which could put troops in Iraq and Afghanistan at the same time and spend enough money to rebuild the economies. Indeed, despite the euphoria for multi-lateralism after the end of Cold War, the South Asian countries were "gravely relying on the assistance and loans provided by the World Bank and developed countries, which in turn resulted in the heavy burden of foreign debts and shortage of foreign exchange reserves and investment capital.

After 9/11, the new strategic development (beginning of the US offensive in Afghanistan) changed the security environment in Asia. US military presence in Uzbekistan and Afghanistan and the new military relationship of the US with Pakistan and India completed the US military involvement in the whole of the Asian continent. Until then South Asia was a gap between the US involvement in West Asia and East Asia. After the US completed its Asian military expansion by filling the gaps left by collapse of Soviet Union under its "war against terror" planning, it felt a need to address another gap which its own larger military involvement had created. The felt US need was primarily due to genuine domestic concerns. The felt need this time was democracy.

For China and the US "the week that changed the world" in February, 1972 when President Nixon visited China had a clear American objective, and that was "to transform the two-power world of the Cold War into a triangle then to manage the triangle in such a way that we would be closer to each of the contenders than they were to each other, thereby maximizing our options". With the disappearance of the Soviet Union, one of the two-power world, despite the initial instability and uncertainty, the US and China appear to move into a maturing stage, and carry out responsibilities particularly in Asia-Pacific region. The following statements of President Bush and Premier Wen confirm how they viewed their role in relation to each other.

Welcoming Chinese Premier Wen Jiabao at the White House on December 9, 2003, President George Bush of the United States of America described the US and China as "partners in diplomacy working to meet the dangers of 21st century." He further added: "As our two nations work constructively across areas of common interest, we are candid about our disagreements. The growing strength and maturity of our relationship allows us to discuss our differences, whether over economic issues, Taiwan, Tibet, or human rights and religious freedom, in a spirit of mutual understanding and respect." Replying to President Bush on the occasion, Chinese Premier Wen said, "Our cooperation in a wide range of areas such as counterterrorism, economy, trade and international and regional issues has effectively safeguarded our mutual interests and promoted peace, stability and prosperity in the Asia Pacific region and the world at large."

The key policy statements above from President Bush and Premier Wen, beyond any doubt, eloquently establishes the importance of Sino-US relationship for the Asia-Pacific region and the world at large over and above the bilateral ties existing between the two great countries. In the period ahead where agenda for democracy is pushed to the front, China-US ties may loose glitters; and China may face all the blames for being a "communist" state. And specifically in the context of South Asia, where the majority belongs to the poor and level of interstate cooperation is low, it is for the people and states of the South Asia to decide either for China-inspired peace with independence and self-governed development or for the US-inspired peace with global democracy and development. Whatever the choice the people and states of South Asia make, the decision of Thirteenth Dhaka SAARC summit to associate China and Japan with SAARC was indeed a very welcome unprecedented geopolitical development. The constructive role played by the small SAARC members in this decision making will certainly help fruitfully maximize comparative advantage of SAARC member's vis-à-vis the new partners (China and Japan).

South Asian states are poor. One major reason for such a condition is they do not have an effective good neighborly policy between themselves. At times certain state's behaviour suggests that it wants to live without neighbours. Mahatma Gandhi has provided an example of a good neighborly policy. In his words of wisdom, "One who serves his neighbours serves all the world."

Since 1978 when the modernization and reform process started, economic growth in China has averaged 9.5 percent per year which remains a truly astounding rate. Similarly, foreign trade has expanded at an annual rate of 15 percent over the same period. As for foreign investment China was able to attract $53.2 billion in 2002 as against $52.7 billion for the United States of America. Indeed, the economic transformation has been so rapid that even renowned investment banking firms like Golsdman Sachs predict that China could be the world's largest economy by 2050 with a GDP of $44.4 trillion ahead of the US GDP of $35 trillion and India's GDP of $27 trillion in the same period.

To correct some of the economic divide of a market based economy so that no part of the country remains left out in the great process of economic transformation, the Chinese government is allocating increasing resources including new investment funds from better off provinces in building new physical and social infrastructure and new industrial establishments in the western region. As a part of this strategy the Qinghai-Tibet railway is completed at a cost of $3.16 billion. Similarly, road network in Tibet is being expanded and improved with links to important cities in other provinces.

China's rapid economic growth has its neighbours change their perception on China. The shift from a "China threat" to "China opportunity" theory opens the alternative to explore the benefits that can be draw from the gigantic China's market-leading to deeper and inner natural and spiritual bonds with China. As the immediate neighbours, as many South Asian scholars and experts have wisely suggested, the SAARC members states should take full advantage of China's achievement, especially China's "western development program," which can facilitate a closer economic and trade interaction specially between Tibet, Xingjian, Sichuan and Yunnan and neighboring South Asian states. Opening of new transport and trade routes and just completed railway line over "the roof of the world" will provide China's western parts with efficient access to neighboring countries leading to a change in geo-political outlook.

The ultimate test of the South Asian ability will lie with its leaders' determination to practically conduct the principle of peaceful co-existence along with its fundamentals in relationship with China. Hopefully the Himalayan twins as if representing north face and south face of Kailash-China and South Asia-cherish more a vision of working together than a division of sphere of influence.

It was this spirit of working together that had inspired the press release that was issued after the international seminar on SAARC and China. China Study Centre, Nepal organized this seminar on 23 December, 2002 in Kathmandu, the venue of SAARC Secretariat. The press release stated: "Based on the papers presented and comments and observations made during the discussion, the participants of the seminar on SAARC and China ...have come to the following consensus." There is a need for institutionalized dialogue mechanism between SAARC and China. The imperative for good neighbourhood and challenges and opportunities of the 21st century in regard to peace, cooperation and development dictate the needs for bold and speedy action to move forward in this direction. In this connection it is necessary to hold follow-up seminar focusing on the specific of the institutionalized dialogue mechanism between SAARC and China.

The SAARC member states may try to expand and intensify their social and economic interaction with China at sub-regional level. The Track II initiative prepares ground for promoting and complementing official level discussion. It is gratifying to note that Thirteenth SAARC summit at Dhaka in November last has gloriously taken initiative for establishing institutionalized dialogue mechanism between SAARC and China. The SAARC member leaders should be commended for their bold and glorious initiative. It is hoped that they will also ensure speedy actions regarding the paraphernalia of China's institutionalized association with SAARC.

What is expected are upcoming SAARC official meetings at various levels will prepare grounds for the SAARC member states to expand and intensify their social and economic interaction with China at sub-regional level. Various sub-regional groupings within SAARC may find, for example, i) eastern Himalayan resource, ii) western Himalayan resources, iii) transportation links and networks, iv) nature tourism and v) spiritual tourism as important themes for sustainable cooperation to the various sub-regional groups within SAARC. It has been learned that attempts have been made to organize seminars on China and South Asian Relations in Colombo. Such activities are encouraging as they promote and compliment official level discussion on inter-regional collaborative dialogue between China and South Asian states.

It will be extremely good if the SAARC member states attempts to expand and intensify their social and economic interaction with China at sub-regional level. A sub-region (based on sub-geographical level-for example, eastern South Asia, western South Asia, and/or function-for example, culture, natural sources or infrastructure) is recognized as a practical mechanism to promote and strengthen SAARC's over all link with China. As more effective, immediate and direct geo-political link between China and South Asia will be through sub-regional grouping of South Asia; members of the South Asian sub-regional grouping will be more dependent on each other to realize the purpose. Whereas for China, this sort of cooperative arrangement will ensure required stability and peace in the frontier regions, for each South Asian sub-region value will be added to tourism, culture, and physical development which will enhance overall quality of life of its people.

CHINA-NEPAL TIES ATTAIN NEW HEIGHTS

This March 10, Nepal proved itself unwilling to allow a repeat of the mass Tibetan demonstrations that were held here from March to September 2008. Although the energy and numbers of last year's demonstrations surrounding the anniversary of the failed Tibetan uprising and Dalai Lama's flight into exile were not present this year, Nepalese riot police still took forcible measures to prevent a group of approximately 200 Tibetan demonstrators leaving the Boudha district of Kathmandu. A British activist named Daisy Karen Wood who attempted to dodge police and enter the Chinese Embassy carrying balloons and a Tibetan flag was quickly arrested. Nepal's desire to quickly suppress events that would embarrass China, its massive northern neighbour, comes as no surprise. Ties between the two countries have been increasing in recent months.

Historically, relations between Nepal and China have been relatively good. For centuries Nepal sent tribute bearing missions to China and acknowledged its superior regional force. The tension that did exist originated out of the perceived threat from India and contention over Tibet, which lies just 114 kilometres from Kathmandu. Following China's refusal to give military assistance to Nepal during the Anglo-Nepalese war of 1814-1816, Nepal invaded Tibet in 1854. China quickly intervened and the Treaty of Thapathali was signed between the two countries in 1856. Nepal recognized China's supremacy in the region and agreed to provide assistance if Tibet was ever invaded by a foreign force.

When an armed British mission arrived in Tibet from India in 1905, however, Nepal did not intervene. Having come under the influence of British India after its loss in the Anglo-Nepalese war, Nepal went as far as to tell China that it would assist the Tibetans if they ever declared independence, provided it was within British interests. When the Tibetans used the chaos of the 1911 Revolution to expel the Chinese, Nepal broke ties with China altogether.

Relations were re-established in 1955 when the Chinese began sending soldiers into Tibet. With the British gone from India, Nepal recognized Tibet as a sovereign part of Chinese territory and in 1960, a year after Tibet's failed uprising and the Dalai Lama's flight into exile, the two countries signed the Treaty of Peace and Friendship, cementing strong ties that continue today.

Now the new "Comprehensive Treaty" will bring the two countries even closer. The treaty puts into place agreements that China will not attack Nepal and will respect its sovereignty, while Nepal will solidify its acceptance of the "One China" policy. Under the policy Tibet, Taiwan, and Hong Kong are stated as indisputable parts of Chinese territory, and Nepal will not allow anti-Chinese activities on its soil. Nepal proved its willingness to fulfil such promises in the days surrounding the 50th anniversary of the March 10, 1959, Tibetan Uprising. The day after a visit by Chinese assistant foreign minister Hu Zhengyue, who arrived in Nepal last month leading a 14-member delegation, 27 Tibetans monks were arrested in Kathmandu. Eighteen were released and nine turned over to the United Nations and deported to India. The streets around the two Chinese embassies in Kathmandu were also closed off, declared "protest-free zones", and staffed with police who had orders to arrest anyone demonstrating nearby. Additional arrests of Tibetan activists were carried out and demonstrators were quickly confronted.

China welcomes these closer relations, with the additional support for its "One China" policy and assistance in controlling the more than 20,000 Tibetan refugees living in Nepal. The refugees, if they ever gave up the aging Dalai Lama's method of peaceful negotiation, could use Nepal's difficulty to control its northern border to launch attacks on Chinese forces in Tibet-something which Khampa fighters did with short-lived US Central Intelligence Agency support in the late 1960s and early 1970s. China views the establishing of closer relations with Nepal as an important step in its competition with India for regional influence. "China now seems to view Nepal as a vital bridge toward South Asia as part of strategy of encircling India," said Nepal expert Sanjay Upadya.

However, Nepal's interest in expanding relations with China is more complicated. The country has long sought to balance the interests of India and China, the two regional powers it lies between. Since the signing of the Indo-Nepalese Treaty of 1950, India has come to heavily dominate Nepalese politics. While the treaty acknowledges Nepal's sovereignty, clauses in the agreement give India a greater amount of control over Nepal than the Maoist government would prefer.

It is the overbearing influence of India that has pushed Nepal's Maoist government decisively towards China. The shift has been so strong that Premier Prachanda went as far as to break the long-standing tradition of Nepalese heads of state making their first foreign trip to India, instead visiting China, ostensibly to attend the opening ceremony of the 2008 Summer Olympic Games in Beijing. The move toward China does not necessarily mean that Nepal is breaking ties with India-the government rather seeks to decrease Indian influence. As Nepalese journalist Narendra Prasad Upadhyaana said, "It is not that China is ideal. It is only to neutralize India. Historically, socially, and culturally Nepal is closer to India. On a political level however the Maoist government wants to avoid being controlled by India as much as possible."

This new partnership with China comes at a time of great necessity for Nepal. The country is facing growing insecurity which many experts in Kathmandu believe could escalate into a crisis within the next year. With the decade-long civil war resulting in the overthrow of the monarchy, Nepal is facing the challenges of a newly democratic nation that has innumerable political groups and organizations vying for a tiny amount of resources amid growing insecurity.

The country's police and army have become polarized, with different groups supporting the Maoists, opposition forces, and even the return of the monarchy. A number of journalists have been attacked in the past six months. Amid simmering discontent within the Maoist Army, which refuses to integrate with the regular army and continues to recruit soldiers, the expected flood of returning immigrants from jobs in the Middle East and Malaysia due to the global financial crisis makes Nepal's immediate future seem grim.

Perhaps the most dangerous threat to the country's stability, however, is the deteriorating situation in the southern Terai region. Members of the Tharu indigenous group recently declared a 14-day strike, shut down roads, and engaged in near daily clashes with police that left four people dead. The Tharus were demanding to be recognized as distinct from the Madhesis, the ethnic group that most indigenous people from the Terai are lumped into. Government negotiation ended the strike only after the situation had become so tense that police were ordered to escort petrol trucks through checkpoints and the price of fruit and vegetables in some Kathmandu markets had nearly doubled.

Though the strike has ended, the Tarai will continue to be an issue for Nepal. The indigenous groups demand that a new constitution divide the country into ethnically based autonomous states, something that could spell disaster as many of the ethnic groups in Nepal do not even acknowledge the others' right to exist. The idea of "ethnic federalism" will not be given up easily though. According to Dr Om Gurung, an indigenous rights leader in Kathmandu, the establishment of ethnically based autonomous federal states was a key promise of the Maoists during the civil war. Recently, however, the government has begun backing away from the promise, and most experts believe that such a system would set the stage for future conflict. Indigenous leaders are adamant, however, that Nepal's diverse nature requires such a system.

Dangerously, after the Maoist victory in the civil war and their subsequent international recognition, organizations in Nepal realized that agitation and violence does indeed work as a means of achieving political goals. With 70 identified armed groups operating across Nepal, most the wings of political organizations, the government and safety of the people are severely threatened. How the indigenous groups will choose to assert themselves if their demands for autonomous states are not met is still unknown.

Unless the government manages to control this growing unrest, the Maoist revolution may in fact prove to have just been the catalyst for a longer struggle for territory, resources, and representation in Nepal that the country will have to face as it struggles over the course of the next year to write a new constitution and make the difficult transition from a country at war to a country at peace.

This is a desire that can be assisted by a closer relationship with China. Over the past years China has proven itself willing to give large amounts of no-strings-attached cash and support for infrastructure building to countries that support its "One China" policy and allow it to expand its growing global influence. This is in contrast with most Western countries which demand that aid goes to specific projects and require greater oversight regarding where the funds end up. While the lack of transparency in Nepal means that much of the aid will be lost due to corruption, there is enough being offered that some effect will be felt by the population.

Along with the $16.4 million donation, after the signing of the "Comprehensive Treaty" China will add an additional 770 kilometres to the Kathmandu-Khasa highway in Tibet, effectively linking Nepal with China's massive internal railway system. Additional roads connecting Tibet and Nepal will be built and Chinese products are increasingly replacing Indian products, something that most Nepalese appreciate because of the lower cost. "China's products are sound to our pockets," said Nepalese journalist Narendra Prasad Upadhyaana.

The additional access to China is also expected to stimulate economic growth in Tibet, something that the Chinese government considers key to making the Tibetans drop their demands for autonomy. Larger groups of tourists coming from Nepal, and Tibetan salt being sold to Nepal, certainly may lessen some of the Tibetans' anger towards China, but it will not quite be the salve that the Chinese government wants it to be. As one Tibetan activist in Kathmandu said, "China does not have human rights. Nepal is following that. They are bending over for China and letting the Chinese control the police and treat the Tibetans here like animals."

The closer relationship with China is also not being viewed favorably by Delhi. Earlier this month several Nepalese opposition politicians left for India, claiming the trip was for health reasons. Their visit coincides with the presence of Nepal's disposed King Gyanendra, who has been in India since last month for a wedding. Although the Indian government allowed the Maoists to overthrow the monarchy, the new preference for China is making India reconsider its support. This is something that the Maoists must have expected. They are, however, reacting nervously to the opposition visit to India. "A new pact is being signed in New Delhi against the Maoist government," said the Janadisha newspaper, a mouthpiece for the Maoist Party. "Delhi is encircling the Maoists," said Nepalese journalist Narendra Prasad Upadhyaana. "India brought them to power and now suddenly they have gone to the Chinese. And India and China still do not have cordial relations."

9 India's Tibet Policy: Need a Change

In recent past there have been some events in Tibet which have put an uncomfortable spotlight on China. Although the Tibetan uprising appears to have been put down for the moment, the Tibet story is not over. Troubles could erupt again. The whole world and the people of China themselves realize that China's Tibet policy has been a failure. A group of eminent Chinese writers and intellectuals have shown the courage to publicly question the Beijing regime's Tibet policy.

The psychological impact of developments in Tibet could be debilitating for China in the long term. It could inspire other disaffected ethnic and other groups in China like the Uighurs to try to coalesce with Tibetan groups, both within China and abroad. The more repression there is within China, the less credible is China's claim of 'peaceful rise.' Tibet may well hold the key both to China's internal stability and Hu Jintao's political longevity. No wonder Beijing is hysterical and considers Tibet a "life-and-death" question. The settlement of the India-China border and the status of Tibet are interlinked issues. Unless there is all-round agreement that Tibet is a part of China, there is only an India-Tibet boundary, not an India-China boundary.

By the crude and aggressive reiteration of its claim to Arunachal Pradesh, China has already ruled out any early settlement of the boundary question with India; recent events in Tibet would only reconfirm Chinese thinking not to settle the border with India unless it has Tibet firmly under its control. Therefore, India should deal with China with this perspective clearly in mind. Although it has already extracted significant concessions from India on Tibet, China remains uncertain and anxious about India's Tibet policy. The Dalai Lama's periodic statements, including recently, that India's policy on Tibet is over-cautious reinforce China's suspicions and fears. The failure of six rounds of talks between the representatives of the Dalai Lama and the Chinese government seem to indicate that the Chinese leaders have made up their minds that a satisfactory solution to Tibet, from China's point of view, is unlikely while the present Dalai Lama is still alive.

China's mistrust of the Dalai Lama has only intensified after the recent troubles. Yet, contrary to what the Chinese Government may be thinking, a post-Dalai Lama situation may become more radicalized, unpredictable and violent. In India's relations with China, Tibet is a key issue that requires skilful handling by India. India has recently taken some welcome tentative steps to review its Tibet policy. The first move was made in January 2008 when the statement issued at the end of Indian Prime Minister's visit to China did not carry any reference to Tibet. It is not clear whether this was a deliberate policy move, or a one-off measure. The widespread disturbances in Tibet in March 2008 provide an opportunity for India to continue with its subtle policy shift. India's official statement on March 15, 2008 was a step in the right direction. Firstly, clearly refuting official Chinese propaganda, it stated that "innocent people" had died in Lhasa. Secondly, by expressing its "hope that all those involved will work to improve the situation and remove the causes of such trouble in Tibet....through dialogue and non-violent means," New Delhi has conveyed its message to Beijing that there is merit in the demands of Tibetans, that the onus is on Beijing to find a solution, and that such a solution requires dialogue, not use of force.

In describing the Dalai Lama as a man of non-violence, Prime Minister Manmohan Singh has clearly conveyed that India does not endorse the harsh and vituperative official Chinese denunciations of the Dalai Lama. China's recent offensive and patronizing approach and behaviour about India's stand on Tibet, including summoning the Indian Ambassador in the middle of the night, required an appropriate riposte. It is good that India has put off Minister Kamal Nath's visit to China. At the same time, India has sought to reassure China that India considers Tibet as "an autonomous region of China." One hopes that in the coming months the Government gives its Tibet policy a clearer strategic direction. While formulating its policy on Tibet, India has to keep in mind that it is uniquely placed vis-à-vis Tibet, and therefore must have a unique policy that conforms to its national interests, irrespective of what the rest of the world says or does. No other country has as important stakes in peace and stability in Tibet as India does.

A Tibet in ferment makes India's Himalayan frontiers unstable and insecure. As a democratic country that is hosting such a large number of Tibetans, India has a legitimate interest in what happens in Tibet. Since developments in Tibet have direct consequences for India, Tibet cannot be, as the Left parties in India make out, just an internal matter of China. If there is a severe crackdown on the Tibetans, it is likely to lead to an increased Chinese military presence in regions close to India's borders, which would have implications for India's own defence planning. It will also inevitably trigger off a fresh influx into India of Tibetan refugees, whom India would find it difficult to turn away on practical and humanitarian grounds. In subsequent official statements and/or through authoritative but deniable unofficial channels, India could emphasize that while it firmly upholds the principles of supporting the territorial integrity of duly constituted states and non-interference in other states' internal affairs, its own experience shows that the peace and stability of multi-racial, multi-religious and multi-cultural societies requires dialogue and accommodation within a democratic framework. Ethnic and separatist problems require political solutions that give every citizen the confidence of being an equal stakeholder in the state. India expects that China would put in place policies that would stabilize Tibet and give the Tibetan diaspora in India the confidence that they can return to their homeland. India needs to take full advantage of an important nuance, perhaps unintended, in India's acceptance of Tibet as a part of China: India has merely conceded that the "territory of the Tibetan Autonomous Region is a part of the People's Republic of China;" it has not accepted that Tibet (whose borders historically and in the minds of the Tibetans extend beyond the Tibetan Autonomous Region) was always a part of China. As a matter of fact, Tibet was quite independent of Chinese rule and had all the attributes of a sovereign state between 1913 and 1950.

Traditionally, thousands of Indian pilgrims have made pilgrimages to Mount Kailash and Mansarovar lakes in Tibet without needing any permission from the Chinese authorities in Beijing. If China can lay claim to Tawang in Arunachal Pradesh on the grounds of its cultural, historical and spiritual links with Tibet, the case for India's claim to Kailash-Mansarovar region on similar reasoning is probably more substantive. Secondly, if at any time in the future the People's Republic of China were to give way to another entity India could well argue that it is not obliged to recognize Tibet as a part of any new political entity of China. Of course, this is a hypothetical scenario, but the Chinese would not miss such nuances and subtleties.

India needs to take a leaf out of China's book in the matter of observance of solemn bilateral commitments. Just as China, contrary to the agreements with India in 2003 and 2005, has re-opened very aggressively its claim to Arunachal Pradesh, has still not fully accepted Sikkim as a part of India, and does not want an early settlement of the boundary question, India too should subtly reopen the whole question of the legitimacy of China's claim to Tibet, which is the basic foundation for China to make any territorial claim on India.

There could be many ways in which India could introduce some nuances in its traditional policy. For example, India could state that it considers Tibet, as an autonomous region, to be a part of the territory of the People's Republic of China – the implication being that it is only if Tibet is a truly autonomous region that India recognizes it as a part of China. Ironically, China, in welcoming the Indian approach during the recent uprising, has given legitimacy to India's unofficial policy shift.

The Chinese should be made aware that subtle shifts in India's Tibet policy will continue, and that India will remove the ambiguities in its Tibet policy only under the following conditions: firstly, if the situation on the ground permits it (very unlikely if

China persists with its present repressive policies); secondly, if there is a definitive settlement of the boundary issue; and, finally, only as a quid pro quo for China recognizing all of Jammu & Kashmir as an integral part of India.

It is time for India to get out of its defensive mindset and timid approach in dealing with China. There are vital national security interests at stake. Relations with China must be handled from a strategic, not a legalistic, perspective. The approach India follows should be multi-dimensional. India does want better relations with China, but it must also evolve a calculated and calibrated policy to put China under some pressure to safeguard its interests and concerns.

CHINA'S CLAIM TO TIBET IS FACTOR IN BORDER DISPUTE

This is perhaps the most militarized Buddhist enclave in the world. Perched above 10,000 feet in the icy reaches of the eastern Himalayas, the town of Tawang is not only home to one of Tibetan Buddhism's most sacred monasteries but also the site of a massive Indian military buildup. Convoys of army trucks haul howitzers along rutted mountain roads. Soldiers drill in muddy fields. Military bases appear every half-mile in the countryside, with watchtowers rising behind concertina wire.

A road sign on the northern edge of town helps explain the reason for all the fear and the fury: The border with China is just 23 miles away; Lhasa, the Tibetan capital, 316 miles; and Beijing 2,676 miles. "The Chinese army has a big deployment at the border, at Bumla," said Madan Singh, a junior commissioned officer who sat with a half-dozen soldiers one afternoon sipping tea beside a fog-cloaked road. "That's why we're here." Though little known to the outside world, Tawang is a flashpoint in relations between the world's two most populous nations. It is the focus of China's most delicate land-border dispute, a conflict rooted in Chinese claims of sovereignty over all of historical Tibet.

In recent months, both countries have stepped up efforts to secure their rights over this rugged patch of land. China tried to block a $2.9 billion loan to India from the Asian Development

Bank on the grounds that part of the loan was slated for water projects in Arunachal Pradesh, the state that includes Tawang. It was the first time China had sought to influence the territorial dispute through a multilateral institution. Then an Indian general announced that the Indian military was deploying extra troops and fighter jets in the area. The growing belligerence has soured relations between the two Asian giants and has prompted one Indian military leader to declare that China has replaced Pakistan as India's biggest threat.

Economic progress might be expected to bring the countries closer. China and India did $52 billion of trade last year, a 34 percent increase over 2007. But businesspeople say that border tensions have infused official deliberations over business deals, dampening the willingness of Chinese and Indian companies to invest in each other's countries. "Officials start taking more time, scrutinizing things more carefully, and all that means more delays and ultimately more denials," said Ravi Bhoothalingam, a former president of the Oberoi Group, the luxury hotel chain, and a member of the Institute of Chinese Studies in New Delhi. "That's not good for business."

The roots of the conflict go back to China's territorial claims to Tibet. Not only does the Dalai Lama, the exiled spiritual leader of the Tibetans, live in the foothills of the western Himalayas with the blessing of the Indian government, but China insists that this swath of northeast India has historically been part of Tibet, and thus should be part of China. Tawang is a thickly forested area of white stupas and steep, terraced hillsides that is home to the ethnic Monpa people, who practice Tibetan Buddhism, speak a language similar to Tibetan and once paid tribute to rulers in Lhasa. The 6th Dalai Lama was born here in the 17th century.

The Chinese army occupied Tawang briefly in 1962, during a war with India fought over this and other territories along the 2,521-mile border. More than 3,100 Indian soldiers and 700 Chinese soldiers were killed and thousands wounded in the border war. War memorials highlighting China's aggressions in Tawang here are big draws for Indian tourists. "The entire border is disputed," said Ma Jiali, an India scholar at the China Institutes of

Contemporary International Relations, a government-supported think tank in Beijing. "This problem hasn't been solved, and it's a huge barrier to China-India relations."

In some ways, Tawang has become a proxy battleground, too, between China and the Dalai Lama, who passed through this valley when he fled into exile in 1959. From his home in the distant hill town of Dharamsala, he wields enormous influence over Tawang. He appoints the abbot of the powerful monastery and gives financial support to institutions throughout the area. Last year, the Dalai Lama announced for the first time that Tawang is a part of India, bolstering the Indian government's territorial claims and infuriating China.

Traditional Tibetan culture runs strong in Tawang. At the Tawang monastery, an important centre of Tibetan learning, monks express apprehension about China's rule over Tibet, which the Chinese army seized in 1951. "I hate the Chinese government," said Gombu Tsering, 70, a senior monk who watches over the monastery's museum. "Tibet wasn't even a part of China. Lhasa wasn't a part of China." Few expect China to try to forcefully annex Tawang, but military skirmishes are a real danger, analysts say. The Indian military recorded 270 border violations and nearly 2,300 instances of "aggressive border patrolling" by Chinese soldiers last year, said Brahma Chellaney, a professor of strategic studies at the Centre for Policy Research, a research organization in New Delhi. Mr. Chellaney has advised the Indian government's National Security Council.

"The India-China frontier has become more 'hot' than the India-Pakistan border," he said in an e-mail. China has grown increasingly hostile to the Dalai Lama after a severe outbreak of ethnic unrest in Tibet. This year, it turned its diplomatic guns on India. China moved in March to block a $2.9 billion loan to India from the Asian Development Bank, a multi-nation group based in Manila that has China on its board, because $60 million of the loan had been earmarked for flood-control projects in Arunachal Pradesh, the state that includes Tawang. The loan was approved in mid-June over China's heated objections.

Weeks after China first tried to block the loan, the chief of the

Indian air force, now retired, told a prominent Indian newspaper that China posed a greater threat than Pakistan. Another official, J.J. Singh, the governor of Arunachal Pradesh and retired chief of the Indian army, said the next month that the Indian military was adding two divisions of troops, totalling 50,000 to 60,000 soldiers, to the border region over the next several years. Four Sukhoi fighter jets were immediately deployed to a nearby air base. Since 2005, when Chinese Prime Minister Wen Jiabao visited India, the two countries have gone through 13 rounds of bilateral negotiations over the issue. A last round was just held last month, with no results. Though China has actually resolved many of its border disputes in recent years, India remains a glaring exception.

THE GOVERNMENT OF TIBET IN EXILE

From July 20 to 23, 1994, Beijing staged the Third Forum on Work in Tibet which recommended the total destruction of an entire civilization flourishing on the Tibetan Plateau for thousands of years. This cultural "empire" once encompassed far-flung areas like Buryatia, Tuva and Kalmykia in Russia; Mongolia; Laddakh, Lahaul-Spiti, Sikkim, and Arunachal Pradesh in India; Mustang, Dolpo and Solo Khumbu in Nepal; Bhutan and parts of western China.

The policy formulated in 1994 in Beijing-and these days pursued with Cultural Revolutionary zeal in Tibet-will mean the annihilation of the spiritual homeland of this shared culture. Implementation of the Third Work Forum is thus having a crippling impact on the traditional culture of millions of non-Tibetans as the well-spring of their cultural inspiration is forcibly drained and there is nothing to replenish the continuous growth and development of this distinct and highly evolved civilization.

Losing Hearts and Minds

The decisions made at the Third Forum rest on two fundamental conclusions which Beijing drew. It realized it was losing out in two vital fields-ideology and propaganda. For a state whose existence is justified by its ideological superiority and the power of its propaganda to shape the thinking of the masses, the implications of this for the future was at best uncertain, at worst dangerous. Beijing concluded it was losing the ideological war because, despite the unrelenting assault on Tibetan Buddhism, Tibetans were as devoted to their traditional beliefs as ever. Beijing has succeeded in physically enslaving the country but it has not won over the hearts, minds and loyalty of the Tibetan populace.

Communist ideology, enforced by the military might of China, had failed to dent the heart of Buddhism. Added to this was the communist authorities' total bafflement at the non-violent policy underpinning the Middle Way Approach advocated by His Holiness the Dalai Lama to resolve the issue of Tibet's future status. For a regime which is based on Mao's dictum that political power grows out of the barrel of a gun, this supposedly eccentric philosophy which says victory lies in captui ng the hearts and minds of people by the power of ideas rather than killing by the power of the gun comes as a bolt from the blue. Much of Beijing's knee-jerk reaction to, and its bafflement at, His Holiness the Dalai Lama's new policy of rapprochement lies at the heart of its new hardline policy.

Beijing considered it was losing the propaganda war because, for one reason or the other, the world's media and its pop culture considered-at least for the moment-Tibet and Tibetan Buddhism their very own cuddly pandas. Despite its financial might China found it extremely difficult to exterminate this image of Tibet and get its voice heard on the Tibetan issue in the court of the international media. In order to address these weaknesses the Third Forum concentrated on two issues. One was to focus on Tibet's economic development in the hope that this would keep Tibetan demonstrations off the streets. This was tantamount to bribing the Tibetans with promises of riches to come if they toed the party line. The other concern was to win the coming and new generations of Tibetans over to the Chinese viewpoint.

Beijing has given up on the present generation of Tibetans as a lost cause. If the coming generations of Tibetans were also lost to the 'Dalai Clique' this, the Chinese concluded, would have dangerous consequences for Chinese rule in Tibet. The 15-year-old Gyalwa Karmapa's dramatic escape from Tibet in

January 2000 was a warning to the Beijing authorities of the erosion of loyalty to China. The Karmapa's flight, and the earlier escape of Agya Rinpoche, the abbot of Kumbum Monastery, came as a huge embarrassment for China, because retaining these high lamas gave China a degree of legitimacy for its rule in Tibet. This is the reason why Beijing is enforcing with greater strictness its 1993 instruction of recalling young Tibetans studying in schools and monasteries run by Dharmasaia in India. This is also the rationale for Beijing closing down schools in Tibet which are privately run by Tibetans.

For these reasons Tibet today is in the throes of a second Cultural Revolution as the Chinese authorities step up their long-term strategy to exterminate Tibet's distinct cultural and ethnic identity. The authorities are pursuing a four-pronged strategy to achieve their final objective. They have stepped up repression while employing their huge propaganda machine to paint a rosy picture of Tibet. They have quickened the pace of economic development to dampen Tibetan nationalism and are simultaneously moving more Chinese settlers onto the Tibetan Plateau to change Tibet's demographic composition and to ease social unrest because of mounting unemployment back in China.

The Third Work Forum on Tibet was convened by the top Chinese leadership and was presided over by President Jiang Zemin. The authorities have now enshrined this Work Forum as the most "important strategic policy to rejuvenate Tibet" and have hailed its directives as the new manifesto for party work on the plateau. The significance of the Third Work Forum lies in the fact that it overturned the more liberal policies laid out for Tibet's "development" by the First and Second Work Forums held in 1980 and 1984.

The first two work forums were initiated by the late Hu Yaobang, then Secretary General of the Chinese Communist Party. This liberal and somewhat maverick leader is credited with masterminding a series of measures to improve the social, economic and political conditions in Tibet. The brief spell of liberalization markedly improved the living conditions of the majority of Tibetans and contributed to a more relaxed intellectual and social climate.

The Third Work Forum reversed these policies and reinstated hardline measures under which Tibet is still reeling today. The Tibetans in Tibet perceive the current repressive policies as a second Cultural Revolution. The question is why did China choose to jettison its earlier more liberal policies and adopt a manifesto which is leading to the systematic destruction of Tibet's distinct culture. The answer lies in domestic and international events which forced China to formulate a series of hardline policies on Tibet which eventually crystallized into the Third Work Forum for Tibet. The world which confronted China in the late 1980s and early 1990s was a frightening one.

Starting from 1987, Tibet was rocked by a string of protest demonstrations, which called for Tibetan independence. One of the largest demonstrations which erupted on March 5, 1989 in Lhasa, forced the authorities to impose martial law on the city. These demonstrations are now seen to have been an inspiration behind the outburst of Chinese students' pro-democracy uprisings. The authorities saw the series of Tiananmen Square demonstrations as a sign of their Central Government losing control, and in an attempt to regain supremacy, the authorities slaughtered-perhaps hundreds if not thousands of students on June 4, 1989. These demonstrations were a chilling replay to the authorities of the May 4, 1919 student demonstrations in Beijing which signalled a political and cultural awakening across the erstwhile Middle Kingdom.

Bejing's fears of losing control were exacerbated by external events which saw the unraveling of the communist world. The Solidarity Movement in Poland, the fall of the Berlin Wall, and the implosion of the Soviet Union fed Beijing's paranoia over threats to the Chinese Communist Party hold on power. Official China's fears were further inflamed by the rapidly changing attitude of the broad masses as they turned back from communism to traditional beliefs like Confucionism, Buddhism, Islam, Christianity and indigenous folk cults. In the eyes of ordinary citizens communism was becoming totally discredited and this, more than anything else, was the biggest nightmare for China's leadership. The leadership's justification for staying in power was being disavowed by the masses. For a one-party dictatorship this historically indicates the first step along the slippery road to dissolution and removal of power.

For these reasons the Chinese leadership then reverted to its earlier view that traditional beliefs were its real enemy. In competing with Buddhism, Confucionism, Islam, Christianity and other isms, communism was losing out in terms of its ability to retain the loyalty and allegiance of the masses. The leadership revived the old aphorisms once served up to the Tibetan people to justify their policies to destroy Tibetan Buddhism during the Cultural Revolution. Bewildered Tibetans were then told that just as there cannot be two suns in the sky, so there cannot be both Buddhism and socialism in Tibet. Inevitably Buddhism then had to give way to socialism. And again, today, religion is being blatantly sublimated to Chinese state power.

These were the fears of the Chinese leaders when they met in Beijing in 1994 to hammer out their new Tibet initiatives. For the Chinese authorities Tibet is an especially sensitive issue because of their conviction that hostile Western forces are using the issue of Tibet to "westernize" China and to lead to its territorial fragmentation. The third generation Chinese leaders came to the conclusion that stability in Tibet was vital to the stability of China as a whole. Earlier, Tibet was merely of peripheral concern to the vital interests of China's sprawling communist empire. Now, with the Third Work Forum, the authorities were saying, "We must clearly understand that we must do our work in Tibet not only for the sake our of own region's stability and development, not only for the interests of our people, but also for the sake of the whole nation's stability and development."

In Tibet, China faced peculiar problems because of the inherent strength of Tibetan Buddhism and the depth of devotion of the populace to His Holiness the Dalai Lama. The sustained burst of religious revival that followed in the wake of the brief spell of liberalization in Tibet confirmed the leadership's worst fears that decades of concerted assault on Tibetan culture and religion had not extinguished the people's traditional beliefs and values. From merely nuisance value, the Chinese leadership now viewed Tibetan

Buddhism as a very real and imminent threat to the stability of Chinese rule in Tibet.

At the same time the Chinese leadership's attitude towards His Holiness the Dalai Lama changed. From being an uncertain ally in the peace process in Tibet, the current Chinese leadership now saw him as a full-blown "enemy". A top-level conclave held in Beijing on March 10, 1993 concluded that, "There are different factions within the Dalai Clique; they are, however, unanimous in their political nature and position. They differ from each other in ideological viewpoints and ways of expressing them. Different strategies must be adopted to use their differences, to deal with them differently in order to divide and destroy them."

Repeated statements by high-level officials describe the struggle against "splittism", the official term for Tibetan independence, as a "life-and-death struggle". At the 1994 annual meeting of the "TAR" Communist Party Committee to brief members on the policy thrust of the Third Work Forum on Tibet, Raidi, deputy Secretary of the Committee said, "Up to now, his (the Dalai Lama's) standpoint on Tibet's independence has never changed, and we must reveal his double-faced true colour. The focal point in our region in the struggle against splittism is to oppose the Dalai Clique. As the saying goes, to kill a serpent, one must first cut off its head."

In short, the Third Work Forum decided that Beijing was in a position to solve the Tibet issue without the Dalai Lama's involvement. It abandoned the earlier liberal policy of including His Holiness the Dalai Lama in any future settlement of Tibet's status. His Holiness the Dalai Lama was clearly singled out as the cause of China's "Tibet problem".

The Third Work Forum also abandoned the policy of granting concessions to Tibet because of the plateau's "special characteristics". This policy had been the cornerstone of recommendations made by the First and Second Tibet Work Forums.

To carry out its new hardline policies in Tibet, Beijing appointed Chen Kuiyuan as the "TAR" Party Secretary in 1992. Chen

Kuiyuan's appointment is significant because he had a track record for being a tough and ruthless administrator. He had already served as the First Secretary of the Chinese Communist Party in Inner Mongolia and is credited with repressing the rebellious Mongols, many of whom refer to him as "the butcher". Chen Kuiyuan was especially recommended to the post by Hu Jintao, the current Vice-President of China, who was then the First Secretary of the Chinese Communist Party in Tibet.

Tackling Tibetan Nationalism

The Third Work Forum policies chalked out for Tibet contained four key elements. China stepped up the scale of repression in Tibet. External propaganda work was escalated. The pace of economic development in Tibet-and its corollary of encouraging more Chinese settlers and businessmen to take advantage of the economic boom on the "roof of the world"-was also increased. In short, Beijing had decided to tackle Tibetan nationalism head-on and observers are still assessing the consequences on both Chinese rule in Tibet and on the populace.

Beijing remains convinced that these key components of its current policy will stabilize Chinese rule over Tibet and solve once and for all, the vexed problem of its negative image over the way Tibet has been handled. One main target of the current policy of repression is Tibetan Buddhism. Chinese leaders are increasingly alarmed by the proliferation of monasteries and temples which the period of liberalization spawned throughout Tibet: they are seen as the bastions of Tibetan nationalism. The authorities have set up "Democratic Management Committees" to control monasteries and nunneries and created "Work Inspection Teams" to supervise the "education" of monks and nuns.

A major thrust is underway to break the bond of loyalty between the clergy in Tibet and His Holiness the Dalai Lama in India. Campaigns like "Strike Hard" and "Patriotic Re-education", unleashed in 1996, are aimed at crippling the rise of Tibetan Buddhism which the authorities suspect is weaning the loyalty of the Tibetan people away from the communist party and towards His Holiness the Dalai Lama. One salient feature of the "Strike

Hard" campaign is how differently it is interpreted in China and Tibet. China's "Strike Hard" campaign was started to weed out corruption. Tibet's version is used as a political tool to eliminate those whom the authorities label "splittists". In Tibet, rather than striking at corruption, the authorities turn a blind eye to this social disease in the hope that it will erode the traditional morality of Tibetans and undermine Tibetan Buddhism.

In fact, at a secret meeting held in December 1999 in Chengdu, capital of Sichuan province, Chen Kuiyuan, the hardline Party Secretary of "TAR" recommended to the Central Chinese Government that an all-out effort must be made to eradicate Tibetan Buddhism and culture from the face of the earth so that no memory of them will be left in the minds of coming generations of Tibetans-except as museum pieces.

Chen Kuiyuan stated that the main cause of instability is the existence of the Dalai Lama and his Government-in-Exile in Dharamsala and these must be "uprooted". He recommended that Tibet, Tibetan people and Tibetan Buddhism-in other words the very name of Tibet-must be destroyed and the "Tibet Autonomous Region" be merged with provinces like Sichuan. While treating Tibetans to boot-heel subjugation at home, internationally China was on an overdrive propaganda blitz. At a brainstorming conclave held on March 10, 1993, Zeng Jian-hui, Vice-Minister of the Propaganda Ministry, told participants, "The propaganda work on the question of Tibet is one of the focal points of the entire external propaganda work...With regard to attacks by the West and the Dalai Clique and their frequent activities, our external propaganda should launch offensive. We should expand our spheres of influence; in particular, we should infiltrate our propaganda into the mainstream life of the West.

"Firstly we should continue to send Tibetan scholars and Tibetan singing and dancing troupes abroad to lecture and perform. Secondly, relevant embassies and consulates should aim at the public opinion and the activities of the Dalai Clique in the countries where they are stationed and utilize speeches, picture exhibitions, special articles and other forms to carry out propaganda work, so as to win over officials and people of those countries... We should reinforce the work of utilizing the power of foreign propaganda. A few years ago, in the light of the situation of that time, we made arrangements for foreign journalists to visit Tibet."

The September 3, 2000 edition of *People's Daily* carried a story headlined "Tibet Welcomes Foreign Journalists for Objective Reporting". It stated that "A senior Tibetan official said Sunday that Tibet welcomes foreign journalists to come for objective and just reporting, but not those who take distorted views. Raidi, Deputy Secretary of the Tibet Autonomous Regional Committee of the Communist Party of China and Chairman of the Standing Committee of the Tibetan Autonomous Regional People's Congress, made the remarks at a meeting here with a press delegation of Thailand." In this context, it is interesting to note that N. Ram, the editor of India's *Frontline* magazine, devoted 36 pages of the September 15, 2000 issue to promote the Chinese line and recommended that the Indian Government expel the Central Tibetan Administration from Indian soil for being the main stumbling block to normal relations between India and China. It is difficult to assess to what extent the views contained in his stupendous reporting marathon are his own.

These editorial outbursts are in line with policy decisions outlined in the early nineties. During a two-day secret conclave in March 1993 in Chengdu, Vice-Minister Zeng Jian-hui, told participants, "All foreigners that we entertain and send to Tibet must have a relatively objective opinion of Tibet. We should use people from abroad to carry out the propaganda on Tibet for us, which is more powerful than if we do it."

Along with its external public relations strategy, China is presently carrying out a potentially much more dangerous policy of speeding up the pace of Tibet's economic development and its related drive to bring more Chinese settlers onto the Tibetan Plateau. Beijing's Western China Development Programme, which incorporates Tibet in its ambit, is devised to shift the focus of China's economic activities from Coastal China to the interior-both to narrow the imbalance in the level of economic development between the two regions and to ease population pressure on the coastal areas which attract millions of migrant workers. The focus of Beijing's Western China Economic Development Programme in Tibet is to exploit the plateau's still untapped minerals and other natural resources and to upgrade Tibet's infrastructure-like roads and telecommunications-to facilitate transportation of these resources to China. The other purpose of the heightened level of economic activity is to divert the Tibetans' attention from their political fate to focus on their livelihood-thus undermining Tibetan nationalism.

The Chinese authorities aim to manipulate the situation in Tibet still further by bringing in more Chinese settlers who would then demographically cement Chinese rule once and for all. These current hardline policies and their implementation in Tibet are impacting the stalled Sino-Tibetan Dialogue and will vitally affect the ability of Tibetans to survive as a distinct people and culture.

Beijing's Flawed Perceptions

The basic flaws in China's new policy in its search to resolve the problem of Tibet is thinking the solution can exclude the involvement of His Holiness the Dalai Lama. The other is in attempting to solve the problem over the heads of Tibet's citizens.

These two fundamental mistakes will exacerbate China's Tibet problem, not solve it. The reason lies in the history of Tibet and in the sentiments of the people. The institution of the Dalai Lamas of Tibet is more than 600 years old, if we start from the birth of the first Dalai Lama in 1391. In the course of its growth and development, the very institution itself came to symbolize fundamental beliefs and the political destiny of the nation. The bond between the Dalai Lamas and the Tibetan people is fundamental and unbreakable; any attempt, however sustained, will never succeed in driving a wedge between the two.

Consequently, China's current policy of forcing Tibetans-especially monks and nuns-to denounce His Holiness the Dalai Lama and pledge loyalty to the Chinese Communist Party will prove counterproductive. In view of this the Third Work Forum's basic assumption that in the case of Tibet time is on the side of China, and that Beijing can stall the problem of Tibet till the demise of the present Dalai Lama whereupon the issue of Tibet will solve itself, is fatally flawed-based as it is on a mistaken perception of the role played by the institution of the Dalai Lamas in the development of Tibetan history.

This assumption, if not reviewed, revised and abandoned, will prove catastrophic for the Chinese leadership and for those who chose to turn their whimsical personal analysis into state policy. The reason is simple. The Chinese Communist Party was founded in the 1920s and came to power in 1949. Within this short span of time the masses have lost faith in communist ideology, and members of the party these days pay mere lip service to the ideological justifications of the party. Conversely, the institution of the Dalai Lamas as a political force is more than 300 years old. These days the Dalai Lama is recognized by Tibetans throughout the world as the heart of Tibetan nationalism. How can a party which has lost its soul outlast an institution which symbolizes the very soul of a people? For these reasons it is imperative for China to review and re-assess its current hardline stance towards Tibet. China must re-start its stalled peace process over Tibet and consider His Holiness the Dalai Lama as a vital and active partner in the procedures. If China does this it will have won a powerful ally and companion along the road to peace, stability and continued prosperity.

CHINA STIFFENS MILITARY INTRANSIGENCE ON INDIA-TIBET BORDER

Introductory Observations

China's military intransigence along the India-Tiber Border seems to have visibly stiffened in the last few months. China's military intransigence does not arise from any military provocations from the Indian side. Legitimate measures by India and Indian Army and India Air Force to improve their defence preparedness along the India-Tibet border cannot be termed by China as provocative, or perceived as such.

Contrarily, despite the India-China "Agreement on Peace and Tranquillity Along the Border" signed in early 1990s, China has indulged in enhanced number of intrusions, transgressions and demolition of unoccupied posts in Indian territory. China has also increased air intrusions into Indian airspace especially in India's Aksaichin Sector. The Indian media, more specifically Indian TV channels have rightly focused on China's growing provocations along the India-Tibet Border. They are doing a good job in awakening and sensitizing Indian public consciousness to Chinese trends of needling and provoking India by unwarranted border incidents. It is patently wrong on the part of the Indian policy establishment and India's strategic analysts to advocate that by doing so, a "war hysteria" is being whipped up.

These are defeatist syndromes more reminiscent of the Nehru era which ultimately emboldened China to inflict the 1962 military debacle on India. Peace is desirable, very much desirable, but not the type of peace which the British PM Chamberlain brought from Munich which led to World War II. India's Prime Minister has always maintained a stony silence on national security threats in the making thus robbing the country of getting the sense as to where the Government stands in meeting threats and challenges from China and Pakistan. In the case of the "Chine Threat" to India, the political leadership and India's policy establishment virtually goes underground in not highlighting China's intentions and threats and further evading making known firm stands if any contemplated.

India cannot afford a 1962 repeat Chinese attack on India's sovereignty and territorial integrity, moreso in light of arrogant threats emanating from China's strategic and military community that "India needs to be taught a military lesson again". India's political leaders, policy establishment and strategic analysts cannot advocate that such Chinese provocative statements against India are emanating from "non-governmental' entities. Do they need to be reminded that China does not boast of "non-governmental entities" in terms of policy articulation. The non-governmental strategic entities are very much a part of China's official machinery and used as conduits to issue warnings and threats which China officially does not want to articulate.

Logically, therefore, we would like to focus attention on the following aspects of China's growing military intransigence on the India-Tibet Border:

- India Was Not China's Neighbour from 1947-1950
- China's Creeping Aggression Against India 1950 Onwards
- China's Reluctance to Reach Border Settlement with India
- China's Revived Upsurge in Military Intransigence: The Contextual Factors
- Indian Public Will Not Accept any Territorial Adjustments with China by Indian Government
- Indian Government's Imperatives for Strong and Assertive Military Preparedness
- Indian Prime Minister's Forthcoming Visit to China Needs to be Postponed.

India Was Not China's Neighbour from 1947-1950

India and Tibet were peaceful neighbours from 1947-1950 on emergence of India as an independent nation. China become India's instantly military adversarial neighbour by its forcible military occupation of the peaceful spiritual kingdom of Tibet. From 1947 – 1950, India under Nehru failed to grasp the menacing trends in the making of the rise of a monolithic Communist China and its hegemonistic designs towards Tibet and Xingjian. Nehru ignored Tibet's cries for help including refusal of support to Tibet to raise in the United Nations the issue of China's threat to Tibet of military occupation. India's strategic diminution in Chinese military perspectives commenced thereafter. This is important to note as China's current perspectives on India continue to be coloured by the same mindset.

CHINA'S CREEPING AGGRESSION AGAINST INDIA 1950 ONWARDS

China was not satisfied with its military occupation of Tibet and adhering to Tibet's traditional boundaries with India. China's military occupation of Tibet and India's supine, submissive and strategically oblivious policies under Nehru from 1950 onwards emboldened China to make demands on India for redrawing and realignment of India's erstwhile borders with Tibet. China forcibly incorporated a major portion of Aksai-chin, an area equal to that of Switzerland, under her control to link Tibet with Xingjian.

Nehru's reaction was to keep the Parliament and the Indian nation ignorant about Chinese aggression for over 5.6 years.

The Indian military establishment starved of defence budget allocation commensurate with the needs to meet the Chinese threat, was emasculated and became the victim of Chinese military humiliation in 1962 due to the incompetence of India's political rulers. An Indian spurt of military build-up in reaction of Chinese aggression of 1962 petered out by 1967 or so. Virtual inertness followed till about 1986-87 when Rajiv Gandhi as PM listening to the advice of Indian military hierarchy made funds available for a forward military build-up in Arunachal Pradesh stemming China's aggression in Sumdorong. China stopped in its tracks. The lesson for India was exercise of firmness of purpose when confronting China.

This military up gradation was brought to a virtual halt by 1991-1993 when India's then Finance Minister now Prime Minister effected cuts in India's defence budgets for nearly a decade. Defence preparedness and upgradation of defence infrastructure against China especially in the North East came to a virtual stop India's spasmodic spurts to improve India's defensive postures along the India-Tibet border therefore did not impose a sustained restraint to China's creeping rhetorical and physical aggression against India. Today, China is now terming Arunachal Pradesh as Southern Tibet and therefore a legitimate target for a future Chinese military action, intruding across in the international border in Sikkim, and upping the ante in the Aksai-chin Sector in Laddakh.

China's Revived Upsurge in Military Intransigence: The Contextual Factors

The major contextual factors prompting China's revived military intransigence along the India-Tibet border can be listed as follows:

- Tibet uprisings and insurgency in Xingjian prompting China's strategic nervousness over its hold on its peripheries.
- India's growing strategic proximity to the United States upsetting the power-balance.

- Upgradation of India's military postures in Aksai-chin sector and Arunachal Pradesh which could be a deterrence to Chinese military adventurisms
- Opening of the Golmud-Lhasa railway facilitating speedy Chinese military buildup in Tibet.

China probably perceives that now maybe the opportune time for China to "teach India a military lesson" before India enhances her global political profile and before India narrows her military differential with China along the India-Tibet border. Current border provocations by China along the India-Tibet Border need to be viewed in this light.

China's Reluctance to Reach Border Settlement with India

China's reluctance to reach border settlement with India on the India-Tibet border arises from:

- Chin's intention to keep alive this issue as a constant strategic pressure-point against India
- Border settlement of the India-Tibet Border would involve physical demarcation by boundary markers, identified and authenticated by both sides.
- Above would rob China the strategic propensity to keep coming up with revised claims on the alignment of the border/LAC.

It is high time India recognizes the futility of continued boundary settlement talks with China. It lulls the Indian establishment into complacency.

Indian Public Will Not Accept any Territorial Adjustments with China by Indian Government

The biggest problem which India faces in facing China squarely is the multiplicity of voices within India pleading that India could swap Aksai-chin with Tawang or carry out adjustments in Tawang to accommodate China. Such voices and views remind one of Munich and Chamberlain. India needs a Winston Churchill to meet the China threat. India's political leaders, policy establishment and strategic analysis should desist from such advocacy as it not only belittles them but more importantly belittles India.

The Indian public will never accept any territorial adjustments with China by any Indian Government. The Indian public will oppose tooth and nail any such misadventure by any Indian Government. Nehru as India's tallest political leader was never forgiven by the Indian public for his misplaced trust in China's peace rhetoric and China then stabbing India in the back. It led to his untimely demise. Other Indian Prime Ministers too should desist from stepping over the similar crevice.

Indian Government's Imperatives for Strong and Assertive Military Preparedness

It is encouraging to note that plans do exist now for an augmented Indian military profile along the India-Tibet border to meat China's large-scale military build-up in Occupied Tibet. The Prime Minister needs a personal over-watch on defence preparedness along the India-Tibet Border. However such an augmentation needs to be done on a fast track basis and not left to the vagaries of India lethargic civil bureaucracy.

India does not have to be apologetic about its legitimate defence preparations along the India-Tibet border. Strong defence preparedness along India's borders is the sovereign right and an inescapable duty of the Indian Government. India's Prime Minister made a bold attempt to visit Arunachal Pradesh some time back, but why did be back-out of visiting Tawang which would been symbolically more assertive. India's Prime Minister failed to send the appropriate message to China. When is the Indian Prime Minister going to visit Leh and Indian territory at Chushul and Pangong Lake? Nehru belatedly did so in 1959 or so to raise the morale of Indian troops guarding India's borders.

Concluding Observations

China's military intransigence along the India-Tibet border arises from strategic and military Chinese arrogance fortified by India's appeasement and supine polices more resembling those of vassal states of China in the past. It is unwarranted on the part of India's political leaders, policy establishment and strategic analysts to term increased media focus on China's military misdemeanors along the India-Tibet border as amounting to generation of "war hysteria" India's strategic image as emerging global power is seriously damaged when responsible Indians start advocating swaps of Indian territory or adjustments in Tawang to accommodate China.

China is "India's Enemy Number One" in Indian strategic perceptions. This is based on China's demonstrated policies of strategic encirclement of India intended to keep India strategically off-balance. China has used India's other arch-enemy Pakistan as a proxy for her designs and strategy against India. China, if serious in altering this Indian perception has to re-cast her South Asian strategy, desist from redefining the boundary alignments along the India -Tibet Border and maintain peace and tranquillity on India's borders.

INDIA SHOULD REVISIT ITS TIBET POLICY

The Indian government's response to the protests in Tibet has been to merely state its "distress" about the situation and reaffirm its position that Tibet is an "internal" affair of China. New Delhi had assured Beijing that its position on the Tibet issue is "clear and consistent" and that this "would not change in the future." The Indian position is based on its traditional opposition to separatist movements and to foreign intervention in support of such movements. Also, given the present dynamics of India-China relations with greater synergy as the goal, New Delhi does not favour supporting the Tibetan cause. However, protests by Tibetans have implications for India as the Tibet issue is entangled with the India-China border dispute.

The Tibet issue is rooted in the histories of the three countries – India, China and Tibet. Tibet has existed throughout history as a distinct civilization with rich culture, language, religion, polity and identity. Through the centuries India and Tibet have maintained strong religious and trade ties, and have shared a peaceful border. But the advent of British power in the Indian subcontinent altered the nature of this relationship.

The British Raj's policy towards Tibet was shaped by the Great Game and the need to prevent Russia from posing a threat to India. It was against this backdrop that the Raj called for the tripartite Simla conference in October 1913, which was attended by representatives from British India (Henry McMahon), Republican China (Chen Yifan) and Tibet (Lonchen Shatra). The goal was to settle the boundary between British India and Tibet on the one hand and between Tibet and China on the other. The result was the Simla Agreement of 1914, which the Chinese representative initialled but only under British pressure. The Agreement divided Tibet into Inner and Outer Tibet. China was given sovereignty over Inner Tibet but only suzerain control over Outer Tibet. And the boundary between India and Tibet was demarcated, with the Raj retaining trading and extra-territorial rights in Outer Tibet.

Independent India inherited this arrangement, which boiled down to sustaining Tibet as a buffer zone with de facto independent status under Chinese suzerainty. In the post-1949 period, when the People's Republic of China came into being, India urged China to let Tibet continue as an autonomous region in line with its historical status, religious, cultural and political identity. However, the entry of 20,000 PLA troops in 1950-51 into Tibet ended its independent status and eventually brought to the fore the India-China border issue.

During his 1954 visit to China, Jawaharlal Nehru had raised the issue of inaccurate border alignment as depicted in some Chinese maps. Premier Zhou Enlai responded that these maps were reproductions of old Kuomintang maps and that his government has had no time to revise them. However, Nehru's December 14, 1958 letter, in which he had once again raised the issue of Chinese maps depicting the border alignment inaccurately, elicited a different response from Zhou. The Chinese Premier wrote back on January 23, 1959 stating that the Sino-Indian border was never delimited and that China has never recognised the McMahon Line.

After the 1962 India-China war, China began to claim some 90,000 square kilometres of Indian territory in the eastern sector and 38,000 square kilometres in the Aksai Chin area. These claims flow directly from China's control over Tibet and its felt need to consolidate its rule over this rebellious territory.

Between 1947 and 1954, India's position on Tibet was based on recognising it as an independent nation. Tibet represented itself as an independent country at the Asian Relations Conference held in New Delhi in March-April 1947. But India subsequently gave up this position on April 29, 1954, when it signed an agreement with China on trade and intercourse between India and Tibet. Under the terms of the agreement, India gave up all extra-territorial rights and privileges that it had inherited from the British Raj and recognised Tibet as part of China. This, in effect, was a unilateral concession without the Indian government gaining anything in return.

In subsequent decades, New Delhi has repeatedly reiterated that Tibet is a part of China, in spite of the latter's encroachment into and extravagant claims over Indian territory, the border war it imposed on India in 1962, and the unresolved border dispute at the centre of which lies Tibet. In effect, such reiteration has meant the dilution of a bargaining card in the border negotiations. In 2003, the Vajpayee government went further than any other government before by stating that the "Tibetan Autonomous Region of China is part of the territory of China." This has two critical implications for Indian security. First, it excluded Inner Tibet (present day Sichuan, Yunnan and Qinghai provinces) from the geographical notion of Tibet, thus recognising Inner Tibet as Chinese land. Second, it provided China a greater opening to advance its claims on Arunachal Pradesh. For, Outer Tibet or the Tibetan Autonomous Region (TAR), according to the Chinese definition, includes Arunachal Pradesh, which it refers to as its 'southern state'.

India has consistently failed to understand nuances in Chinese diplomatic practice and negotiating tactics. China is tackling the Tibet problem at two levels. One, it is involving the Dalai Lama's representatives in fruitless talks, while also disparaging him as a 'splittist' who aims to disintegrate China. Two, it is arm-twisting India by repeatedly claiming that Arunachal Pradesh is part of China. Here, it is worth noting that at the sixth round of talks with Tibetan representatives Chinese negotiators had conveyed that the Dalai Lama should accept Arunachal Pradesh as part of China, which the Dalai Lama has refused to accept. China is not seriously considering a resolution to the Tibet issue or the border dispute with India. It is simply buying time till the Dalai Lama passes away, after which, it hopes, the Tibetan movement would fizzle out. This would also further weaken India's bargaining position on the border negotiations while at the same time gaining for itself greater manoeuvrability.

The presence of the Dalai Lama in India along with 120,000 Tibetan refugees spread across 35 settlements is leverage for India. But India has so far steadfastly avoided using the Tibetan card. Given the intricate linkage between the Tibet issue and the border dispute, India needs to revise its policy on Tibet. Its present policy of appeasement and unilateral concessions has not stopped China from claiming Indian territory. Chinese maps continue to show Arunachal Pradesh as part of China, and Jammu and Kashmir as falling outside India. Some Chinese maps still do not represent Beijing's revised position on Sikkim.

The latest unrest among Tibetans provides an opportunity for India to revisit and revise its Tibet policy. First, India should make it clear to the Chinese government that developments in Tibet are a concern for India and that it cannot remain unaffected by developments there. Second, on the border issue, instead of merely restating that all of Arunachal Pradesh is an integral part of its territory, India should make it very clear that these are non-negotiable. Third, upholding its democratic principles as well as its cultural affinity with the Tibetans, India should impress upon the Chinese that while it does not support political activity by Tibetans in its soil, it also cannot suppress peaceful demonstrations by them. Fourth, India should move away from its 'over-cautious' and diffident policy on Tibet and adopt a more independent stand that takes into account its national interests.

10 Transfer of Missiles by China

Transfers of missiles, missile technology and components, missile production facilities and equipment, and technical training by China to countries in the developing world have caused many in the West to worry that China is contributing to dangerous missile proliferation. Of particular concern are the transfers of ballistic and cruise missiles capable of functioning as delivery systems for weapons of mass destruction (WMD) to countries of proliferation concern, including Pakistan, Iran, Syria, Iraq, Libya, and North Korea. Western nonproliferation specialists are especially worried about China's perceived willingness to transfer production technology and expertise, which enables countries in the developing world to produce advanced missiles indigenously.

In its missile sales, as with its conventional arms sales in general, China has followed three arms export principles:

(1) The weapons exported must be meant for legitimate self-defence

(2) The weapons must contribute to regional stability

(3) The weapons must not be intended for interference in another country's internal affairs.

According to former Chinese missile engineer Hua Di, "Chinese-made [ballistic missiles] were never launched in any military conflict in the world." In the past, China has stated that the focus of nonproliferation efforts should be on the restriction of WMD themselves, not on their delivery systems. China further argued that if one type of delivery system is to be restricted (e.g. ballistic missiles), then other delivery systems, such as combat aircraft, ought to be restricted as well. China has previously criticized the international agreement on the restriction of ballistic missile exports, the Missile Technology Control Regime (MTCR) on these grounds. China has also been sharply critical of unilateral US sanctions imposed for alleged Chinese violations of MTCR guidelines, especially with regards to its application on states that are not members of the MTCR, such as China.

In response to US pressure and sanctions imposed in 1991 for alleged agreements to transfer M-11 missiles and technology to Pakistan, as well as M-9 missiles and technology to Syria, China issued a unilateral pledge to abide by MTCR guidelines. However, this pledge was called into question in 1993, when the US again imposed MTCR-related sanctions on China for M-11 technology transfers to Pakistan. The US agreed to lift these sanctions in October 1994, when China reaffirmed and clarified its commitment to MTCR guidelines in a joint statement with the US on missile proliferation. However, reports continued to circulate that China was possibly still involved in certain transfers of missile production technology to countries of proliferation concern.

On 21 November 2000, the Chinese Foreign Ministry issued a policy statement on missile nonproliferation pledging that new stringent laws would be issued that would include such regulations as license application and review, end-user certifications, and a "catch-all" clause. On the same day, the State Department announced that it was waiving sanctions on Chinese entities for the past sales of missile technologies to entities in Iran and Pakistan and resuming discussions with China on extending the 1995 US-China Agreement on International Trade in Commercial Launch Services. The MFA statement did not specifically refer to the MTCR or its control list, nor did it mention when China would issue the new export control law, leaving some experts to argue that this represented a loop-hole in the bilateral accord.

Despite the November 2000 pledge, Beijing and Washington continued to bicker about the issue. The US government claimed that a Chinese company had shipped missile technology to Pakistan in violation of the bilateral agreement. In September 2001 the US government again imposed economic sanctions on the accused Chinese company, and the Bush administration invoked a ban on new licenses for U.S. companies to put their satellites on Chinese rockets or transfer satellite technology. The apparent gap between Beijing's words and deeds can be contributed to a number of factors. Many analysts believe that China has viewed the implementation of export control pledges as a tool in winning concessions from the US on issues such as arms transfers to Taiwan and missile defence. Another obvious problem with all of China's export controls, not only the missile related ones, is insufficient domestic infrastructure, which can hinder effective and comprehensive implementation.

More recently, in a major policy development, China finally promulgated the long-awaited regulations on missile-related transfers. In August 2002 China got closer to meeting US demands for stronger controls on its missile exports when it issued new regulations and a control list for the export of missile technology. This demonstrates Beijing's new official stance on the appropriateness of restricting proliferation of WMD delivery systems, and has indicated an understanding of the need to abide by the growing international norm aimed at controlling the missile trade. The new regulations were announced at the start of a visit to Beijing of Deputy Secretary of State Richard Armitage. According to a Washington Post article:

"Beijing's decision to publish the rules appeared intended to further strengthen ties with the United States that have been improving since China backed the U.S.-led war on terrorism after the Sept. 11 attacks. U.S. officials have made it clear that weapons proliferation is a 'make-or-break issue' in relations with China..." The 2002 regulations and control list are relatively comprehensive and in some fields are stricter than MTCR guidelines. The regulations also follow the MTCR's "presumption of denial" approach, requiring specific approval and an export license for exports to authorized end-users. In a press briefing on the new regulations, Liu Jieyi, Director General of Arms Control and Disarmament at the Ministry of Foreign Affair stated:

"The Regulations reflect the 'catch-all' principle in export control where there is a risk of proliferation. ... The Regulations specially stipulate that if an exporter knows or should know that the missile-related items or technologies to be exported will be used by the receiving party directly in its program for developing missiles that can be used to deliver weapons of mass destruction, the exporter is still required to apply for export license even if the items and technologies do not figure in the Control List. Furthermore, the competent departments may decide, on an Ad Hoc basis, to exercise export control on specific items and technologies not contained in the Control List."

However, when Liu was asked about whether China would continue exporting relevant technologies to Pakistan and Iran he stated: "I am not sure about the factual basis of what you were suggesting in your question. China has been implementing a very strict policy on the non-proliferation of missiles and missile-related items and technologies.... The Regulations and Control List will be strictly enforced. Since we are talking about Regulations promulgated by China, I don't think it's fair and polite to bring other countries into discussion."

Initial reaction from Washington after China's announcement was low-key. Reports indicated that the US leadership recognized the new regulations as a step forward, but would hold off with their judgment until China proved its commitment to enforce its new rules. State Department spokesman Richard Boucher stated that: "It is an important part to have the regulations in place, it is an equally important part to see that they are enforced." However, CIA Director, George Tenet, testified to the Senate Intelligence Committee on February, 11, 2003 that Chinese firms were not complying with export controls. In his testimony, he remarked that:

"China vowed in November 2000 to refrain from assisting countries seeking to develop nuclear-capable ballistic missiles, and last August Beijing promulgated new missile-related export controls. Despite such steps,...Chinese firms remain key suppliers of ballistic and cruise missile-related technologies to Pakistan, Iran, and several other countries—and Chinese firms may be backing away from Beijing's 1997 bilateral commitment to forego any new nuclear cooperation with Iran. We are monitoring this closely."

CHINA'S MISSILE EXPORTS AND ASSISTANCE TO THE MIDDLE EAST

China's missile trade with various countries in the Middle East has been a subject of substantial concern in Western nonproliferation circles. China has reportedly transferred missiles, missile technology, materials, and production assistance to a number of Middle Eastern countries, including Iraq, Turkey, Libya, Egypt, Saudi Arabia, and the United Arab Emirates. In some cases, Chinese trade activities have been masked using cover names for businesses. The Shandong Arts and Crafts Co. reportedly sold Iraq test equipment for inertial guidance systems. In another case where trade activities were obfuscated, a North Korean company based in China allegedly sold Egypt specialty steel used in the making of missiles. However, the most serious sources of concern in this region, from a nonproliferation standpoint, are Chinese missile trade and cooperation with Iran and Syria.

Allegations of Chinese M-9 ballistic missile transfers to Syria in the early 1990s contributed to the US decision to impose Missile Technology Control Regime (MTCR)-related sanctions on China in 1991. China's transfers of anti-ship cruise missiles and ballistic missiles to Iran, along with related components, technology, and materials, has been a source of continuing friction. Of particular concern, from a nonproliferation perspective, are Chinese transfers of production technology and expertise that contribute to indigenous missile programs. Transfers of production technologies could contribute to Iran's production of medium and long-range missiles which are banned by the MTCR.

China has generally denied an extensive missile technology trade with the Middle East, although it has on several occasions conceded that certain transfers, previously denied, had taken place. As early as 1989, China denied that it sold missiles to the Middle East despite US information to the contrary. For example, on 12 December 1989, a Chinese Foreign Ministry spokesman stated, "Except for Saudi Arabia, where a small number of mid-range missiles were sold, China has never sold, nor is planning to sell, missiles to any Middle East country."

Throughout the 1990s, China insisted that its missile sales to the Middle East are modest and responsible. Since 1991, China has pledged to abide by MTCR guidelines and parameters in all its missile technology exports, although that commitment has been called into question on several occasions. As of 1999, the central issue of concern regarding missile exports to the Middle East are Chinese sales of missile technologies to Iran which could be used for non-MTCR compliant systems.

MISSILE TECHNOLOGY CONTROL REGIME (MTCR)

Summary

The Missile Technology Control Regime (MTCR) is a set of guidelines regulating the export of missiles, unmanned air vehicles (UAVs), and related technology for those systems capable of carrying a 500 kilogram payload at least 300 kilometres, as well as systems intended for the delivery of weapons of mass destruction (WMD). The MTCR was formed in 1987 by the G-7 partners, and is an informal voluntary arrangement, not a treaty or an international agreement. The MTCR consists of common export policy applied to a common list of controlled items. Each member implements its commitments in the context of its own national export laws. In addition to the MTCR's members, a number of countries unilaterally observe — or "adhere to" — the Guidelines.

The MTCR considers "missiles" to include: ballistic missiles, space launch vehicles (SLVs) and sounding rockets. UAVs include: cruise missiles, drones, and remotely piloted vehicles (RPVs). The MTCR Guidelines specifically state that the Regime is "not designed to impede national space programs or international cooperation in such programs as long as such programs could not contribute to delivery systems for weapons of mass destruction." The MTCR was originally concerned only with nuclear capable delivery systems. In January 1993, the Partners extended the guidelines to cover delivery systems capable of delivering all WMD (nuclear, chemical, and biological).

The MTCR's annex of controlled equipment and technology is divided into "Category I" and "Category II" items. It includes equipment and technology, both military and dual-use, that are relevant to missile development, production, and operation. According to the Guidelines, export of Category I items is subject to a presumption of export denial. Category I includes complete rocket systems, unmanned air-vehicle systems such as cruise missiles, target and reconnaissance drones, specially-designed production facilities for these systems; and certain complete subsystems. Category II covers a wide range of parts, components and subsystems such as propellants, structural materials, test equipment and facilities, and flight instruments. These items may be exported at the discretion of the MTCR Partner government, on a case by case basis, for acceptable end-uses. They may also be exported under government-to-government assurances, which provide that they not be used on a missile system capable of delivering a 500 kilogram payload to a range of at least 300 kilometres.

November 2000 Pledge

On 21 November 2000, the Chinese Foreign Ministry issued its most stringent and specific policy statement on missile nonproliferation to date. The Chinese government promised, for the first time, to issue export control laws covering missile technologies. In the past, Chinese officials have stated that its controls on missile exports were governed by internal documents and not public laws. The Chinese pledged that the new laws would include such regulations as license application and review, end-user certifications, and a "catch-all" clause. The Chinese statement did not, however, specifically reference the MTCR or its control list and the statement did not mention when China would issue the new export control law. Some experts argued that the latter elements represented a loop-hole in the accord. The Chinese government also denied that it engaged in illegitimate trade with either Iran or Pakistan. The *China Daily* reports Chinese Foreign Ministry spokesman, Sun Yuxi refuting US allegations that China supplied Iran and Pakistan with missiles. Sun denounced the allegations as "rumors with ulterior motives." Sun said the PRC had exercised strict control on the export of missile technologies.

On the same day, the State Department announced that it was waiving sanctions on Chinese entities for the past sales of missile technologies to entities in Iran and Pakistan. These exports, which date back to 1992, violated the 1990 Missile Control Act which calls for sanctions on entities engaged in export of MTCR-controlled items. The sanctions were for the export of both MTCR category I and category II items. The US also pledged to resume discussions with China as soon as possible on extending the 1995 US-China Agreement on International Trade in Commercial Launch Services. Under this accord, US companies can export satellites to China for launch on Chinese rocket boosters.

Old Problems Arise

The November 2000 deal did not hold for very long. On 1 September 2001 the US government imposed economic sanctions on a Chinese company for shipping missile technology to Pakistan in violation of a bilateral agreement in November 2000 and US law. The US government said that the China Metallurgical Equipment Corporation in late 2000 and early 2001 shipped missile technology to Pakistan that would assist its Shaheen 1 and Shaheen 2 programs. The sanctions, under the 1990 Missile Control Act, ban US companies from doing business with the Chinese entity for two years. The Bush administration has also invoked a ban on new licenses for U.S. companies to put their satellites on Chinese rockets or transfer satellite technology. These transfers were subsequently confirmed in September CIA report on global proliferation developments.

The Chinese government vociferously denied a Chinese company had shipped proscribed missile technology to Pakistan. The Foreign Ministry spokesman said: Over a period of time, the US has repeatedly alleged that MECC was engaged in missile proliferation activities according to its so-called "intelligence information". In-depth investigations by the Chinese side indicate that MECC has never engaged in any activities as alleged by the United States and the US allegation is groundless. However, the US side is bent on making the erroneous decision based on its wrong intelligence information, in disregard of the constructive position and the investigation results of the Chinese side. Such a US move is totally groundless and irresponsible, which the Chinese side can never accept.

The Foreign Ministry called for the US to immediately lift the sanctions. China threatened repercussions of the sanctions were not lifted. "China strongly urges the US side to immediately withdraw its wrong decision, so as to avoid any damage to Sino-US cooperation in non-proliferation. Otherwise, the US side should bear all the responsibilities for the consequences arising therefrom."

2002 Regulations

In the aftermath of the September 11th terrorist attacks, US-China relations showed signs of improvement. Beijing extended its support to the US-led campaign against global terrorism. However, the Bush administration continued to stress that the issue of nonproliferation and export control was essential to further improvements in bilateral relations. In an effort to resolve bilateral tension, in August 2002 Beijing announced new export control regulations and an expanded control list, fulfilling its November 2000 pledge to issue export control laws covering missile technologies. The announcement coincided with a visit by Deputy Secretary of State Richard Armitage to Beijing, and was seen as an aspect of preparations for President Jiang Zemin's upcoming visit to the US in October 2002.

The new regulations included both the MTCR's "presumption of denial" approach, end-user certifications, and a "catch-all" clause. The new regulations appeared to mark a realization in China's leadership of the dangers of the proliferation of WMD and their delivery systems to its own security, as well as an attempt to remove this issue as a barrier to bilateral cooperation. The 2002 regulations and control list are comprehensive and closely follow the MTCR. The discrepancies with the MTCR were explained by senior Chinese diplomat Liu Jieyi as: "If you compare the List with MTCR, you will find that the categorization is a bit different for the sake of easy administration.

There are items not contained in MTCR in the List. So in this respect, this List covers a wider area than MTCR. Of course there is also a very limited number of MTCR items that are not in the list because they are not really that relevant, either because we don't have them, or they have never come into the picture, or because our experts do not know exactly what they are. Some discrepancies, however, may still allow for license-free export of some technologies that would be useful for countries to establish indigenous missile programs.

The US response to the regulations was cautious, with many in the Bush administration taking a "wait-and-see" approach before making a final judgment as to whether Beijing had fully committed itself to comprehensive implementation of these regulations. In an example of this cautious attitude, State Department spokesman Richard Boucher stated that: "It is an important part to have the regulations in place, it is an equally important part to see that they are enforced." On 9 May 2003, the U.S. expressed its dissatisfaction with China's implementation of its new export control regulations and control list by imposing sanctions on North China Industries Corporation (Norinco) for allegedly supplying missile technology to Iran. The sanctions barred all exports to the US by Norinco and its subsidiaries, and forbade any contracts between the company and US government agencies. The measure was expected to have more of an impact than previous sanctions; in 2002, Norinco exported an estimated $100 million worth of products to the US.

11 Missile Exports and Assistance to Pakistan by China

For the United States, China's missile exports and assistance to Pakistan have been a serious proliferation concern over the years and remain a contentious issue in Sino-US relations. US intelligence reports have revealed that China has transferred complete M-11 missiles, missile related technology, and manufacturing assistance to Pakistan. The US is concerned that Chinese missile transfers could lead to instability in South Asia as India and Pakistan continue to engage in a regional arms race, heightening the risk of military confrontation between the two countries. In this context, proliferation of ballistic missiles into this region is particularly destabilizing, more so in the aftermath of the nuclear tests of May 1998. Chinese missiles and/or technology might also be re-transferred to third parties, further undercutting international nonproliferation efforts.

The United States has made and continues to make serious efforts to dissuade China from transferring missiles, components, and missile related technology to Pakistan. Washington has engaged Beijing in a series of negotiation seeking to obtain Chinese pledges to abide by the Missile Technology Control Regime (MTCR) guidelines and eventually to become a member of the regime. For these purposes, the US has both applied consistent diplomatic pressures, offered economic incentives, and imposed economic sanctions on China. While China made pledges in 1991 and 1994 to the US promising to comply with the main provisions of the MTCR and halt all sales of complete MTCR-class missile systems, it has tended to interpret these pledges narrowly and has continued missile technology transfers and manufacturing assistance to Pakistan, including a second missile factory. More recently, China has also implicitly linked its MTCR commitments to issues of increasing salience to its own security concerns, namely, theatre missile defence (TMD), US arms sales to Taiwan, and US intention to deploy national missile defence (NMD) and amend the ABM Treaty.

Given the deterioration of Sino-US relations in the aftermath of the NATO bombing of the Chinese embassy, the release of the Cox Report and allegations of Chinese nuclear espionage, the growing tension over the Taiwan issue in the aftermath of Chen Shuibian's election to Taiwan's presidency; and the passage in the House of the Taiwan Security Enhancement Act and the proposed China Nonproliferation Law, bilateral cooperation in arms control and nonproliferation may continue to stagnate. Sino-Pak missile cooperation could remain an irritant to US-PRC relations for some time to come. In this context, recent US intelligence reports alleging continued Chinese transfers of missile technology and technical expertise to Pakistan could impede efforts to mend US-China bilateral relations in the aftermath of the bombing of the Chinese embassy in Yugoslavia.

Responsible Factors

There are various strategic, commercial, and foreign policy rationales behind Chinese missile exports and assistance to Pakistan. China and Pakistan have enjoyed a solid strategic relationship since the 1960s. Over the years China has provided Pakistan with a wide range of major conventional weapons systems and the two countries have also developed a close partnership in various defence cooperation programs. While this strategic relationship initially grew out of the mutual needs of China and Pakistan in countering the Soviet and Indian security threats, respectively, it continues to serve the two countries' national security interests in the post-Cold War era. Pakistan relies on China as a trusted ally in dealing with India from a position of military weakness; Beijing values its close ties with Islamabad both to extend its influence to South Asia and to balance against India. Commercially, as China began its economic reform and opening up in the early 1980s, defence industries and arms exporting companies were under tremendous pressure to tap into the lucrative international arms market. Pakistan became a valued customer for Chinese arms. Finally, given US concern about and emphasis on missile proliferation issues, Beijing has also found it useful to exploit them as bargaining leverage in dealing with Washington on issues important to China: US arms sales to Taiwan, TMD deployment in East Asia, among others.

China reportedly began discussing possible sales to Pakistan of M-11 missiles and related technology in the late 1980s. The contract for the M-11 sale was reportedly signed in 1988. In April 1991, the United States announced that it had discovered the transfer of an M-11 missile even though China insisted it had never shipped the system to Pakistan. In May 1991, the US imposed sanctions against China. In November 1991, Secretary of State James Baker reached an agreement with then Chinese Foreign Minister Qian Qichen in which Beijing verbally agreed to abide by "the guidelines and parameters of the MTCR" in exchange for the lifting of the sanctions imposed earlier that year. (However, China's pledge said nothing about adhering to the MTCR's annex.) After China sent Washington a letter in February 1992 affirming its earlier MTCR assurance in writing, the sanctions were lifted in March 1992.

However, this commitment did not end the controversy. The September 1992 US decision to sell 150 F-16 fighters to Taiwan led China to withdraw from P-5 talks on conventional arms transfers. In December 1992 reports surfaced that China had transferred 34 complete M-11 systems to Pakistan, in apparent violation of its earlier [1991] pledge. China and Pakistan both denied that the transfer had taken place. In August 1993, the Clinton Administration imposed MTCR related sanctions on China after determining that China had again engaged in missile trade with Pakistan.5 China denounced the sanctions, calling the US decision "a wrong judgment based on inaccurate intelligence" and threatened to scrap its promise to abide by the MTCR.

The impasse was finally in October 1994 when the two countries issued a joint statement on missile proliferation. In the joint statement, the United States agreed to lift sanctions and in return China promised *to ban all exports* of ground-to-ground missiles exceeding the primary parameters of the MTCR. (The MTCR only calls for a "strong presumption of denial" for such exports.) China also agreed to accept the concept of "inherent capability" which binds China from exporting any missile that is inherently capable of delivering a 500 kg payload over 300 km. This standard would prohibit future exports of the M-11 missile. The US waived the sanctions in November 1994.

Persistent US diplomatic efforts since 1994 have also led China to clarify its MTCR commitment. Beijing has both reaffirmed its obligations to permanently curtail its missile cooperation with Pakistan and indicated that it is actively studying joining the MTCR as a full member. However, serious questions about China's missile export controls remain. Although China promulgated regulations on conventional arms transfers in 1997, it is not clear if they cover missiles and missile-related technology transfers. While an internal control list restricting missile exports exists, Beijing has not revealed its scope, contents, and the extent to which it approximates that contained in the MTCR annex. Developments of the last few months have again derailed the meager progress that had been made between the two Sino-US summits. The release of the Cox Report, the US bombing of the Chinese embassy in Belgrade, and US intentions with regard to national missile defence (NMD) and theatre missile defence (TMD) have effectively put any prospect of China's joining the MTCR on hold. Increasingly, Beijing is demanding a linkage between its MTCR membership and broader issues of US arms sales to Taiwan, and the development, and future deployment of TMD in Northeast Asia. China's continuing transfers of missile technology to Pakistan and Iran may be a means of gaining leverage over the US. However, if China concludes that its fundamental security interests are threatened, it might step up these activities.

Sino-US disagreements over Chinese missile-related activities and missile nonproliferation continue. China has not accepted the MTCR annex and US efforts to get China to adopt legally binding export controls on MTCR items have yet to lead to the publication of regulations on missile exports (although Chinese officials insist they have an internal control list). In addition, suspicion of continued Chinese assistance to the Pakistani missile production facility at Rawalpindi persists and this raises serious questions of Beijing's sincerity in abiding by its pledges. During and immediately after the Sino-US summit of June 1998, Beijing indicated that it was "actively studying" MTCR membership and renewed once more its missile nonproliferation pledge on curbing its missile technology transfers and assistance to South Asia in the Jiang-Clinton Joint Statement. However, given the recent negative developments in bilateral relations (e.g., the Cox Report, the embassy bombing, TMD), it is not clear that these disagreements will get resolved any time soon. Policy Issues

Chinese missile transfers to Pakistan raise a number of issues for US nonproliferation policy and Sino-US relations. First, China's missile exports and assistance can undermine international missile nonproliferation efforts, in particular the objectives of the MTCR. China's most serious confrontations with the United States over ballistic missile proliferation have involved Chinese transfers of complete M-11 missiles and missile-related technology to Pakistan. The M-11 is a single stage, solid fueled missile with a reported range of 290 km and a payload of 800 kg. While technically the M-11 missiles do not fall within the MTCR parameter, they have the inherent capability of being able to deliver a 500 kg payload over 300 km. The fact that China has resisted joining the MTCR as a formal member, coupled with its ambiguous interpretation and implementation of its bilateral commitments, raises questions as to the seriousness of Chinese commitment to arms control and nonproliferation.

US concerns over Chinese missile exports to Pakistan focus mainly on regional stability and the potential of further proliferation to other regions where the US has important strategic interests, including the Middle East and the Persian Gulf. The introduction and improvement of ballistic missiles into South Asia could result in a fierce arms race between India and Pakistan, which in turn could be highly destabilizing given the perennial animosity between the two countries; the recent conflicts in Kargil only heightens such concerns. Given the short distances between major population centres of the two countries, poor intelligence, and short warning time, there would be great temptation to launch preemptive strikes in crisis situations. A more serious concern is the mating of nuclear warheads and other WMD with missiles. The further proliferation of ballistic (and cruise) missiles to countries such as Iran, Syria, and Libya could enable these countries to seriously threaten US interests in the Middle East and the Persian Gulf.

Furthermore, China's missile exports and assistance to Pakistan represent a major bone of contention in Sino-US bilateral relations and has the potential to limit and undermine bilateral cooperation in other areas. Over the last decade, Chinese proliferation behaviour, bilateral trade issues, Taiwan and human rights controversies have been the four key obstacles to better US-China relations. US efforts to change Chinese behaviour through both economic incentives and sanctions have achieved noticeable but limited results. While the US has made strong efforts to persuade China to join the MTCR, China continues to resist and remains critical of the regime, in particular its charge that the regime is discriminatory in nature and its exclusion of high-performance aircraft. Continued controversy over Chinese missile-related transfers and assistance to Pakistan points to serious differences between Washington and Beijing with regard to regional security. While the US tends to compartmentalize nonproliferation issues on their own merits, the Chinese have insisted that proliferation issues cannot be separated from underlying security causes.

Finally, differences in interests exist and this may account for the difficulty for a final resolution of the issue. Washington seeks to stem proliferation of WMDs and their delivery systems to the Middle East, the Persian Gulf, and South Asia out of its interests for secure supplies of oil, the security of Israel, and stability on the subcontinent. Beijing, on the other hand, regards its nuclear and missile exports as an important source of foreign exchange as well as a means of gaining influence in these regions. China's refusal to adopt IAEA full-scope safeguards (FSS) may be due to concerns that such measures would deprive it of potential nuclear markets. Regarding continued missile technology transfers and assistance to Pakistan, Beijing's motive may be more strategic than commercial. Islamabad has remained an important factor in Beijing's strategic calculations regarding South Asia and a useful counterweight to India.

Three issues confront the Clinton administration: the credibility of Chinese commitments to missile nonproliferation; whether the US should impose sanctions on China as required by domestic laws; and balancing the management of bilateral relations and the enforcement of nonproliferation legislation. The charges about renewed Chinese missile technology cooperation with Pakistan occurred at a particularly sensitive moment as Beijing and Washington are resuming both the security and arms control dialogues; as the Senate is to begin debates on PNTR on China, with some senators proposing the "China Nonproliferation Law" bill and seeking to amend the bill with provisions requesting annual review of Chinese missile proliferation activities; and as the deadline of a task force investigation of the 1992 Chinese sale of 34 M-11 missiles is approaching or may have already been passed. While both China and the Clinton administration have the incentives to reach a compromise to avoid sanctions, the room for such an outcome remains limited.

New Developments

Suspicions persist regarding China's continued missile cooperation with Pakistan. It has been speculated that the Shaheen-1 IRBM, which Pakistan tested in April 1999, is actually modeled on Chinese M-9 missiles. A February 1999 CIA report stated that "Chinese and North Korean entities continued to provide assistance to Pakistan's ballistic missile program during the first half of 1998. Such assistance is critical for Islamabad's efforts to produce ballistic missiles...China's involvement with Pakistan will continue to be monitored closely." A September 1999 National Intelligence Council (NIC) report stated that "Pakistan has Chinese supplied M-11 short-range ballistic missiles..." This is the first time that the US government has publicly verified that China actually supplied Pakistan with these missiles. The NIC report referred to the transfer of 34 M-11 missiles delivered in November 1992, but there is no evidence that China has resumed the transfer of complete missile systems to Pakistan. However, an unclassified CIA report to

Congress released in February 2000 suggests that "some [Chinese] ballistic missile assistance [to Pakistan] continues."

Following the September 1999 NIC Report Republican Senator Jesse Helms, chairman of the Senate Foreign Relations Committee, threatened to block the appointment of Acting Assistant Secretary of State for Nonproliferation Affairs Robert Einhorn to a permanent position unless the Clinton administration formed a task force to impose sanctions on China. A task force was formed and given a six month deadline to make a determination, which is expected to be in late May or June 2000. US and Chinese reportedly have been meeting to reach a compromise to avoid sanctions. China is unlikely to become a full member of the MTCR, but a compromise on strengthening China's nuclear export controls may be possible.

The recent US intelligence reports suggest that despite Chinese pledges to the contrary, it has continued to provide Pakistan with specialty steels, guidance systems and technical expertise in the latter's effort to develop long-range ballistic missiles. These and other allegations have apparently led to the proposal by Republican Senator Fred Thompson and Democratic Senator Robert G. Torricelli of legislation aimed at monitoring Chinese missile proliferation activities and mandating automatic sanctions should "credible evidence" indicates that specific Chinese exports and transfers have taken place. US Assistant Secretary of State for Nonproliferation Robert Einhorn traveled to Beijing in early June to seek commitment from China not to export missiles and missile technology to Iran and Pakistan. The July meetings in Beijing between Chinese officials and John Holum, Undersecretary of State for Security and Arms Control, and Secretary of Defence William Cohen are expected to focus heavily on China's alleged missile assistance to Pakistan.

On 21 November 2000, the State Department announced that it was waiving sanctions on Chinese entities for the past sales of missile technologies to entities in Iran and Pakistan. These exports, which date back to 1992, violated the 1990 Missile Control Act which calls for sanctions on entities engaged in export of MTCR-controlled items. The sanctions were for the export of both MTCR category I and category II items. The US also pledged to resume discussions with China as soon as possible on extending the 1995 US-China Agreement on International Trade in Commercial Launch Services. Under this accord, US companies can export satellites to China for launch on Chinese rocket boosters. [State Department Statement on Chinese Missile Sanctions, November 2000]

In response to these actions, the Chinese Foreign Ministry issued its most stringent and specific policy statement on missile nonproliferation to date. China stated.

"China is opposed to the proliferation of weapons of mass destruction...China has no intention of assisting, in any way, any country in the development of ballistic missiles that can be used to deliver nuclear weapons (i.e., missiles capable of delivering a payload of at least 500 kg to a distance of at least 300 km.)"

This statement appears to build on China's past commitment in the 1998 US-China Joint Statement on South Asia not to provide missile technologies to Pakistan or India. As part of the recent commitment, the Chinese government importantly promised, for the first time, to issue export control laws covering missile technologies. In the past, Chinese officials have stated that its controls on missile exports were governed by internal documents and not public laws. The Chinese pledged that the new laws would include such regulations as license application and review, end-user certifications, and a "catch-all" clause. The Chinese statement did not, however, specifically reference the MTCR or its control list and the statement did not mention when China would issue the new export control law. Some experts argue that these latter elements represent a loop-hole in the accord. The Chinese government also denies that it engaged in illegitimate trade with either Iran or Pakistan. The *China Daily* reports Chinese Foreign Ministry spokesman, Sun Yuxi refuting US allegations that China supplied Iran and Pakistan with missiles. Sun denounced the allegations as "rumors with ulterior motives." Sun said the PRC has exercised strict control on the export of missile technologies.

According to CIA Director General Tenet, whatever the current policy of Beijing on missile assistance to Pakistan, previous aid has enabled Islamabad to move rapidly toward serial production of solid propellant engines. Future assistance cannot be ruled out. The concern is that continued development of the Shaheen-II will require additional Chinese assistance.

In August 2001, concerns about China's contiinued missile technology assistance to Pakistan reemerged. According to a report in the *Washington Times*, a Chinese company has sent a shipments of missile components to Pakistan. The leaked intelligence information noted that the China National Machinery & Equipment Import & Export Corp., known as CMEC, reportedly supplied the missile components for Pakistan's Shaheen-1 and Shaheen-2 missile programs. A U.S. spy satellite reportedly detected the latest shipment as it arrived by truck at the mountainous Chinese-Pakistani border May 1. It was one of 12 missile component transfers sent by ship and truck detected by U.S. intelligence agencies since the beginning of the year.

After bilateral consulations failed to resolve this dispute, in September 2001 the US government imposed economic sanctions on a Chinese company for shipping missile technology to Pakistan in violation of a bilateral agreement in November 2000 and US law. The US government said that the China Metallurgical Equipment Corporation in late 2000 and early 2001 shipped missile technology to Pakistan that would assist its Shaheen 1 and Shaheen 2 programs. The sanctions, under the 1990 Missile Control Act, ban US companies from doing business with the Chinese entity for two years. The Bush administration has also invoked a ban on new licenses for U.S. companies to put their satellites on Chinese rockets or transfer satellite technology. These transfers were subsequently confirmed in September CIA report on global proliferation developments.

The Chinese government vociferously denied a Chinese company had shipped proscribed missile technology to Pakistan. The Foreign Ministry spokesman said:

Over a period of time, the US has repeatedly alleged that MECC was engaged in missile proliferation activities according to its so-called "intelligence information". In-depth investigations by the Chinese side indicate that MECC has never engaged in any activities as alleged by the United States and the US allegation is groundless. However, the US side is bent on making the erroneous decision based on its wrong intelligence information, in disregard of the constructive position and the investigation results of the Chinese side. Such a US move is totally groundless and irresponsible, which the Chinese side can never accept.

The Foreign Ministry called for the US to immediately lift the sanctions. China threatened repercussions of the sanctions were not lifted. "China strongly urges the US side to immediately withdraw its wrong decision, so as to avoid any damage to Sino-US cooperation in non-proliferation. Otherwise, the US side should bear all the responsibilities for the consequences arising therefrom."

12 China's Asian Military Doctrine

China's National People's Congress (NPC) Standing Committee is currently deliberating a new law on "National Defence Mobilization". The law envisages various emergent actions if the country's "state sovereignty, unification, territorial integrity or security were threatened", and provides for expropriation of civilian resources if required. The NPC Standing Committee, a version of China's Parliament, takes up a draft law for discussion only after this had received the sanction of the Politbureau of the Chinese Communist Party (CCP), the country's preeminent political body. The brief statement on the law carried by the Global Times (April 21, 2009), has very wide interpretation of conditions or threat that would call upon the activation of the details in the law.

Appropriation of civilian resources in case of a war or the threat of a major war, is not new. The civilian infrastructure like airports, ports, communication system have been incorporated in the People Liberation Army's (PLA) simulated and actual exercises in the past also. Engineering of extreme nationalism or ultra-nationalism has been resorted to by the state against foreign powers, especially the USA over the last decade where a situation of confrontation had arisen. It began with the US bombing of the Chinese Embassy in Kosovo in 1999, where US Missions in China were attacked by the people.

The Cultural Revolution (1966-1976) unleashed by Mao Zedong, included ultra-nationalism and anti-foreigner indoctrination as part of it political agenda. The ten-year long upheaval put the country back by 50 years, according some political assessments after the demise of Mao. But while Mao's Mantra was defence against historical foreign exploitation, the new doctrine appears as offence against foreign countries through power diplomacy to establish Chinese supremacy in the world, starting with Asia. The implication of such a policy on China's Asian neighbours needs no emphasis.

China Defence White Paper 2008, released in January, was apparently a precursor to what was coming. A so-called exercise in military transparency as demanded by the USA, the European Union and Japan among others, hardly gave any realistic account of defence spending, foreign acquisitions or indigenous production. It, however, deliberately gave clear but teasing indications about where its military thrust was going. It was evident that its military might was set to gallop not only in the traditional hard equipment area, but cyber warfare, informization and space supplemented military superiority using no contact destructive weapons including laser, electromagnetic and radiation weapons.

Targets, both specific and in general, are gradually being identified. In March, the official Chinese news agency, the China News Network (CNN) said that the US and Japan were joining hands with the ASEAN countries to oppose China in the South China sea, and India's "look east" policy was a bid to enlarge its say in the affairs of the area. The report also said that China must strengthen its military strength in the region to the level of a deterrent force. Simultaneously, tension has been rising over the ownership of the Spratly group of islands in the South China sea claimed as a whole by China as its sovereign territory, and partially claimed by others in the region. Both Malaysia and the Philippines have reiterated their claims on some of the islets and reefs of this group which are in their continental shelves. The Philippines also enacted a law in March this year to make their claims official as per the UN Laws of the Seas. China has refuted these claims and warned Manila against it.

The Sprately islands area is estimated to have rich gas deposits though no realistic survey has been made yet. The South China sea is a very important strategic shipping route which Chinese want to control. It has proposed joint development of the resources there, but under the conditions its sovereignty over the area is accepted by the others.

China is increasingly feeling that its carefully crafted policy over decades to dominate Asia without any challenge is being threatened by India's development into a global power of considerable acceptance from a sub-continental cage. It has watched three Indian steps very carefully. First was the establishment of the tri-services command in the Andamans, development of the Indian Navy, and the counter-piracy and rescue exercises of the Indian navy with South East Asian countries in the South China Sea and the Malacca Strait. The next was the Indian nuclear test in May 1998, and the resilience it demonstrated to hold its nuclear position against international pressures, finally to be accepted as a de facto nuclear power. It saw in the NDA government led by the BJP the determination to carve India's name in the international ranks.

The third was the Indo-US nuclear deal and the Indo-US strategic partnership under the UPA government led by the Congress. Beijing opposed the Indo-US nuclear agreement till the end, but had to withdraw in the face of Indian diplomacy backed by the global recognition of an emerging India as a benevolent force of temperance and balance. Within the above parameters, China perceived an India-US-Japan-Australia challenge to China's Asia and Asia Pacific Kingdom. It had neutralized Australia for a brief period, but got caught recently in its intelligence and economic subversion of Canberra. It is also aware that most of the South East Asian countries which were overwhelmed by Chinese power waves, may look to the new strategic developments to stand up to face Chinese domination.

A sense of frustration appears to be creeping in Beijing, and they appear to be considering the need for military force backed power projection. At the same time, the Chinese are trying to work with the USA using the global economic meltdown, to construct a bilateral relationship to ensure Washington that China's military and economic power are still decades behind that of the USA.

An article written by Senior Chinese expert Zheng Youngnian

currently a visiting adjunct and director of the Centre for East Asian Studies at the Singapore National University, claims Asia is China's "great backyard", and China's rise must first be in Asia only by acquiring the capabilities to resolve various issues in the continent – an euphemism for intervention in the hot spots. The article suggests that while China has won a significant position in the world by its investments and involvement in Latin America and Africa, to be really effective it must acquire the preeminent position in Asia and, if need be, through power diplomacy and power projection. Zheng advocates the use of power to resolve emerging hot spots that can rise to a crisis level and destabilize China's stability, security and territorial integrity. He further cautions that while relations with major powers cannot be ignored, as the same time small countries cannot be neglected in any way.

Zheng's article was also published in the Singapore daily United Morning Post giving it wide publicity in south East Asia and the Asia Pacific region. The message is unmistakable and would raise concerns in Asia, especially for countries which have territorial disputes with China and those harbouring any intention of forming an alliance to stand up to China. These developments culminated with the Chinese naval review on April 23, 2009 in which an unprecedented fifty-six Chinese submarines, destroyers, frigates, missile boats and aircraft were displayed to invited foreign navies including the Indian and US navies. The naval parade was led by two Chinese nuclear submarines which were kept secret from foreigner till now.

For countries like the USA and Russia the display was to suggest the Chinese navy was far behind theirs. But to the Asian navies it was a different message of power, with their naval commander-in-chief Admiral Wu Shengli proclaiming earlier this month that China would develop a new generation of warships and aircraft to give it much longer range capabilities. The Chinese warships deployed in waters off the Somali coast in anti-piracy operation is the first display of the Chinese navy's long-range capabilities with the ability to operate for extended durations on its own.

On a separate issue, Prof. Yang Haisheng of Sichuan University observed that India should not consider the entire Indian Ocean region as its own backyard and shut off China's co-operation with countries of the region. In 1993, the then head of the PLA's General Logistic Department, Zhou Nanqi, had said the Indian Ocean is not India's Ocean. China's strategy to acquire port facilities for its navy in Pakistan, Myanmar, Bangladesh and Sri Lanka is well known to the international strategic community. Nobody would grudge China acquiring a large navy and aircraft carriers to guard its sea borders and secure its shipping from piracy. But when the real intention is the dominate Asia and impose its unreasonable demands through military power diplomacy, it is another thing. This is certainly going to provoke an arms race in Asia. Japan, South Korea and Australia have already begun to respond. India still remains in some kind of a hole, many a time pushing strategic threats from China under the carpet.

CHINA: CRITICAL COMMENTS OF SCHOLARS ON INDIAS MILITARY STRATEGY

Appearance of several articles in the state-controlled Chinese language media on the military developments in India since the end of 2004 in the Peoples Republic of China (PRC), suggest that the subject has become important, if not of immediate concern, for Beijing from a strategic point of view. Such assessments, which appear to be coming at irregular intervals from scholars of prominent think tanks in the country, do not however conceal Chinas underlying fears over the likely long term security implications for the region including the PRC, arising from the evolving defence policy formulations in India. Setting the stage for a reevaluation of Indias military strategy, an authoritative periodical (Contemporary International Relations, in Chinese language, believed to be close to the PRCs Ministry of State Security, October 2004) observed that India has shifted to an active defence policy.

A subsequent comment in the Reference News (Can Kao Xiao Xi, Chinese language, restricted circulation, February 17, 2005) while highlighting the increases in Indias defence budget, remarked that this may lead to Indias going all out to import weapons from abroad. Injecting the China factor into the matter, a viewpoint noticed later (Reference News, March 2, 2005) described Indias objective was to overtake the PRC in military expansion.

The next prominent coverage which came after a gap, citing New Delhis big military procurement contracts with Moscow, concluded (China Comments News Agency, January 24, 2006) that the world attention is now focused on how India is developing its arms and equipment and consolidating its military position in the South Asian Sub-Continent and the Indian Ocean.

A very recent signed article contributed by Professor Zhang Weiwei (PRC Foreign ministry-affiliated China Institute of International Studies, February 6, 2006) has spelled out Chinas perceptions of Indias current military strategy. Identifying the three main components of Indias current strategy as strengthening military structure, realizing military modernization and becoming a global military power, the article pointed out that Indias present objectives are to become a military power on par with China, France and the UK. Political and Military leaders, however, consider that from a long term point of view, India wants to achieve a military balance with China, the USA and Russia. Though India stands in no comparison with any of these three countries in the field of military technology, it aims to have a turn around in this field by 2010.

Professor Zhang added that as part of changing strategy, India aims to establish its hegemony in South Asia, control the Indian Ocean and extend its influence to the far-flung South China Sea and Pacific regions. Explaining the first factor, he said that Pakistan is the only country in South Asia having the strength to challenge India, but through waging wars with Pakistan three times, India has already weakened latters military potential. At present, India enjoys an edge over Pakistan in fields like conventional weapons and war capabilities, excepting in the nuclear sector. With geographic and other conditions favouring it, India could expand its strategic space in the region when compared to Pakistan. Opinions therefore point out that India has already become a super power in South Asia and the requirement for India now is only to continue the consolidation of such position.

Commenting on Indias efforts to build a blue water Navy and control the Indian Ocean, the Chinese scholar pointed out that in the Post-September 11 period, the region extending from West Asia to Southeast Asia including the Indian Ocean came under the definition of territory vital to Indias global strategy. Energy security has become important for India. Accordingly, India is enforcing a policy to control vital Sea Lanes of Communications whether it is Hormuz or Malacca Straits.

Elaborating the third component, i.e. Indias efforts to influence South China Sea and Pacific Regions, Professor Zhang opined that it meant a shift in New Delhis emphasis from South Asia to Asia-Pacific. The shift is also to be seen as part of developing Look East policy of India, seeking to strengthen links with Southeast Asian nations including the Philippines, Vietnam and Myanmar as well as the East Asian big powers like China and Japan. Separately, under its active military diplomacy, Indias military links with Russia (ally), the US (natural ally), Japan (to reach a balance in the Asian situation), China and Southeast Asian nations are growing.

Identifying another objective of India under its current military strategy as entering the nuclear club, the scholar stated that for New Delhi as the status of a nuclear weapon power is essential for the countrys comprehensive national strength; political, economic and diplomatic factors alone may not be adequate for India in attaining such strength. The Indian Government claims to have the right to use nuclear weapons and it is ominous, according to the scholar. Indias development of nuclear weapons is primarily meant to get world recognition to its big power status and it can therefore be expected that New Delhi will continue to maintain the nuclear programme in its agenda, he concluded.

Professor Zhang at the same time perceived the following as constraints for India in pursuing its current military strategy weak economic basis, lack of military technological strength and insufficient capacity to produce advanced weapons. India remains strategically important globally as an Indian Ocean power, a major player to the East of unstable West Asia and a big nation southwest of China which allow it to be fit for the big power strategies like that of the US. But in future, Indias emergence may not be acceptable to the USA. In particular, the US may find the Indias long term objective to achieve naval domination over the Indian Ocean as a challenge to its own global strategic interests.

Admittedly, the articles appearing in the Chinese language media on Indias current military strategy do not seem to indicate a hardening of Chinese stand on the subject, at least for the moment. Relations with India continue to be strategically important for China and no definite anti-India trend (notwithstanding revival of references to Indias hegemony in South Asia) can be discerned in the writings, which are mainly meant for the Chinese speaking domestic population. The importance however lies in the fact that the Chinese scholars have been allowed to deliberate on Indias military, a topic sensitive for bilateral relations. In contrast, the PRCs English language press has so far remained cautious in their comments on India. Future trends will be interesting to watch.

13 National Defence of China

The 21st century marked a tremendous changes and adjustments across the world. Peace and development remain the principal themes of the times, and the pursuit of peace, development and cooperation has become an irresistible trend of the times. However, global challenges are on the increase, and new security threats keep emerging. Economic globalization and world multi-polarization are gaining momentum. The progress toward industrialization and informationization throughout the globe is accelerating and economic cooperation is in full swing, leading to increasing economic interdependence, inter-connectivity and interactivity among countries.

The rise and decline of international strategic forces is quickening, major powers are stepping up their efforts to cooperate with each other and draw on each other's strengths. They continue to compete with and hold each other in check, and groups of new emerging developing powers are arising. Therefore, a profound readjustment is brewing in the international system.

In addition, factors conducive to maintaining peace and containing war are on the rise, and the common interests of countries in the security field have increased, and their willingness to cooperate is enhanced, thereby keeping low the risk of worldwide, all-out and large-scale wars for a relatively long period of time. World peace and development are faced with multiple difficulties and challenges. Struggles for strategic resources, strategic locations and strategic dominance have intensified. Meanwhile, hegemonism and power politics still exist, regional turmoil keeps spilling over, hot-spot issues are increasing, and local conflicts and wars keep emerging.

The impact of the financial crisis triggered by the U.S. subprime mortgage crisis is snowballing. In the aspect of world economic development, issues such as energy and food are becoming more serious, highlighting deep-seated contradictions. Economic risks are manifesting a more interconnected, systematic and global nature. Issues such as terrorism, environmental disasters, climate change, serious epidemics, transnational crime and pirates are becoming increasingly prominent. The influence of military security factors on international relations is mounting. Driven by competition in overall national strength and the development of science and technology, international military competition is becoming increasingly intense, and the worldwide revolution in military affairs (RMA) is reaching a new stage of development. Some major powers are realigning their security and military strategies, increasing their defence investment, speeding up the transformation of armed forces, and developing advanced military technology, weapons and equipment. Strategic nuclear forces, military astronautics, missile defence systems, and global and battlefield reconnaissance and surveillance have become top priorities in their efforts to strengthen armed forces.

Some developing countries are also actively seeking to acquire advanced weapons and equipment to increase their military power. All countries are attaching more importance to supporting diplomatic struggles with military means. As a result, arms races in some regions are heating up, posing grave challenges to the international arms control and nonproliferation regime. The Asia-Pacific security situation is stable on the whole. The regional economy is brimming with vigor, mechanisms for regional and sub-regional economic and security cooperation maintain their development momentum, and it has become the policy orientation of all countries to settle differences and hotspot issues peacefully through dialogue. The member states of the Shanghai Cooperation Organization (SCO) have signed the Treaty on Long-Term Good-Neighborly Relations, Friendship and Cooperation, and practical cooperation has made progress in such fields as security and economy.

The conclusion of the ASEAN Charter has enabled a new step to be taken toward ASEAN integration. Remarkable achievements have been made in cooperation between China and ASEAN, as well as between ASEAN and China, Japan and the Republic of Korea. Cooperation within the framework of the East Asia Summit (EAS) and the South Asian Association for Regional Cooperation (SAARC) continues to make progress. The Six-Party Talks on the Korean nuclear issue have scored successive achievements, and the tension in Northeast Asia is much released. However, there still exist many factors of uncertainty in Asia-Pacific security. The drastic fluctuations in the world economy impact heavily on regional economic development, and political turbulence persists in some countries undergoing economic and social transition. Ethnic and religious discords, and conflicting claims over territorial and maritime rights and interests remain serious, regional hotspots are complex.

At the same time, the U.S. has increased its strategic attention to and input in the Asia-Pacific region, further consolidating its military alliances, adjusting its military deployment and enhancing its military capabilities. In addition, terrorist, separatist and extremist forces are running rampant, and non-traditional security issues such as serious natural disasters crop up frequently. The mechanisms for security cooperation between countries and regions are yet to be enhanced, and the capability for coping with regional security threats in a coordinated way has to be improved. China's security situation has improved steadily. The achievements made in China's modernization drive have drawn worldwide attention. China's overall national strength has increased substantially, its people's living standards have kept improving, the society remains stable and unified, and the capability for upholding national security has been further enhanced. The attempts of the separatist forces for "Taiwan independence" to seek "de jure Taiwan independence" have been thwarted, and the situation across the Taiwan Straits has taken a significantly positive turn. The two sides have resumed and made progress in consultations on the common political basis of the "1992 Consensus," and consequently cross-Straits relations have improved.

Meanwhile, China has made steady progress in its relations with the developed countries, strengthened in all respects the good-neighborly friendship with its neighboring countries, and kept deepening its traditional friendship with the developing countries. China is playing an active and constructive role in multilateral affairs, thus notably elevating its international position and influence. China is still confronted with long-term, complicated, and diverse security threats and challenges. Issues of existence security and development security, traditional security threats and non-traditional security threats, and domestic security and international security are interwoven and interactive.

China is faced with the superiority of the developed countries in economy, science and technology, as well as military affairs. It also faces strategic maneuvers and containment from the outside while having to face disruption and sabotage by separatist and hostile forces from the inside. Being in a stage of economic and social transition, China is encountering many new circumstances and new issues in maintaining social stability. Separatist forces working for "Taiwan independence," "East Turkistan independence" and "Tibet independence" pose threats to China's unity and security. Damages caused by non-traditional security threats like terrorism, natural disasters, economic insecurity, and information insecurity are on the rise.

Impact of uncertainties and destabilizing factors in China's outside security environment on national security and development is growing. In particular, the United States continues to sell arms to Taiwan in violation of the principles established in the three Sino-US joint communiques, causing serious harm to Sino-US relations as well as peace and stability across the Taiwan Straits. In the face of unprecedented opportunities and challenges, China will hold high the banner of peace, development and cooperation, persist in taking the road of peaceful development, pursue the opening-up strategy of mutual benefit, and promote the building of a harmonious world with enduring peace and common prosperity; and it will persist in implementing the Scientific Outlook on Development in a bid to achieve integration of development with security, persist in giving due consideration to both traditional and non-traditional security issues, enhancing national strategic capabilities, and perfecting the national emergency management system. At the same time, it will persist in pursuing the new security concept featuring mutual trust, mutual benefit, equality and coordination, and advocating the settlement of international disputes and hotspot issues by peaceful means. It will encourage the advancement of security dialogues and cooperation with other countries, oppose the enlargement of military alliances, and acts of aggression and expansion. China will never seek hegemony or engage in military expansion now or in the future, no matter how developed it becomes.

National Defence Policy

China pursues a national defence policy which is purely defensive in nature. China places the protection of national sovereignty, security, territorial integrity, safeguarding of the interests of national development, and the interests of the Chinese people above all else.

China endeavors to build a fortified national defence and strong military forces compatible with national security and development interests, and enrich the country and strengthen the military while building a moderately prosperous society in all aspects. China's national defence policy for the new stage in the new century basically includes: upholding national security and unity, and ensuring the interests of national development; achieving the all-round, coordinated and sustainable development of China's national defence and armed forces; enhancing the performance of the armed forces with informationization as the major measuring criterion; implementing the military strategy of active defence; pursuing a self-defensive nuclear strategy; and fostering a security environment conducive to China's peaceful development. According to the needs of national security and the level of economic and social development, China pursues a three-step development strategy to modernize its national defence and armed forces step by step in a well-planned way.

This strategic framework is defined as follows: Promoting the informationization of China's national defence and armed forces. Taking informationization as the goal of modernization of its national defence and armed forces and in light of its national and military conditions, China actively pushes forward the RMA with Chinese characteristics. It has formulated in a scientific way strategic plans for national defence and armed forces building and strategies for the development of the services and arms, according to which it will lay a solid foundation by 2010, basically accomplish mechanization and make major progress in informationization by 2020, and by and large reach the goal of modernization of national defence and armed forces by the mid-21st century. Overall planning of economic development and national defence building. Sticking to the principle of coordinated development of economy and national defence, China makes overall plans for the use of its national resources and strikes a balance between enriching the country and strengthening the military, so as to ensure that its strategy for national defence and armed forces building is compatible with its strategy for national development. It makes national defence building an organic part of its social and economic development, endeavors to establish scientific mechanisms for the coordinated development of economy and national defence, and thus provides rich resources and sustainable driving force for the modernization of its national defence and armed forces. In national defence building, China makes it a point to take into consideration the needs of economic and social development and insists on having military and civilian purposes compatible with and beneficial to each other, so as to achieve more social benefits in the use of national defence resources in peacetime. Deepening the reform of national defence and armed forces. China is working to adjust and reform the organization, structure and policies of the armed forces, and will advance step by step the modernization of the organizational form and pattern of the armed forces in order to develop by 2020 a complete set of scientific modes of organization, institutions and ways of operation both with Chinese characteristics and in conformity with the laws governing the building of modern armed forces.

China strives to adjust and reform the systems of defence-related industry of science and technology and the procurement of weapons and equipment, and enhance its capacity for independent innovation in R&D of weapons and equipment with better quality and cost-effectiveness. China endeavors to establish and improve the systems of weaponry and equipment research and manufacturing, military personnel training and logistical support that integrate military with civilian purposes and combine military efforts with civilian support.

In addition, China makes an effort to establish and improve a national defence mobilization system that is centralized and unified, well structured, rapid in reaction, and authoritative and efficient. Taking the road of leapfrog development.

Persisting in taking mechanization as the foundation and informationization as focus, China is stepping up the composite development of mechanization and informationization. Persisting in strengthening the military by means of science and technology, China is working to develop new and high-tech weaponry and equipment, carry out the strategic project of training talented people, conduct military training in conditions of informationization, and build a modern logistics system in an all-round way, so as to change the mode of formation of war-fighting capabilities. Persisting in laying stress on priorities, China distinguishes between the primary and the secondary, and refrains from doing certain things, striving to achieve leapfrog development in key areas. China persists in building the armed forces through diligence and thrift, attaching importance to scientific management, in order to make the fullest use of its limited defence resources. China implements a military strategy of active defence. Strategically, it adheres to the principle of featuring defensive operations, self-defence and striking and getting the better of the enemy only after the enemy has started an attack. In response to the new trends in world military developments and the requirements of the national security and development strategy, China has formulated a military strategic guideline of active defence for the new period. This guideline aims at winning local wars in conditions of informationization. It takes into overall consideration the evolution of modern warfare and the major security threats facing China, and prepares for defensive operations under the most difficult and complex circum-stances.

Meeting the requirements of confrontation between war systems in modern warfare and taking integrated joint operations as the basic approach, it is designed to bring the operational strengths of different services and arms into full play, combine offensive operations with defensive operations, give priority to the flexible application of strategies and tactics, seek advantages and avoid disadvantages, and make the best use of our strong points to attack the enemy's weak points. It endeavors to refine the command system for joint operations, the joint training system and the joint support system, optimize the structure and composition of forces, and speed up the building of a combat force structure suitable for winning local wars in conditions of informationization. This guideline lays stress on deterring crises and wars. It works for close coordination between military struggle and political, diplomatic, economic, cultural and legal endeavours, strives to foster a favourable security environment, and takes the initiative to prevent and defuse crises, and deter conflicts and wars. It strictly adheres to a position of self-defence, exercises prudence in the use of force, seeks to effectively control war situations, and strives to reduce the risks and costs of war. It calls for the building of a lean and effective deterrent force and the flexible use of different means of deterrence.

China remains committed to the policy of no first use of nuclear weapons, pursues a self-defensive nuclear strategy, and will never enter into a nuclear arms race with any other country. This guideline focuses on enhancing the capabilities of the armed forces in countering various security threats and accomplishing diversified military tasks.

With the focus of attention on performing the historical missions of the armed forces for the new stage in the new century and with raising the capability to win local wars in conditions of informationization at the core, it works to increase the country's capabilities to maintain maritime, space and electromagnetic space security and to carry out the tasks of counter-terrorism, stability maintenance, emergency rescue and international peacekeeping. It takes military operations other than war (MOOTW) as an important form of applying national military forces, and scientifically makes and executes plans for the development of MOOTW capabilities. China participates in international security cooperation, conducts various forms of military exchanges and promotes the establishment of military confidence-building mechanisms in accordance with this guideline. This guideline adheres to and carries forward the strategic concept of people's war. In accordance with this guideline, China always relies on the people to build national defence and the armed forces, combines a lean standing force with a powerful reserve force, and endeavours to reinforce its national war potential and defence strength.

China is working to set up a mechanism for unified and efficient national defence mobilization, stepping up the mobilization of economy, science and technology, information and transportation, and making improvements in the building of the reserve force. China is striving to make innovations in the content and forms of people's war, exploring new approaches of the people in participating in warfare and support for the front, and developing new strategies and tactics for people's war in conditions of informationization. Moreover, the People's Liberation Army (PLA) subordinates its development to the overall national construction, supports local economic and social development, and consolidates the unity between the PLA and the government, and between the PLA and the people.

PLA : Its Reform and Development

In the great historical course of China's reform and opening-up over the past three decades, the PLA has invariably taken modernization as its central task, continuously engaged in reform and innovation, comprehensively advanced revolutionization, modernization and regularization, and made important contributions to safeguarding national sovereignty and security, and maintaining world peace. In recent years, the PLA has accelerated RMA with Chinese characteristics, and pushed forward its military, political, logistical and equipment work in a coordinated way, in an effort to achieve sound and rapid development.

Thirty Years of Reform and Development

From the late 1970s and into the 1980s, the PLA set out on the road of building a streamlined military with Chinese characteristics. According to the scientific judgment that peace and development had become the principal themes of the times, it made a strategic shift in its guiding principle for military building from preparations for "an early, large-scale and nuclear war" to peacetime construction, and advanced its modernization step by step in a well-planned way under the precondition that such efforts should be both subordinated to and in the service of the country's overall development. It set the general goal of building a powerful military, revolutionary in nature, modernized and regularized, and blazed a trail for building a lean military with Chinese characteristics. It underwent significant adjustment and reform, and streamlined the size of its armed forces by a million troops, thereby taking an important step forward in making itself streamlined, combined and efficient.

Entering the 1990s, the PLA began to vigorously promote RMA with Chinese characteristics. It established the military strategic guideline of active defence for the new era, based on winning local wars in conditions of modern technology, particularly high technology. It began to adopt a strategy of strengthening the military by means of science and technology, and a three-step development strategy in modernizing national defence and the armed forces, and promoted the coordinated development of national defence and economy. Regarding RMA with Chinese characteristics as the only way to modernize the military, it put forward the strategic goal of building an informationized military and winning informationized wars.

Driven by preparations for military struggle, it accelerated the development of weaponry and equipment, stepped up the development of the arms and services of the armed forces, as well as forces for emergency mobile operations, optimized its system and structure, and reduced the number of personnel by 700,000. As a result, its capability of defensive operations increased remarkably. At the new stage in the new century, the PLA has been striving to create a new situation in its modernization drive at a new historical starting point. With the Scientific Outlook on Development as an important guiding principle for national defence and armed forces building, it has acted in accordance with the strategic thought of balancing economic and national defence development and integrating efforts to enrich the country and strengthen the military. It has been dedicated to performing its new historical missions and improving its capabilities to counter various security threats and accomplish diversified military tasks. It has accelerated the composite development of mechanization and informationization, vigorously conducts military training in conditions of informationization, and boosts innovation in military theory, technology, organization and management, to continuously increase the core military capability of winning local wars in conditions of informationization and the capability of conducting MOOTW.

Improving the Military Training

Regarding military training as the basic approach to furthering the comprehensive development of the military and raising combat effectiveness, the PLA is working to reform training programs, methods, management and support, and create a scientific system for military training in conditions of informationization.

Increasing training tasks. The PLA is intensifying strategic- and operational-level command post training and troop training in conditions of informationization, holding trans-regional evaluation exercises with opposing players, conducting whole-unit night training and carrying out integrated exercises for logistical and equipment support. Moreover, it is attaching more importance to MOOTW training in counter-terrorism, stability maintenance, emergency response, peacekeeping, emergency rescue and disaster relief.

Deepening training reform. The PLA is creating a task list for military training in conditions of informationization, developing a new edition of the Outline for Military Training and Evaluation, and promoting the application of innovations made in training reform. It is also reinforcing the joint training of the services and arms, strengthening functional training, giving prominence to command and coordinate training and the studies of ways of fighting, and improving training in regional cooperation. It is improving on-base training and simulated training, promoting web-based training, and conducting training with opposing players. It is also reforming training evaluation mechanisms, making training standards stricter, and enforcing meticulous management of the whole process and all aspects of military training.

Conducting training in complex electromagnetic environments. The PLA is spreading basic knowledge of electromagnetic-spectrum and battlefield-electromagnetic environments, learning and mastering basic theories of information warfare, particularly electronic warfare. It is enhancing training on how to operate and use informationized weaponry and equipment, and command information systems. It is working on the informationizing of combined tactical training bases, and holding exercises in complex electromagnetic environments.

Strengthening Ideological and Political Work

The PLA insists on putting ideological and political work first, and pushing forward the innovative development of ideological and political work, to ensure the Party's absolute leadership over the armed forces, the scientific development of the military, the all-round development of the officers and men, the increase of combat capabilities and the effective fulfillment of historical missions.

In January 2007 the General Political Department of the PLA issued the Guideline for the Ideological and Political Education of the Chinese People's Liberation Army (Trial). This guideline spells out clearly that such education refers to the work by the Communist Party of China (CPC) to arm the military with political theories and provide it with ideological guidance; scientifically regulates such education for all kinds of PLA forces and personnel; and further strengthens the development of rules and regulations for such education. Pursuant to the guideline, units whose ratios of political education to military training are 3 to 7 and 2 to 8 should devote 54 and 42 workdays, respectively, to political education each year. The PLA persists in arming its officers and men with the theory of socialism with Chinese characteristics, educates them in its historical missions, ideals, beliefs, fighting spirit and the socialist concept of honor and disgrace, and carries forward the fine traditions of obeying the Party's orders, serving the people, and fighting bravely and skillfully. The PLA's ideological and political education adheres to six principles: to be guided by scientific theories, to put the people first, to focus on the central task and serve the overall interests, to aim at concrete results, to educate through practical activities, and to encourage innovation and development.

Following these principles, the PLA has flexibly applied and innovatively developed educational forms and means, improved radio, television and network educational facilities, and built military history museums, cultural centres, "homes of political instructors," study rooms, and company clubs and honours exhibitions.

In April 2008 the Central Military Commission (CMC) approved the Regulations of the Chinese People's Liberation Army on the Work of Servicemen's Committees, which was jointly issued by the Headquarters of the General Staff, the General Political Department, the General Logistics Department and the General Armament Department. The document has institutionalized political democracy, economic democracy and military democracy for grass-roots units in the new situation. The servicemen's committee is an organization through which the grass-roots military units practice democracy in political, economic and military affairs and through which the servicemen exercise their democratic rights and carry out mass activities.

THE ARMY

As the basis of the PLA, the Army is a service mainly conducting land operations. It consists of such arms as infantry, armor, artillery, air defence, aviation, engineering, signals, chemical defence and electronic countermeasures (ECM), as well as various specialized service units.

Background

The PLA was founded on August 1, 1927, and comprised only the Army in its early days. For a long time the Army was mainly composed of infantry. During the Agrarian Revolutionary War (1927-1937) a small number of cavalry, artillery, engineering and signals troops were added.

The Liberation War (1946-1949) witnessed the advent of tank and chemical defence forces. In the 1950s the Army set up leading organs for such arms as artillery, armor, engineering and chemical defence.

Since the 1980s the structure of the Army has changed dramatically, with the creation of the aviation and ECM arms and the establishment in 1985 of Army combined corps. After 81 years of development, the Army has grown from a single arm into a modern army with various arms. It has become a powerful service capable of conducting both independent and joint operations with the Navy, Air Force and Second Artillery Force.

Structure and Organization

The Army has no independent leading body, and its leadership is exercised by the four general headquarters/departments. The seven military area commands exercise direct leadership over the Army units under them.

The Army includes units of mobile operational, garrison, border and coastal defence, and reserve troops. The organizational order of these units is combined corps, division (brigade), regiment, battalion, company, platoon and squad. Directly under a military area command, a combined corps consists of divisions or brigades, and acts as a basic formation at the operational level. Directly under a combined corps, a division consists of regiments and acts as a basic formation at the tactical level.

Directly under a combined corps, a brigade consists of battalions, and acts as a formation at the tactical level. Normally under a division, a regiment consists of battalions, and acts as a basic tactical unit. Normally under a regiment or brigade, a battalion consists of companies, and acts as a tactical element at a higher level. A company consists of platoons, and acts as a basic tactical element. The Army mobile operational units include 18 combined corps and some independent combined operational divisions (brigades).

Force Building

In recent years, in line with the strategic requirements of mobile operations and three-dimensional offense and defence, the Army has been moving from regional defence to trans-regional mobility. It is gradually making its units small, modular and multi-functional in organization through appropriate downsizing and structural reform. It is accelerating the development of aviation, light mechanized and information countermeasure forces, and gives priority to the development of operational and tactical missile, ground-to-air missile and special operations forces, so as to increase its capabilities for air-ground integrated operations, long-distance maneuvers, rapid assaults and special operations.

The Army has made great progress in building its arms. The armored component has been working to enhance the integration of information systems with weapon platforms, deploy new major battle tanks, and develop heavy, amphibious and light mechanized forces. The proportion of armored mechanized divisions/brigades in combined operational divisions/brigades has further increased. The artillery component has been working to develop a three-level operational command system and deploy a series of advanced weapons and equipment, and new types of ammunition, such as operational and tactical missiles and large-caliber self-propelled gun-howitzers.

It has established a preliminary system for all-range precision strikes. The air defence component has been working to deploy a series of advanced field ground-to-air missiles, and new types of radar and intelligence command systems, and to establish and improve an air defence operations system combining reconnaissance, early warning, command and control, and information countermeasures and interception.

The engineering component has been working to accelerate the establishment of a system of both specialized and multifunctional engineering support forces which can be used both in peacetime and wartime. It has developed relatively strong capabilities in the fields of accompanying support, rapid barrier breaching, comprehensive protection, counter-terrorist explosive ordnance disposal, emergency rescue and disaster relief. The chemical defence component has been working to develop new types of protection forces. It has established a preliminary integrated system of nuclear, biological and chemical early warning, reconnaissance and monitoring, protection command and protection forces.

The Army aviation wing is one of the combat arms of the Army, and has a three-level (general headquarters/departments, theaters and combined corps) administration system. In recent years it has been working to shift from being a support force focusing on transportation missions to being an integrated combat force focusing on air assault missions; it has stepped up training in fire assault, aircraft-borne operations, air mobility and air service support; and actively participated in counter-terrorism, stability maintenance, border closure and control, emergency rescue, disaster relief and joint exercises. The purpose is to build a well-equipped and multifunctional Army aviation force which is appropriate in size and optimal in structure.

The border and coastal defence force of the Army, under the leadership of general headquarters/departments, military area and provincial military commands, is the mainstay for safeguarding national sovereignty and territorial integrity, and maintaining security and stability in border and coastal areas. In recent years, adhering to the principles of placing equal emphasis on land and sea, strengthening border defence by means of science and technology, giving priority to key projects and promoting coordinated development, the border and coastal defence force has focused on combat readiness, and comprehensively enhanced its reconnaissance and surveillance, command and control, quick response and defensive operations capabilities.

It has consistently strengthened the defence and protection of major directions and sensitive regions, watercourses and sea waters in border and coastal areas. It has intensified border control and management, and participated in emergency-handling and disaster-relief missions. It has carried out extensive exchanges and cooperation on border defence with neighboring countries, and dealt with border and coastal affairs proactively and appropriately. As a result, it has made important contributions to peace and stability, reform, opening-up, and social and economic progress in border and coastal areas.

THE NAVY

The Navy is a strategic service of the PLA, and the main force for maritime operations. It is responsible for such tasks as safeguarding China's maritime security and maintaining the sovereignty of its territorial waters, along with its maritime rights and interests. The Navy is mainly composed of submarine, surface ship, aviation, Marine Corps and coastal defence wings.

History of Development

The Navy was founded on April 23, 1949. From 1949 to 1955 it set up the surface ship force, coastal defence force, aviation, submarine force and Marine Corps, and established the objective of building a light maritime combat force. From 1955 to 1960 it established the Donghai Fleet, Nanhai Fleet and Beihai Fleet, successively. From the 1950s to the end of the 1970s the main task of the Navy was to conduct inshore defensive operations. Since the1980s, the Navy has realized a strategic transformation to offshore defensive operations. Since the beginning of the new century, in view of the characteristics and laws of local maritime wars in conditions of informationization, the Navy has been striving to improve in an all-round way its capabilities of integrated offshore operations, strategic deterrence and strategic counterattacks, and to gradually develop its capabilities of conducting cooperation in distant waters and countering non-traditional security threats, so as to push forward the overall transformation of the service. Through nearly six decades of development, a modern force for maritime operations has taken shape, consisting of combined arms with both nuclear and conventional means of operations.

Structure and Organization

In time of peace, the Navy adopts a leadership system which com-bines operational command with building and administration, and which mainly consists of the Navy Headquarters, fleets, test bases, educational institutions, and an armaments academy. There are three fleets under the Navy, namely, the Beihai Fleet, Donghai Fleet and Nanhai Fleet, which are headquartered respectively in Qingdao of Shandong Province, Ningbo of Zhejiang Province, and Zhanjiang of Guangdong Province. Each fleet has under its command fleet aviation, support bases, flotillas, maritime garrison commands, aviation divisions and marine brigades. At present, the Navy has eight educational institutions, namely, the Naval Command College, Naval Engineering University, Naval Aeronautical Engineering College, Dalian Naval Academy, Naval Submarine College, Naval Arms Command College, Naval Flying College and Bengbu Naval School for Non-commissioned Officers.

The submarine force is equipped with nuclear-powered strategic missile submarines, nuclear-powered attack submarines and conventional submarines, all organized into submarine bases and submarine flotillas. The surface ship force mainly consists of destroyers, frigates, missile boats, mine sweepers, landing ships and service ships, and is organized into flotillas of destroyers, speedboats, landing ships and combat support ships, as well as maritime garrison commands. The aviation wing mainly consists of fighters, fighter-bombers, bombers, reconnaissance aircraft, patrol aircraft and helicopters, all organized into aviation divisions. The Marine Corps is organized into marine brigades, and mainly consists of marines, amphibious armored troops, artillery troops, engineers and amphibious reconnaissance troops. The coastal defence force is mainly organized into coastal missile regiments and antiaircraft artillery regiments, and mainly consists of shore-to-ship missile, antiaircraft artillery and coastal artillery troops.

Force Building

In line with the requirements of offshore defence strategy, the Navy takes informationization as the orientation and strategic priority of its modernization drive, and is endeavoring to build a strong navy. It deepens reforms and innovations in training programs and methods, highlights training in maritime integrated joint operations, and enhances integrated combat capability in conducting offshore campaigns and the capability of nuclear counterattacks. It organizes in a scientific way operational training, tactical training, specialized skill training and common subject training, focuses on the integrated training of joint operations elements in conditions of informationization and explores methods of training in complex electromagnetic environments. It also attaches importance to MOOTW, training and actively participates in bilateral and multilateral joint training exercises.

Upgrading weaponry and equipment, and optimizing the weaponry and equipment system. Efforts are being made to build new types of submarines, destroyers, frigates and aircraft, forming a preliminary weaponry and equipment system with second-generation equipment as the core and the third generation as the backbone. The submarine force possesses underwater anti-ship, anti-submarine and mine-laying capabilities, as well as some nuclear counterattack capabilities. The surface ship force has developed a surface striking force represented by new types of missile destroyers and frigates, and possesses maritime reconnaissance, anti-ship, anti-submarine, air-defence, mine-laying and other operational capabilities. The aviation wing has developed an air striking force represented by sea-attack aircraft, and possesses reconnaissance, anti-ship, anti-submarine and air-defence operational capabilities. The Marine Corps has developed an amphibious operational force represented by amphibious armored vehicles, and possesses amphibious operational capabilities. The coastal defence force is represented by new types of shore-to-ship missiles and possesses high coastal defence operations capability.

Optimizing the logistical support system, and improving maritime integrated support capabilities. Aiming at enhancing its integrated logistical support capabilities, the Navy has preliminarily built a logistical support system with shore-based logistical support as the foundation and sea-based logistical support as the mainstay, and meshes the two into an integrated whole. It has stepped up the building of ship bases, berthing areas, supply points, docks and airfields. As a result, a shore-based support system is basically in place, which is coordinated with the development of weaponry and equipment, and suited to war-time support tasks. The Navy has gradually deployed new types of large integrated supply ships, medical ships and ambulance helicopters, and succeeded in developing many types of maritime support equipment and a number of key technologies, leading to significant progress in the modernization of the maritime support force.

Enhancing the capabilities and quality of naval officers and men, and training qualified military personnel. The Navy has adopted a personnel training model in which commanding officer candidates receive integrated education for academic credentials and separate pre-assignment education, and is making efforts to improve the pre-assignment training system for officers. The personnel training of the Navy highlights the uniqueness of the service, and stresses the cultivation of practical capabilities. To raise officers' competence for handling their assignments, the Navy is striving to improve the personnel training programs of its educational institutions and implement assignment-oriented curricula. It is also endeavoring to expand the scale of training for NCOs and foster intermediate and senior NCOs qualified for technically complex posts.

THE AIR FORCE

The Air Force is a strategic service of the PLA, and the main force for carrying out air operations. It is responsible for such tasks as safeguarding the country's territorial air space and territorial sovereignty, and maintaining a stable air defence posture nationwide. It is mainly composed of aviation, ground air defence, airborne, signal, radar, ECM, technical reconnaissance and chemical defence sections.

History of Development

The Air Force was founded on November 11, 1949. The years from 1949 to 1953 witnessed the establishment of an Air Force leading organs in the CMC and in each of the military area commands; the creation of the fighter, bomber, attacker, reconnaissance and transport, airborne forces and a number of educational institutions; and the organization of the Air Force of the Chinese People's Volunteers to take part in the War to Resist U.S. Aggression and Aid Korea (1950-1953). The Air Force was merged with the Air Defence Force in 1957, by adopting a system combining air operations with air defence. In the 1960s and 1970s the Air Force formed the guiding principle of giving priority to the development of air defence forces, and gradually grew into an air force for territorial air defence. Since the 1990s the Air Force has been in a phase of rapid development. It has deployed third-generation combat aircraft, third-generation ground-to-air missiles, and a series of relatively advanced and computerized weapons and equipment. It has stepped up the development of military theories with strategic theories at the core, and introduced a strategic concept that the Air Force should be capable of both offensive and defensive operations. As a result, the Air Force has begun its transition from territorial air defence to both offensive and defensive operations. After nearly six decades of development, the Air Force has initially developed into a strategic service comprising more than one wings. It now has relatively strong capabilities to conduct air defensive and offensive operations, and certain capabilities to execute long-range precision strikes and strategic projection operations.

Structure and Organization

In peacetime, the Air Force practices a leadership system which combines operational command with building and administration, and which consists of the Air Force Headquarters, air commands under military area commands, corps-level (division-level) command posts, divisions (brigades) and regiments. The Air Force has under it an air command in each of the seven military area commands of Shenyang, Beijing, Lanzhou, Jinan, Nanjing, Guangzhou and Chengdu. It has also under it an airborne corps as well as various institutions of education, research and experimentation. Under each air command at the military area command level are aviation divisions, ground-to-air missile divisions (brigades and regiments), antiaircraft artillery brigades (regiments), radar brigades (regiments), ECM brigades (regiments and battalions), and other specialized service units. In key areas there are also corps-or division-level command posts. The Air Force has also a number of educational and training institutions, including the Air Force Command College, Air Force Engineering University, Air Force Aviation University, Air Force

Radar College, Air Force College at Guilin, Air Force College at Xuzhou, Air Force School for Noncommissioned Officers at Dalian and seven flying colleges.

An aviation division usually consists of regiments, groups and squadrons, and has such types of aircraft as fighters, attackers, fighter-bombers, bombers, transports and combat support aircraft. It has under it aviation regiments and related stations. The aviation regiment is the basic tactical unit. With battalions as the basic fighting units, the ground-to-air missile force is usually organized into divisions, regiments and battalions or into brigades (regiments) and battalions. With batteries as basic fighting units, the antiaircraft artillery force is usually organized into brigades (regiments), battalions and companies. The airborne forces are organized into corps, divisions, regiments, battalions and companies.

Force Building

To meet the requirements of informationized warfare, the Air Force is working to accelerate its transition from territorial air defence to both offensive and defensive operations, and increase its capabilities for carrying out reconnaissance and early warning, air strikes, air and missile defence, and strategic projection, in an effort to build itself into a modernized strategic air force.

Taking into full account preparations for combat and its own transformation and development, the Air Force is exploring training systems and methods tailored to the development of the latest generation of weaponry and equipment. It stresses technical and tactical training in complex environments, combined training of different arms and aircraft types, and joint training; conducts mission-oriented and confrontational training; and is increasing on-base, simulated and web-based training. It is working to optimize the tripartite pilot training system composed of flying colleges, training bases and combat units, and intensifying the training of aviation units in counter-air operations, air-to-ground attacks and joint operations. It is deepening reforms and innovations in institutional education by improving the system of discipline, and making innovations in teaching programs, means and methods. It is strengthening on-the-job training, and exploring a new model of personnel development, namely the triad of institutional education, training in units and professional military education. For this purpose, the Air Force Military Professional University was established in July 2008.

To satisfy the strategic requirements of conducting both offensive and defensive operations, the Air Force attaches importance to developing new types of fighters, air and anti-missile defence weapons, and command automation systems. It has deployed some relatively advanced computerized equipment, and air-to-air and air-to-ground precision-guided munitions, upgraded the electronic information systems of the equipment on active service, and improved the basic networks for intelligence and early warning, command and control, and communications. It has in the main established a major battle weaponry and equipment system with third-generation aircraft and ground-to-air missiles as the mainstay, and modified second-generation aircraft and ground-to-air missiles as the supplement.

Centring on the improvement of the capabilities and quality of its personnel, the Air Force pursues a road of personnel development which takes new-and high-tech talents as the driving force, makes breakthroughs in critical areas and aims at overall improvement. It makes overall plans for training command, staff, flight and technical support personnel. It has fostered a group of core personnel with a good command of information technology and a contingent of new types of high-caliber personnel as represented by inter-disciplinary commanding officers, first-rate pilots, leaders in scientific and technological research, and technical experts.

To raise its integrated support capabilities, the Air Force attaches importance to the development of logistical and equipment support systems. It endeavours to improve the support facilities of airfields and positions; strengthen its logistical forces for rapid construction of air defence projects, bomb elimination at and rapid repair of airfields which have suffered attack, and aviation medical support; develop and deploy the second generation of specialized logistical equipment; create a storage and supply network for special-purpose materials; and build step by step bases capable of supporting multiple types of aircraft. The Air Force is also stepping up efforts to deepen the reform of the equipment support mode; improve the layout of support networks for the supply, maintenance and technical support of ammunition and material; and make support equipment smaller in size, more versatile in function and fitter for field operations.

THE SECOND ARTILLERY FORCE

The Second Artillery Force is a strategic force under the direct command and control of the CMC, and the core force of China for strategic deterrence. It is mainly responsible for deterring other countries from using nuclear weapons against China, and for conducting nuclear counterattacks and precision strikes with conventional missiles.

The Second Artillery Force sticks to China's policy of no first use of nuclear weapons, implements a self-defensive nuclear strategy, strictly follows the orders of the CMC, and takes it as its fundamental mission the protection of China from any nuclear attack. In peacetime the nuclear missile weapons of the Second Artillery Force are not aimed at any country. But if China comes under a nuclear threat, the nuclear missile force of the Second Artillery Force will go into a state of alert, and get ready for a nuclear counterattack to deter the enemy from using nuclear weapons against China. If China comes under a nuclear attack, the nuclear missile force of the Second Artillery Force will use nuclear missiles to launch a resolute counterattack against the enemy either independently or together with the nuclear forces of other services. The conventional missile force of the Second Artillery Force is charged mainly with the task of conducting medium-and long-range precision strikes against key strategic and operational targets of the enemy.

THE PEOPLE'S ARMED POLICE FORCE

As a component of China's armed forces and subordinate to the State Council, the People's Armed Police Force (PAPF) is under the dual leadership of the State Council and the CMC. The PAPF consists of the internal security force and various police forces. The border public security, firefighting and security guard forces are also components of the PAPF. The PAPF is charged with the fundamental task of safeguarding national security, maintaining social stability and ensuring that the people live and work in peace and contentment.

NATIONAL DEFENCE RESERVE BUILDUP

China firmly relies on the people for national defence, and seeks to strengthen the buildup of the national defence reserve incompliance with the requirement of being able to deal with both emergencies and wars.

Reserve Force Buildup

With active servicemen as its backbone and reserve officers and men as its foundation, the reserve force is an armed force formed in line with the unified structure and organization of the PLA. It is under the dual leadership of the PLA and local Party committees and governments.

The reserve force was founded in 1983. In August 1986 it formally became a part of the PLA. In May 1995 the NPC Standing Committee adopted the Law of the People's Republic of China on Reserve Officers. In April 1996 the CMC began to confer military ranks on reserve officers. The Law of the People's Republic of China on National Defence promulgated in March 1997 explicitly stipulates that China's armed forces consist of the active-duty force and the reserve force of the PLA, the People's Armed Police Force and the militia.

After 25 years of buildup and development, the reserve force has become an important component of the national defence reserve. It is made up of the Army Reserve, Navy Reserve, Air Force Reserve and the Second Artillery Force Reserve. The Army Reserve breaks down into infantry, artillery, antiaircraft artillery, antitank artillery, tank, engineering, chemical defence, signals, coastal defence and other specialized forces. The Navy Reserve is mainly composed of reconnaissance, mine-sweeping and mine-laying, radar observation and communications and other specialized forces. The Air Force Reserve mainly comprises ground-to-air missile, radar and other specialized forces. The Second Artillery Force Reserve mainly consists of the specialized missile support force and special equipment maintenance force.

In line with the unified structure and organization of the PLA, the reserve force has reserve divisions, brigades and regiments, and corresponding leading organs. Reserve units are organized mainly on a regional basis. Divisions are set up in provinces and brigades (regiments) in prefectures (autonomous prefectures or prefecture-level cities). A division (brigade) can be set up in a region covering more than one prefecture (autonomous prefecture or prefecture-level city), and a regiment in a region covering more than one county (county-level city or district).

In recent years, the reserve force has made new strides in organization building and military training. It has gradually enlarged the pool of reservists, improved its organizational methods, and actively explored new organizational models, such as industrial, trans-regional and community-based organizations. It conducts and manages training according to the training program and law, so as to regularize training. As stipulated in the Outline for the Military Training and Evaluation of the Reserve Force, one third of the authorized strength of a unit must undergo 30 days of training annually. Training tasks are based on possible wartime assignments and the caliber of the reservists. The reserve force is in the process of shifting its focus from quantity and scale to quality and efficiency, and from a combat role to a support role. The goal is to enable the reserve and active forces to cooperate closely with each other, to complement each other, and to develop in a coordinated way.

Militia Force Building

Militia work is under the unified leadership of the State Council and the CMC, and the leadership of local Party committees, local governments as well as the local military commands. The General Staff Headquarters supervises militia work nationwide. The military area commands are responsible for militia work in their respective jurisdictions. Provincial military commands, prefectural military commands and people's armed forces departments of counties (county-level cities or districts) are the organs of military leadership and command, and responsible for the militia work in their respective jurisdictions. The grass-roots people's armed forces departments established in town-ships (towns), urban sub-districts, enterprises and public institutions are responsible for organizing and carrying out militia work. Local Party committees and governments at all levels make overall plans and arrangements for militia work.

In recent years China has persisted in reform and innovation in militia force buildup, adjusted its size and structure, and upgraded its weaponry and equipment. The organizational structure has optimized to increase the capabilities of the militia to support combat and emergency response forces, and to gradually shift the centre of its responsibilities from rural areas to cities, areas along communication lines and other key areas. Importance has been attached to establishing militia organizations in emerging enterprises and high-tech industries to increase the technology content of the militia force. Investment in weaponry and equipment has been increased to systematically and organically provide a series of new types of militia air defence equipment such as air defence artillery and portable air defence missiles in key areas. Equipment for emergency response and stability-maintenance operations has been improved. Some types of weapons have been upgraded. During the Eleventh Five-Year Plan period (2006-2010) the number of militia personnel is scheduled to be reduced from 10 million to eight million.

In May 2007 the General Staff Headquarters released a new edition of the Outline for the Training and Evaluation of the Militia. The new outline adds over a hundred training tasks in dozens of categories covering specialties of the Navy, Air Force and Second Artillery Force, marking a shift from traditional single-service to multi-service/arm specialized militia training. Based on the principles of integrating resources, pooling strengths, organizing training level by level and conducting trans-regional training, the military training of the militia has a four-level organizational system: The provincial military commands are the backbone; the prefectural military commands are the main body;

the people's armed forces departments are the basis; and the grass-roots people's armed forces departments are the supplement. The militia is improving its technology-based training, and promoting on-base, simulated and web-based training step by step. Prominence is given to such tasks as rapid mobilization of specialized detachments, coordination with active units and operations in complex electromagnetic environments. In addition, efforts are being made to enhance training in emergency response and rescue. The aim is to raise the militia's capabilities in combat operations, emergency rescue, disaster relief, crisis response and social stability maintenance.

DEFENCE EXPENDITURE

Guided by the principle that defence expenditure should grow inline with the demands of national defence and economic development, the Chinese government decides on the size of defence expenditure in an appropriate way, and takes a road of national defence and armed forces modernization featuring lower cost and higher efficiency.

In the past three decades of reform and opening up, China has insisted that defence development should be both subordinated to and in the service of the country's overall economic development, and that the former should be coordinated with the latter. As a result, defence expenditure has always been kept at a reasonable and appropriate level. From 1978 to 1987, as the nation shifted its focus to economic development, national defence received a low input and was in a state of bare sustenance. During this period the average annual increase of defence expenditure was 3.5 percent, while that of GDP was 14.1 percent and that of the state financial expenditure was 10.4 percent. The shares of China's annual defence expenditure in its GDP and in the state financial expenditure dropped respectively from 4.6 percent and 14.96 percent in 1978 to 1.74 percent and 9.27 percent in 1987. From 1988 to 1997, to make up for the inadequacy of defence development and maintain national security and unity, China gradually increased its defence expenditure on the basis of its sustained economic growth. During this period the average annual increase of defence expenditure was 14.5 percent while that of GDP was 20.7 percent and that of the state financial expenditure was 15.1 percent. The shares of China's annual defence expenditure in its GDP and in the state financial expenditure continued to drop. From 1998 to 2007, to maintain national security and development and meet the requirements of the RMA with Chinese characteristics, China continued to increase its defence expenditure steadily on the basis of its rapid economic growth. During this period, the average annual increase of defence expenditure was 15.9 percent, while that of GDP was 12.5 percent and that of the state financial expenditure was 18.4 percent. Although the share of China's defence expenditure in its GDP increased, that in the state financial expenditure continued to drop on the whole.

China's GDP was RMB 21,192.3 billion in 2006 and RMB 25,730.6 billion in 2007. The state financial expenditure was RMB 4,042.273 billion in 2006 and RMB 4,978.135 billion in 2007, up 19.1 percent and 23.2 percent respectively over the previous year. China's defence expenditure was RMB 297.938 billion in 2006 and RMB 355.491 billion in 2007, up 20.4 percent and 19.3 percent respectively over the previous year. The shares of China's annual defence expenditure in its GDP and in the state financial expenditure in 2006 were roughly the same as those in 2007, being 1.41 percent and 7.37 percent in 2006 and 1.38 percent and 7.14 percent in 2007. China's defence expenditure mainly comprises expenses for personnel, training and maintenance, and equipment. Expenses for personnel and training and maintenance account for two thirds of the defence expenditure. In 2007, the defence expenditure was used to cover the expenses of the active force (RMB 343.439 billion), the reserve force (RMB 3.693 billion) and the militia (RMB 8.359 billion). China's defence budget for 2008 is RMB 417.769 billion.

In the past two years, the increased part of China's defence expenditure has primarily been used for the following purposes: (1) Increasing the salaries and benefits of servicemen. Along with the rise of the income of civil servants and the living standards of both urban and rural residents, China has increased the relevant allowances and subsidies of servicemen to ensure the parallel improvement of their living standards. (2) Compensating for price rises. With the rise of the prices of food, building materials, fuel, etc., China has accordingly increased the boarding subsidies and other funds closely related to servicemen's life as well as the expenses on education, training, petroleum, oils and lubricants for the armed forces, and improved the working and living conditions of border and coastal defence forces, units in remote and tough areas, and grass-roots units. (3) Pushing forward the RMA. China has augmented the input into military informationization and moderately increased the funds for equipment and supporting facilities, so as to raise the defence capabilities in conditions of informationization.

Both the total amount and per-service-person share of China's defence expenditure remain lower than those of some major powers. In 2007 China's defence expenditure equaled 7.51 percent of that of the United States, 62.43 percent of that of the United Kingdom. China's defence expenses per service person amounted to 4.49 percent of that of the United States, 11.3 percent of that of Japan, 5.31 percent of that of the United Kingdom, 15.76 percent of that of France and 14.33 percent of that of Germany. As for the share of defence expenditure in GDP, that of China was merely 1.38 percent, while that of the United States was 4.5 percent, that of the United Kingdom 2.7 percent, and that of France 1.92 percent.

The Chinese government has established defence expenditure reporting and publishing mechanisms. Since 1978 the Chinese government has submitted a financial budget report to the NPC and published the total amount of the defence budget each year. The relevant data of China's defence expenditure has been made public in the China Economy Yearbook since 1981, and in the China Finance Yearbook since 1992. And since 1995 the composition and main purposes of China's defence expenditure have been published in the form of government white papers.

ARMS CONTROL AND DISARMAMENT

The Chinese government has always attached importance to and been supportive of international efforts in the field of arms control, disarmament and non-proliferation. China has taken concrete measures to faithfully fulfil its relevant international obligations.

China is committed to, along with the international community, consolidating and strengthening the existing international arms control, disarmament and non-proliferation mechanisms pursuant to the purposes and principles of the Charter of the United Nations and other universally recognized norms governing international relations, and to the preservation of international strategic stability and promotion of the common security of all countries.

Nuclear Disarmament

China holds that all nuclear-weapon states should make an unequivocal commitment to the thorough destruction of nuclear weapons, undertake to stop research into and development of new types of nuclear weapons, and reduce the role of nuclear weapons in their national security policy.

The two countries possessing the largest nuclear arsenals bear special and primary responsibility for nuclear disarmament. They should earnestly comply with the relevant agreements already concluded, and further drastically reduce their nuclear arsenals in a verifiable and irreversible manner, so as to create the necessary conditions for the participation of other nuclear-weapon states in the process of nuclear disarmament.

China supports the early entry into force of the Comprehensive Nuclear Test-Ban Treaty, and will continue to honor its moratorium commitment on nuclear testing. China supports the preparatory work for the entry into force of the Treaty by the Preparatory Commission of the Comprehensive Nuclear Test-Ban Treaty Organization, and has contributed to the establishment of the International Monitoring System (IMS).

China has always stayed true to its commitments that it will not be the first to use nuclear weapons at any time and in any circumstances, and will unconditionally not use or threaten to use nuclear weapons against non-nuclear-weapon states or in nuclear-weapon-free zones. China calls upon other nuclear-weapon states to make the same commitments and conclude an international legal instrument in this regard. China has already signed all relevant protocols which have been opened for signature of various nuclear-weapon-free zone treaties, and has reached agreement with the ASEAN on relevant issues of the Protocol of the Treaty on the Southeast Asia Nuclear-Weapon-Free Zone. China welcomes the Treaty on a Nuclear-Weapon-Free Zone in Central Asia signed by the five Central Asian countries.

China values the role of the Conference on Disarmament (CD) in Geneva, and supports efforts in the CD to reach a comprehensive and balanced program of work, so as to enable the CD to start substantial work on such issues as the Fissile Material Cut-off Treaty (FMCT), prevention of an arms race in outer space, nuclear disarmament and security assurance to non-nuclear-weapon states.

China maintains that the global missile defence program will be detrimental to strategic balance and stability, undermine international and regional security, and have a negative impact on the process of nuclear disarmament. China pays close attention to this issue.

Prohibition of Biological and Chemical Weapons

China observes in good faith its obligations under the Biological Weapons Convention (BWC), and supports the multilateral efforts aimed at strengthening the effectiveness of the Convention.

China has actively participated in the meetings of the parties to the Convention and the meetings of experts in a pragmatic manner. China has already established a comprehensive legislation system for the implementation of the Convention, set up a national implementation focal point, and submitted its declarations regarding confidence-building measures to the Implementation Support Unit of the Convention in a timely fashion. China has also strengthened bio-safety, bio-security and disease surveillance, and actively carried out related international exchanges and cooperation.

China earnestly fulfils its obligations under the Chemical Weapons Convention (CWC) by setting up implementation offices at both central and local levels, submitting timely and complete annual declarations, subsequent declarations regarding newly discovered chemical weapons abandoned by Japan in China and information on the national protection program. China has received more than 170 on-site inspections by the Organization for the Prohibition of Chemical Weapons (OPCW).

The Analytical Chemistry Research Laboratory of the Institute of Chemical Defence became the first OPCW-designated laboratory in China in 1998, followed by the Toxicant Analysis Laboratory of the Academy of Military Medical Sciences, which became an OPCW-designated laboratory in 2007.

In May 2008 China and the OPCW jointly held a training course on protection and assistance in Beijing. With a view to accelerating the destruction of chemical weapons abandoned by Japan in China, China has assisted Japan in carrying out more than 100 on-site investigations, and excavated more than 40,000 items of chemical weapons abandoned by Japan. China urges Japan to earnestly implement its obligations under the Convention, and start the actual destruction of chemical weapons abandoned by Japan in China as soon as possible.

Non-Proliferation

China firmly opposes the proliferation of weapons of mass destruction (WMD) and their means of delivery, and actively takes part in international non-proliferation efforts. China holds that an integrated approach should be adopted to address both the symptoms and root causes of proliferation.

The international community should devote itself to building a global and regional security environment featuring stability, cooperation and mutual trust, and earnestly maintaining and strengthening the authority and effectiveness of the international non-proliferation regime. In this regard, double standards must be abandoned. All states should resort to dialogue and negotiation to resolve differences in the field of non-proliferation. The relations between non-proliferation and the peaceful use of science and technology should be properly addressed, with the aim of preserving the right of peaceful use of each state while effectively preventing WMD proliferation.

China has joined all international treaties and international organizations in the field of non-proliferation. It attaches great importance to the role of the Treaty on the Non-proliferation of Nuclear Weapons (NPT), the Biological Weapons Convention (BWC) and the Chemical Weapons Convention (CWC) in preventing the proliferation of WMD. China supports the role played by the UN in the field of non-proliferation, and has conscientiously implemented the relevant resolutions of the UN Security Council.

China is dedicated to the denuclearization of the Korean Peninsula, and firmly promotes the Six-Party Talks process on that issue. China facilitated the adoption of "Initial Actions for the Implementation of the Joint Statement" and the "Second-Phase Actions for the Implementation of the Joint Statement" respectively in February and October 2007.

14 Myths and Realities of China's Military Power

Given the atmosphere of suspicion and distrust that so often characterizes U.S.-China relations, it is vitally important that Chinese foreign policy and military capabilities be calmly and carefully assessed. Unfortunately, images of China as a potential threat tend to dominate in public discussions of China policy. Negative images of China stem in part from memories of the Tiananmen massacre that still loom large in the minds of most Americans.

The alleged spy scandals and accusations of theft of American nuclear secrets are also factors. China is widely seen as taking a hard line in its relations with the U.S. on such issues as human rights and arms sales. Although Chinese military capabilities have improved recently, these advances are modest, and China will remain a weak military power for a long time.

Despite the worst-case scenario painted by the Cox report two years ago, China remains a small nuclear power with only minor capabilities. There is no evidence that it has tested—let alone integrated—any stolen American technology into its nuclear forces. China has only about 20 Inter-Continental Ballistic Missiles (ICBMs)—each armed with only a single warhead—that can reach the continental United States, and its one nuclear-powered ballistic missile submarine has apparently been nonoperational for several years. In recent years China has purchased a variety of weapons systems from the Russians. Representing a significant improvement over most Chinese equipment, these weapons include advanced SU-27 fighters and SU-30 ground attack aircraft, S-300 SAM antiship missiles, Kilo-class submarines, and Sovremenny-class destroyers. China has also introduced new weapons systems of its own design, including tanks, short-range ballistic missiles, and the Song-class submarine.

China, however, continues to rely on outdated technology to equip most of its armed forces. The SU-27s and SU-30s are China's first fifth-generation, modernized combat aircraft. But most of the Chinese Air Force's combat aircraft are obsolete. China has about 30 SU-30s but relies on over 1,500 J-6 and Q-5 ground attack planes and some 700 J-7s. These designs date back to the early 1950s and 60s. Although older planes are being phased out, it will be more than a decade before China's Air Force reaches the current technological level of Taiwan's combat aircraft. The bulk of China's armored forces still features tanks based on Soviet designs from the 1950s. The Sovremenny-class destroyers are designed to attack American aircraft carriers and are far more advanced than anything else in the Chinese Navy. China has only two such destroyers, and the rest of its navy remains technologically backward.

China is at least two decades away from being able to deploy a fully functional carrier with aircraft. The new Kilo and Song submarines are indeed a significant improvement for the Chinese Navy, but it will be years before China finishes replacing its older, less advanced submarines. Moreover, the Chinese armed forces continue to suffer from significant deficiencies in training and recruitment standards. The Chinese have yet to conduct a full-scale combined arms training exercise that would allow them to fully integrate the new weapons systems that they have acquired. Although worrisome, the 17.7% increase in China's 2001 defence budget is more of a political signal to the U.S. and Taiwan than an indication of substantially improving Chinese military capabilities.

Except for a brief skirmish with Vietnam over a disputed South China Sea islet in 1988, China has not resorted to the use of force since its disastrous attack on Vietnam in 1979. By and large, China has acted as a satisfied power, having increased economic ties with all its neighbours and negotiated border agreements with most neighboring countries. Only in the case of Taiwan is there a real danger of conflict. Beijing has been quite clear that it is willing to use force if Taiwan declares its independence. However, China lacks the amphibious assault capabilities it would need to land a sufficient force on Taiwan (where there are only a few, easily defended places to land troops). Taiwan's Air Force is far smaller but much more modern than China's. China could place a naval blockade on Taiwan or use its growing arsenal of missiles to try to coerce Taiwan into surrendering, but neither approach would guarantee success. Although China's M-9 and M-11 missiles look threatening, they lack the precision needed to knock out all of Taiwan's defenses, and China's submarine force is still in the early stages of modernization. A military and economic siege would take months to succeed. The cost to China itself would be immense, and the U.S. would have plenty of time to consider how to react. In sum, impressions of the Chinese threat are exaggerated, with respect to both China's capabilities and its intentions.

Problems with Current U.S. Policy

Key Problems

- Washington is moving away from its policy of deliberate ambiguity toward Taiwan's defenses. This limits future U.S. options and increases the possibility that the United States and China will stumble into a crisis.
- U.S. perceptions tend to exaggerate the extent of Chinese capabilities.
- U.S. policy on TMD and NMD has the potential to be destabilizing.

The main problem with current China policy is the growing tendency in the U.S. to overestimate Chinese military capabilities and China's potential threat to U.S. national security. Current plans to proceed with National Missile Defence (NMD) and Theatre Missile Defence (TMD) systems are largely based on this overestimation of the China threat. Given that NMD currently enjoys a fair amount of support on both sides of the aisle in Congress, it is likely to be implemented in some form. The Bush administration contends that the capabilities of NMD will be sufficient to provide protection from "rogue" states but modest enough to not threaten the Russians and Chinese. From the Chinese perspective, however, NMD represents a substantial threat to its national security. Chinese officials argue that Washington has greatly exaggerated the rogue state threat, and there is widespread suspicion that NMD's real objective is to neutralize China's nuclear deterrence capability.

Indeed, the proposed NMD system would be more than adequate to eliminate any deterrence credibility from China's meager ICBM force. This would leave China without any second-strike capability in the event of a confrontation with the United States. If the U.S. proceeds with NMD, then China will likely decide to improve its own nuclear capabilities. One option for China would be to increase its arsenal of missiles in an attempt to overwhelm any missile defence the Americans build. China could also upgrade its missiles with multiple-entry warheads, thereby increasing the number of warheads aimed at the United States. It might even do both. However, any plan by China to increase the size or capability of its nuclear forces would likely also increase sentiment among U.S. policymakers that China is indeed a potential threat to America's security. Thus, the deployment of NMD could easily trigger a series of events that would trap the U.S. and China in a classic security dilemma of mutual misperceptions.

Extending a missile shield to Japan and Taiwan may also be destabilizing. Washington regards TMD as necessary in northeast Asia to defend Japan (and U.S. forces stationed there) against a North Korean missile threat. A TMD system could also help Taiwan resist a potential attack from China. (See Missile Defence and China by Wade Huntley and Robert Brown, FPIF, January 2001.) Beijing, which sees TMD as a threat to its territorial integrity, argues that such a system would encourage Taiwanese independence and otherwise foster the political separation of Taiwan from mainland China. China's most obvious response would be to increase the number of its battlefield missiles, so it could overwhelm any Taiwanese missile defence system. Less obvious to many American observers is that China is also concerned about TMD in Japan. Within China's military, TMD is seen as a potential first step in the remilitarization of Japan. Far from creating greater stability in the region, TMD systems in East Asia may set off an arms race.

Arms sales to Taiwan also remain problematic. The Taiwan Relations Act (TRA) commits the U.S. to offer arms for Taiwan's self-defence. Over the past decade the U.S. has sold Taiwan 126 F-16s as well as Patriot antimissile systems, eight Knox-class frigates, seven Perry-class frigates, M-60A3 tanks, and electronic equipment. Combined with arms purchases from France, these sales have substantially improved Taiwan's defence capabilities. The Taiwanese government is currently seeking further arms purchases from the U.S., including four Aegis-class destroyers, designed to provide air defence for Taiwan's Navy. Other items reportedly on the list include submarine hunting aircraft, missiles, AIM-120 air-to-air missiles, ship-to-ship missiles, antiaircraft missiles, and submarines.

The Aegis-class destroyers have come to assume enormous symbolic value as a litmus test of the degree of U.S. political support for Taiwan. From both the Chinese and Taiwanese perspectives, any sale of Aegis destroyers would signal that the United States is moving closer to a de facto military alliance with Taiwan, rendering Washington a potential enemy in Beijing's eyes. Ironically, for all the controversy over the proposed sale, the Aegis is not necessarily the best military choice for Taiwan. These ships will do little to counter China's newer submarines, which represent Taiwan's primary threat. Taiwan would be better off buying antisubmarine weapons, which are also less politically offensive to Beijing.

Worst-case scenarios and ideological considerations are pushing the U.S. in the direction of providing Taiwan with more than is necessary for its defence. This creates a negative reaction in China and reinforces Beijing's perception of the U.S. as a potential enemy. China, in turn, is taking a more hard-line stance toward the U.S.—thereby confirming Washington's suspicions of Beijing.

Washington is also moving away from its traditional policy of deliberate ambiguity toward a more clear-cut commitment to Taiwan's defence in advance of any actual crisis. This limits future

U.S. options and increases the possibility that the United States and China will stumble into a crisis that neither country wants or desires. This is especially worrisome in light of renewed congressional pressure to end or sharply curtail military exchanges between the U.S. and China. These exchanges have come under criticism, because they are perceived by some as rewarding China, despite its bad human rights record, and because the exchanges have not produced as many positive results as had been hoped. However, mutual misperceptions about military capabilities and intent are most likely to occur in the absence of communication. The April 2001 spy plane controversy, for example, was aggravated by a lack of trust on both sides. If the Bush administration decides to end the exchange program, there is a risk of fostering even greater mistrust between the two powers and increasing the chance of more dangerous incidents in the future.

Highlights

BRAHMAPUTRA DAMS: GOVT WAS ALERTED, DIDN'T MOVE

With new evidence emerging to suggest that China has begun constructing a dam on its side of the Brahmaputra the National Remote Sensing Agency (NRSA) and National Technical Research Organisation (NTRO) are taking a hard look at the Chinese plans before the matter can formally be taken up with Beijing. Official sources said that the NTRO, using NRSA data, had alerted the Government in May 2008 about nine suspected locations along the river on the Chinese side. The NTRO had informed the Committee of Secretaries about increased infrastructure activity near the Great Bend where the Brahmaputra takes a steep turn to enter India. Citing "open sources", NTRO had even indicated 2009 could see "commencement" of construction work in the Great Western River Diversion Project.

Reports on Chinese plans to divert Brahmaputra water have been taken note of ever since 2003. In 2005, Li Ling's book 'How Tibet's water will save China' detailed plans to divert about 200 BCM of water from Tibet, including 120 BCM from the Brahmaputra basin on the Chinese side. The CoS has been monitoring this aspect since 2006. Sources said that the CoS met several times — in October 2006, September 2008, October 2008 and February 2009 — to discuss reports of Chinese plans to build a dam on the Brahmaputra. At one stage, the CoS was informed that the Great Western River Diversion Project had "moved from discussion to planning stage".

Despite a CoS recommendation, the Government did not constitute a Group of Ministers. The CoS recommended a GoM to fast-track storage projects in Arunachal Pradesh to take care of any "adverse construction" on the Chinese side. But only a high-level group of senior officials and experts was formed to expedite projects in Arunachal Pradesh. Assam Chief Minister Tarun Gogoi has said that his government was "seriously concerned" over the construction of a dam by the Chinese as "we apprehend it will affect Assam and dry up Brahmaputra and other water resources downstream." Gogoi said he would meet the Prime Minister and Union Water Resources Minister and ask them to take up the issue with Beijing.

In New Delhi, BJP president Rajnath Singh was said to have raised the dam-construction matter in a meeting with Chinese Ambassador Zhang Yan. According to a release issued by his office, Singh also said that "China's repeated claims on Arunachal Pradesh amounted to repeated interference in India's internal affairs". He said the "BJP was solidly behind the Union Government in its diplomatic efforts to resolve bilateral issues with its northern neighbour". Zhang Yan was quoted as having said that China wanted to have cordial relations with India but "there were some historical issues to be resolved".

INDIA TO CHECK IF CHINA IS BUILDING BRAHMAPUTRA DAM

While increasingly distrustful of China's intentions, the government refrained from questioning Beijing's denial that it was engaged in constructing a dam on Brahmaputra which could impact ecology in the northeastern states. Reacting to a fresh report questioning China's denial, the MEA here said, "India and China agreed in November 2006 to establish an Expert Level Mechanism to discuss trans-border river issues in an institutional way. Three meetings have been held so far.... The Chinese side has categorically denied that there is a plan to build any such large scale diversion project on the Brahmaputra river."

However, it said the government would "ascertain whether there are recent developments that suggest any change in the position conveyed to us by the government of China". The fact about China building dams on the Brahmaputra to divert water to its parched northeast regions was first highlighted by TOI. In

November 2006, India and China set up an experts committee on transborder rivers.

China has continued to deny that it was building dams on Brahmaputra which would result in diversion of waters crucial for India's northeast. Yet, exactly a year ago, PM Manmohan Singh, meeting Chinese president Hu Jintao on the sidelines of the ASEM summit in Beijing, devoted most of his conversation to the question of Brahmaputra and Chinese actions on it. The PM confirmed that this was his focus during the conversation. There are indications that China may have put the plan in high gear. In April 2009, China's Gezhouba Corporation, one of the country's biggest engineering and construction companies, won a 1.14 billion yuan bid for the hydropower plant in Zangmu, in the middle of the Brahmaputra river. The company's website said it would be responsible for "designing, constructing and running the project that supplies 3.4-million cu m of concrete and 8-million-ton aggregate for the water power station. The project is expected to last until the end of December 2015."

Zangmu is only the first dam to be built. China plans to build four more dams at Jiacha, Zongda, Lengda, Jiexu and Langzhen. The Chinese are also building another hydropower project with large-scale dams in Tibet, which has already seen tens of thousands of Tibetans protesting against the building of hydro projects on the Brahmaputra. It needed the Chinese Public Security Bureau and Peoples Armed Police to fire at the crowd, killing six women. China has already dammed the Mekong rover and the resulting siltation has created a huge problem for lower riparian states in Thailand, Cambodia, etc.

INSIDE STORY OF SINO-INDIAN BORDER TALKS

A briefing to the domestic audience in China about the Sino-Indian border issue has always been a rare event; marking one such occasion is a very recent detailed review of the subject, done by a Chinese analyst who appears to be authoritative and well versed with the ongoing border negotiations between the two sides. The review can certainly be looked upon as a link to understand how China's border policy towards India is evolving;

it would sure be of great interest to experts on the subject in general and for India specifically, its significance would need no emphasis, at a time when the country's Minister for External affairs has just returned home from Beijing after holding talks with his Chinese counterpart on a host of issues including border. The Chinese analyst Zhuhua observes on Sino-Indian Border talks as follows:

Sikkim-No Chinese Formal Statement Recognising it as Part of India

The analyst states that the Sino-Indian Memorandum on Nathula as a border trade point (2003) has signified China's "de facto" recognition of India's sovereignty over Sikkim. Quoting Indian side, Zhuhua mentions that at the time of border talks, Beijing handed over a 'new' official map to them showing Sikkim as a State of India. Foreign press reports pointed out that India as a quid pro quo, reiterated its recognition of the Tibet Autonomous Region as part of the People's Republic of China (PRC) and its policy of not permitting any anti-China political activity by the Tibetans in India and also, internal opinions in China justified the changed stance of China on Sikkim on the basis of the need for Beijing to "struggle side by side with compromise" in order to win "support in other fronts". The analyst further points out that the Chinese Foreign Ministry website has deleted Sikkim from its list of "Countries and Regions" and its spokesperson has mentioned that Sikkim is no longer a problem in bilateral relations. Thus, overall, Sikkim has ceased to appear as 'a historical legacy' for China. The Blog at the same time notes that the Chinese Government has never issued any formal statement recognising Sikkim as part of India's territory", about which New Delhi has expressed dissatisfaction".

Briefing to the Chinese on the Border Issue

Giving a background to the border issue for the benefit of viewers in China, Zhuhua observes that there are two lines concerning the Sino-Indian border-a traditional customary line and a line of actual control. The former came into being before the modern era and relying on traditional practices and governance, some borders came into being. The line of actual control provides the basis for India's position. Alleging that in the year 1913, British India's official McMahon concocted the so called McMahon line, pushing Indian control up north of the customary line by 100 kms, the analyst says that in this way 90,000 Sq kms of territory which were under Chinese jurisdiction, was taken over by India. Adding that the Sino-Indian agreement on taking Political Parameters as basis to settle the border dispute in 2005, takes into account 'history and current situation' factors, the Blog points out that the same has facilitated the distinguishing of the two lines mentioned above.

According to the Blog, the total disputed border area between China and India comes to about 125, 000 sq kms of land. In the Western Sector, the disputed territory is about 30,000 sq kms in Aksai Chin, located at the junction of Western parts of Xinjiang and Tibet regions. This territory is basically within the framework of the traditional and customary borderline and is under China's control now. In the Middle sector, the disputed land is about 2000 kms located in areas, northwest of China-Nepal border. Sikkim is in this region.

Zhuhua further observes that the main and biggest dispute concerns the Eastern Sector-involving 90, 000 sq km territory lying between south of McMahon line and north of the traditional customary line. This territory is "at present" is under the de facto control of India. Noting that the Sino-Indian border war in 1962 was the result of the Indian Government's 'forward strategy', the analyst adds that the area of this disputed region is three times that of Taiwan, six times that of Beijing and ten times that of Malvenas island, disputed by Britain and Argentina. It is flat and rich in water and forest resources. Tawang, home place of Sixth Dalai Lama, is located in this region. On December 1,1962, Chinese troops withdrew to 20 kms from the McMahon line; subsequently however India disregarded Chinese proposals and re-occupied areas held by the PLA before withdrawal. India even pushed its control up north, to areas beyond the pre-war border positions of the Chinese troops. It established North East Frontier Agency and in 1986, made it as one of India's 24 states. The analyst then points out that the migration of 7 million people into this territory at India's behest, was meant to make formation of the new state a 'fait accompli', compelling China into a 'passive' state. This fact of migration will continue to be the basis to 'fine tune' the Sino-Indian border negotiations.

Border Issue-Outlook for Future

Quoting former PRC Ambassador to India Zhou Gang, the analyst finds that out of the three steps needed to reach a solution on the border-first an agreement on principles, second discussions and the last settlement on the ground-only the first step has now been completed. Real difficulties are ahead in respect of the other two and in this regard, the high pressure on both nations coming from public sentiments domestically, stands out. Involved in these sentiments are issues such as sovereignty, national dignity, lives of border residents and resources. The question as to how the two nations are going to deal with public sentiments, will determine the future course of border talks. The Blog in this connection then gives weight to what Professor Wang Hungwei of the Chinese Academy of Social Sciences has said – "India's Prime Minister Nehru had in the past made mistaken projections about China to the Indian public as a 'devil' and it would be hard for the present leaders in India to retreat from Nehru's views. For the PRC, McMahon line, stands as a symbol of imperialist aggression on the country, which also remains a part of education on history in China. The Blog feels that India is all along adopting a hard position on the boundary and refers to assessments by Chinese experts that even if leaders of the two countries are prepared to recognise the territories controlled by each other as border, the Indian Parliament may not approve the same. India has vested interests and it tries to convince its people of the government's stand by hook or crook. On China's attitude, mentioning again what Zhou Gang has said, the analyst opines that the same has been restrained and rational.

Zhuhua, referring to the views of qualified analysts in China, further says that it would not be possible for China to recover the lost 90000 sq kms of territory in the border, by relying on negotiations. An unidentified researcher of the PRC Foreign Ministry is quoted as saying that a question facing China is whether it can make concessions to India in the Eastern Sector. If China does so, it would amount to Beijing's recognition of McMahon line and acceptance of the 1962 conflict as a Chinese war of aggression. The researcher further feels that the key to border solution lies in achieving a breakthrough in the matter of deciding on the status of McMahon line. That would pose a test for both the Chinese and Indian governments. There are also scholars in China who caution about the impact of the agreement on political parameters on the PRC. For e.g, they say that the 'watershed principle' in reality has McMahon line as basis and should thus be prevented.

Implications

What the analyst has said indicate that the theme of pending Chinese 'de jure' recognition of Sikkim.as part of India, has now reached the level of domestic comments. Without briefings from the Government, the same cannot happen. This gives rise to questions whether or not Beijing is signalling a retreat from its declared position on Sikkim, or is it meant to pressurise India during border negotiations, especially on the issue of Tawang in Eastern Sector. Also, a new dispute on what is now known as 'finger area' in the Sikkim border seems to have arisen. What clarifications Beijing gave to the visiting Indian Minister on Sikkim, remain unclear. Secondly, Zhuhua's blog is noteworthy for its revelation of what the Chinese foreign ministry thinks-it would be difficult for the PRC to make any territorial concessions to India in the Eastern Sector due to historical factors. The overall picture thus points to the likelihood of a prolonged course of border talks. The boundary question may not affect the present comfort level in bilateral ties, as both sides agree to look beyond the border dispute in promoting relations with each other. One cannot be optimistic, however, about the likely scenario in the long run, considering the damage potentials of the unsolved core issues including that of border.

ANALYSIS OF INDIA-CHINA BORDER DISPUTE: MUCH HYPE, SMALL GAINS (RC)

India and China, notwithstanding the media hype, appear to have made only small gains in narrowing their differences over the alignment of the Line of Actual Control along the 545-km long stretch in the former's central sector, covering the Himachal Pradesh and Uttar Pradesh boundaries with Tibet. The two sides had exchanged maps, giving their understanding of the LAC in the sector at the Expert Group meeting in November 2000. The latest EG meeting on June 28-29 was called to reconcile the differences. But the differences persist; the group will meet in December to resolve them. The LAC is the line up to which troops of the two sides exercise effective control. It has not been demarcated. But the term was first used by then Chinese Premier Zhou Enlai, well before the 1962 war, in a letter written in 1959 to then prime minister Jawaharlal Nehru. The Chinese put forward the line as its understanding of the de facto positions on the two sides. Beijing claimed India and China did not have a delineated boundary, but there was a well-recognised LAC.

This was strange logic since in vast portions of the difficult mountain border, forces of neither side were continually present. Instead, a historically derived and traditional boundary existed. Diplomatically, it was a useful Chinese ploy to secure a new boundary alignment seen to be important for its security. Between 1956, 1960 and 1962, Chinese maps were to show three distinct and advancing LACs, especially in the Laddakh sector, as its forces captured new territory across the Kuen Lun, the Aksai Chin plateau and the Karakoram ranges. The LAC established after the 1962 war has remained more or less stable, but has not been demarcated. For nearly three decades after the war, India considered it an illegitimate line created through aggression.

How did India agree to move away from attempting to settle the boundary dispute to a demarcation of the LAC? In the post-1976 normalisation phase, the Indian position has evolved through three distinct stages. Through the years up to 1987, New Delhi searched for an acceptable boundary deal. This was given up in 1987, following little movement and the eruption of a crisis over the Sumdorong valley.

In December 1988, then prime minister Rajiv Gandhi visited China to open a new chapter of détente. Over the next decade, India and China sought to enhance politico-military dialogue and build comprehensive ties in order to create the conditions for a fair boundary settlement. The 1993 and 1996 agreements, peace, tranquillity and confidence building measures were results of this phase. While overall ties grew during this period, confidence did not. Through each of these stages, China stuck to its wide territorial claims and refused to budge from any part of the occupied territories. Beijing also evinced little interest in an early settlement of territorial issues. Meanwhile, its overall military and economic power underwent a quantum jump and its nuclear and missile collaboration with Pakistan fundamentally altered India's strategic environment. India's Pokhran tests in May 1998 inaugurated the latest phase of the relationship and a new attempt to find the basis for stable, non-conflicting, long-term ties. Given the vast and continuing differences between the two countries, and the fact China officially claims the entire state of Arunachal Pradesh besides occupying a very large part of northeast Laddakh, India has had to make hard choices. Early delineation of the LAC has therefore emerged as an option for stabilising the border regions and securing a working boundary that the military forces on both sides would respect.

However, the settlement of the LAC will not be easy as the Chinese have initiated nerve-sapping bargaining over where the Line ought to be. The first exchange of maps occurred seven years after the 1993 agreement to maintain peace and tranquillity along the LAC. The central sector is the smallest and least complicated of the three sectors through which the border runs; it was expected that fixing the LAC here would be relatively simple. The eastern and western sectors are much longer and more complicated. The dispute in the central sector revolves around the possession of the Barahoti grazing grounds and a few smaller areas. This problem, which has existed since 1960, could not be settled in this round of talks. It will be taken up again in December. Meanwhile, the Joint Working Group, which will meet in the interim, could give both countries some direction that would guide them towards facilitating an agreement.

The non-issue of Tawang

Some media reports have harped on a trade-off in the eastern sector that gives Tawang to China in return for its recognition of the rest of the boundary. This is a non-issue under the current agenda. The two sides have yet to exchange their maps in this sector. Moreover, Tawang is lodged well south of the Indian side of the LAC and the Chinese recognise this. There are some pockets along the eastern line, where perceptions differ, but Tawang is not among them. But the Sumdorong Chu valley along the Arunachal border, where a conflict nearly broke in 1986-87, is. The two sides had, in 1996, agreed to pull back their forces from the disputed area by 200 metres on either side, pending a final clarification of the LAC. This will be done once the central sector is settled and the EG moves towards an exchange of maps in the other two sectors.

The Dynamics of a Relationship

An agreement on the less complicated central sector would have a positive effect on India-China relations. But the agreement needs to be reached early, without the searing bouts of bargaining that is typical of diplomatic negotiations with China. External Affairs Minister Jaswant Singh had stressed, during his visit to Beijing in July 1999, the need for an early delineation of the LAC in order to improve the post-Pokhran II political atmospherics, prevent accidental conflicts as might have happened in 1986-87, and expand understanding. With economic ties not large enough to determine the dynamics of Indo-China relations, stabilising the security dimension was deemed to be a feasible alternative. The LAC demarcation is vital if both nations are to facilitate cross-border trade and road communications, especially across Laddakh and Xinjiang, Sikkim, West Bengal and the rest of northeast India.

Finally, the effectiveness of the 1993 and the 1996 political and military CBM agreements critically depend on the delineation of the LAC. India has indicated it wants stable and growing ties with China and is not averse to reasonable compromises. The Chinese initiative so far has stressed on economic cooperation and 'friendly' political ties, but has been woefully short of substance in areas that shape the dynamics of the relationship. The long frontier with India remains China's last major unsettled land border. True, the border with Tajikstan and small segments of the Russian border have yet to be demarcated. But her border with India border is not only long, it is also caught up her Tibetan and overall Asian strategy.

Given the fact that security and strategic factors dominate the relationship, the People's Liberation Army remains the major shaper of China's India policy. A coalition of hardline forces have deeply influenced boundary policy, resulting in endless negotiations that lead nowhere, resulting in very negative consequences for her relations with India.

India's relations with the other major powers — the United States, Russia, Japan — are growing. There are indications that China is increasingly concerned about the strategic implications of India's evolving relationship with the United States. One way it could reduce its anxiety is by becoming more pro-active and moderate in its stance towards a settlement of the LAC and the boundary.

The more China haggles over marginal gains in territory, remains inflexible over its 'claims' and continues to be insensitive to India's security interests, the more it loses diplomatically in New Delhi. India-US relations have a dynamics well beyond the 'China issue.' Beijing's policies will determine its importance and content in India's relations with the US and other Asian powers.

CHINA-INDIA BORDER DISPUTE HOTS UP OVER USE OF MULTILATERAL INSTITUTION

A new twist has been introduced into the vexed land border dispute between India and China, with the latter trying to block a 2.9 billion dollar Asian Development Bank (ADB) loan to India on the grounds that part of the loan was destined for water projects in Arunachal Pradesh, the state that includes the disputed area of Tawang.

This is the first time that China has sought to influence the territorial dispute through a multilateral institution. This move plus aggressive border violations byu China has prompted the Indian Army to deploy extra troops and fighter jets in the area as a counter measures.

Based on the information of New York Times, one former Indian Air Force chief has declared China and not Pakistan as India's biggest threat. Perched above 10,000 feet in the icy reaches of the eastern Himalayas, Tawang is the biggest tinderbox in Sino-Indian relations. According to the NYT, in recent months, both countries have stepped up efforts to secure their rights over this rugged patch of land.

It is a conflict rooted in Chinese claims of sovereignty over all of historical Tibet. From India's point of view, Tawang is an integral part of the country and to safeguard it, a huge Indian military buildup is on. Army trucks have been hauling howitzers along rutted mountain roads.

Soldiers drill in muddy fields. Military bases appear every half-mile in the countryside, with watchtowers rising behind concertina wire. With the border with China just 23 miles away; Lhasa, the Tibetan capital, 316 miles; and Beijing, 2,676 miles, the Indian side is of the view that with the PLA engaged in big deployment at the border, at Bumla, there is a necessity to do the same on its side of the border.

China and India did 52 billion dollars worth of trade last year, but businesspeople say border tensions have been infused with official interference, damping the willingness of Chinese and Indian companies to invest in each other's countries. The NYT quotes Ravi Bhoothalingam, a former president of the Oberoi Hotel Group and a member of the Institute of Chinese Studies in New Delhi, as saying: " Officials start taking more time, scrutinizing things more carefully, and all that means more delays and ultimately more denials. That's not good for business."

Tawang is a thickly forested area of white stupas and steep, terraced hillsides that is home to the Monpa people, who practice Tibetan Buddhism, speak a language similar to Tibetan and once paid tribute to rulers in Lhasa. The Sixth Dalai Lama was born here in the 17th century. The Chinese Army occupied Tawang briefly in 1962, during a war with India fought over this and other territories along the 2,521-mile border. More than 3,100 Indian soldiers and 700 Chinese soldiers were killed and thousands wounded in the border war.

In some ways, Tawang has become a proxy battleground, too, between China and the Dalai Lama, the exiled spiritual leader of the Tibetans, who passed through this valley when he fled into exile in India in 1959. Last year, the Dalai Lama announced for the first time that Tawang is a part of India, bolstering the India's territorial claims and infuriating China. Few, however, expect China to try to annex Tawang by force, but military skirmishes are a real danger, analysts say. The Indian Army has recorded 270 border violations and nearly 2,300 instances of "aggressive border patrolling" by Chinese soldiers last year.

According to Brahma Chellaney, a professor of strategic studies at the Centre for Policy Research, "The India-China frontier has become more 'hot' than the India-Pakistan border." "The China-India border has got to be one of the most continuously negotiated borders in modern history. That shows how intractable this dispute is," said M. Taylor Fravel, an associate professor of political science at the Massachusetts Institute of Technology who is a leading expert on China's borders.

CHINA-INDIA BORDER DISPUTE – A PERSPECTIVE

The whole gamut of Sino-Indian relations have revolved around the unresolved boundary row between the two neighbours, culminating in the 1962 conflict. Years later there appeared to be a thaw in relations with trade ties between the two countries improving. However, the relations have been far from normal and India had more than adequate reasons to be suspicious of Chinese intentions and motives particularly in relation to the border issue. It is necessary to delve into history in order to determine why resolution of this dispute has been difficult.

India and China have for long found it difficult to resolve the border dispute which has impeded normal ties between the two Asian giants for about four and half decades. The cause of the conflict in 1962 was a dispute over the sovereignty of the widely-separated Aksai Chin (in Kashmir) and Tawang in Arunachal Pradesh border regions. Tawang district is located around latitude 27° 45′ N and longitude 90° 15′ E in North-West Arunachal Pradesh. Tawang was the scene of intense fighting during the 1962 Sino-Indian War. Chinese troops had then occupied Tawang and destroyed portions of the monastry. After the Chinese troops withdrew, Tawang was once again under Indian administration. Aksai Chin in Kashmir's Laddakh region is the other disputed territory which is at present under the control of the Chinese. This article primarily focuses only on the disputed border area in Tawang, Arunachal Pradesh.

The core issue: The status of Tibet is central to the border dispute for the simple reason that for two millennia, there never was a border between India and China. Lt Cmdr Calvin James Bernard of the US Navy in his paper titled "China-India Border War (1962)" stated that the roots of the conflict goes back to the 18th century, when both China and British India asserted claims to desolate, remote mountain areas between China and India.

Military expeditions, intrigue and unproductive diplomatic exchanges marked decades of relations between the two countries. Rather than resolving the border issue, Chinese and British Indian actions only set the stage for conflict.

According to Mohan Guruswamy, the roots of India's problem with China go back a couple of centuries when Emperor Napoleon and Tsar Alexander met in July 1807. As the Russian empire began its eastward expansion, which many felt would culminate in the conquest of India, there was a shadow contest for political ascendancy between the British and Russian empires. The Russians' desire for an empire and a warm water port did not diminish and so the game continued. The British response to meet the Russian threat was to establish a forward defensive line in the northern region so that a Russian thrust could be halted well before the plains of Hindustan. This called for making Afghanistan and Tibet into buffer states and for fixing suitable and convenient borders with these states. In other words, British India did not have a border with China.

It is only in October 1950, when Communist China's troops entered Tibet to 'liberate' the Roof of the Word that suddenly India acquired a new neighbour. Tibet was always a buffer between the Chinese and the British Empire. In 1914 at Simla an agreement came to be signed between the Dalai Lama's Representative and Sir Henry McMahon to define the border between Tibet and India. The McMahon Line came into being. The border agreement was arrived at bilaterally during the tripartite Convention between British India, China and Tibet. Though the Chinese subsequently refused to ratify the Convention, they did not object to the bilateral accord between Delhi and Lhasa. The Chinese were more concerned by the demarcation of their border with Eastern Tibet. The Chinese Premier Zhou Enlai (or Chou-en-lai) convinced Nehru that the British were 'imperialists' and therefore all treaties or agreements signed by them were 'imperialist treaties.' The inference drawn by the clever Chinese premier was that the McMahon line was an imperialist creation and therefore not acceptable by New China: The Chinese Premier conveniently presumed and told India's ambassador to China K N Panikkar that India had no intention of claiming special rights arising from the unequal treaties of the past. Nehru while concurring that the British were imperialists could not follow Zhou's conclusion on the McMahon Line. However, he did not want to raise the issue first. Since nothing was heard from the Chinese side about the issue of the frontier, Nehru deduced that McMahon Line was a foregone conclusion.

In 1954 the Panchsheel Agreement (known as Agreement on Trade and Intercourse between Tibet Region of China and India) came to be signed between the two countries. This agreement too was silent about the border. The Chinese Premier Zhou did not bring up the topic of the border till the end of the fifties. And by that time it was a bit too late for India as the Aksai Chin was fully in possession of the Liberation Army. The Chinese stand was unequivocal that it had never accepted the McMahon line and NEFA belonged to them. Zhou's visit to India in 1960 was followed by several rounds of detailed discussions which were held between June and December. While India presented detailed maps and documents proving its claims, the Chinese hardly gave any evidence of their 'possessions.'

Post 1962

Nathu La: September 1967

In 1965, two significant events took place on the Sino-Indian border. The first was the warning issued to India about Chinese sheep not being allowed to graze on their side of the border by India. This happened in September 1965 when the Indo-Pak war was simmering on India's western border.

At the same time, in September-December 1965, the PLA sent probing missions on the entire Sikkim-Tibet border. According to one account, there were seven border intrusions on the Sikkim-Tibet border between September 7 and December 12, 1965, involving the PLA. In all these border incursions, the Indian side responded "firmly" without provoking the other. Though details of casualties of these PLA border incursions are not reported, there were reports indicating that the PLA suffered "heavy" casualties against "moderate" loss by India.

Two years later, in September 1967, in spite of their setbacks in 1965, the PLA launched a direct attack on the Indian armed forces at Nathu La, on the Sikkim-Tibet border. The six-day "border skirmishes" from September 7-8 to 13, 1967, had all the elements of a high drama, including exchange of heavy artillery fire, and the PLA soldiers tried to cross the border in large numbers. Again the attack was repulsed at all points by the Indian troops.

Sumdorong Chu Incident of June-October 1986

In 1986 China decided to flex its muscles again with India. In mid-1986, it came to the notice of India that the PLA had built a helipad at Wandung in Sumdorong Chu Valley referred to as Sangduoluo He in the Chinese media in Arunachal Pradesh. India reacted swiftly and the PLA had an eyeball-to-eyeball confrontation with the India Army in Sumdorong Chu Valley of Arunachal Pradesh in August 1986. After a week of tense moments both sides mutually agreed to withdraw their forces inside their respective territories and create a no man's land.

In August '87, Indian and Chinese troops moved their respective posts slightly apart in the Sumdorong Chu Valley, following a meeting of the field commanders. During the 8th round of border talks on November '87, it was decided to upgrade the talks from the bureaucratic to the political level. Following then Prime Minister Rajiv Gandhi's visit to China in 1988, a Joint Working Group (JWG) was set up to discuss, among other things, the alignment of the LAC. In 1993, an agreement was inked between the foreign ministers of the two countries on the reduction of troops along the LAC. This was possibly first of the Confidence Building Measures (CBMs).

It was decided to pull back from respective forward check posts in the Sumdorong Chu Valley from a situation of "close confrontation" and in 1994, the Indian External Affairs Ministry described the situation as one of "close proximity" where the respective posts were 50-100 yards apart. Following the JWG meeting in April 1995, the two sides agreed to a simultaneous withdrawal of their troops from the four border posts-two Indian and two Chinese-in the Sumdorong Chu Valley. As of June 1999, the valley was unoccupied by either the Indian army or Chinese, and their respective posts in the area were close to a kilometre apart.

A View from China

According to a leading Chinese scholar on India Ma Jiali, China's claim to the whole of Arunachal Pradesh may only be a negotiating ploy. However, he added that the demand for Tawang might well be non-negotiable.

According to Ma Jiali, the disputed area in Arunachal Pradesh is very large. Tawang was the birthplace of the 6th Dalai Lama, Tsangyang Gyatso. The Tibetan people thus have very strong religious sentiments towards Tawang. It must be noted that in 1938, the Survey of India published a map of Tibet, which showed the Tawang tract as part of that country.

Even the first edition of Jawaharlal Nehru's Discovery Of India showed the Indo-Tibetan boundary as running at the foot of the hills. The Tibetans did not accept this 'annexation' of the Tawang tract and challenged the British attempts to expand their government into this area. But they tacitly accepted the rest of the McMahon demarcation. It is clear that, but for the Tawang tract, there is little basis for the Chinese claim on the whole of Arunachal Pradesh. According to other Chinese scholars, India should accept the Chinese view that McMahon Line was illegal and unacceptable and once it is done, the border settlement would be easy. Scholars have also warned that "substantial adjustments" would have to be made if the border issue between India and China is to be resolved.

The hint here is towards major concessions by India on Tawang. As far as the other sector of dispute, namely, Aksai Chin is concerned the Aksai Chin road is strategically too important for the Chinese, as it is the only link between its two western provinces of Tibet and Xinjiang. Thus the question of relinquishing the occupation of this area does not arise.

It is important to appreciate that there have been subtle changes in the Chinese position on the border dispute. At a point of time it was felt that the North-East was the bargaining chip or the 'pressure' for a de jure control of Aksai Chin. Today, while Aksai Chin has become non-negotiable, China seeks concessions from India on Tawang. The pressure on Tawang has been kept up by raking up issues of the entire state of Arunachal Pradesh and even Sikkim. China is in no hurry to resolve the issue. One reason could be the repeated incursions into Tawang could provide legitimacy to China for exercising de facto control over the territory. But at the core is also the assessment that the time for striking a deal with India is not now and when that would be would depend on how the mandarins assess the respective strengths of the two sides and whether China holds the upper hand.

Don't ignore the Sun Yuxi factor: Just a week ahead of Chinese President Hu Jintao's state visit to India in November 2006, Beijing's envoy to New Delhi Sun Yuxi claimed that Arunachal Pradesh was a Chinese territory. "In our position the whole of what you call the state of Arunachal Pradesh is Chinese territory, and Tawang (district) is only one place in it. We are claiming all of that—that's our position," he told the news channel CNN-IBN just days ahead of the Chinese President's visit to India. Sun was the man who drove Beijing's policy of stirred up tensions along the border in Arunachal. From incursions into the state, to demolition of Indian army observation posts along the Bhutan border and objections to road building in Sikkim, Sun carried out his mission with a bullheadedness that drove South Block to silent fury and prompting them to demand the recall of the envoy.

The South Block was infuriated by Sun's manipulation of the bilateral talks on border issue: from Aksai Chin in Laddakh to thousands of miles east in Arunachal, where India's insecurities ran the deepest.

The Indian government angrily rejected the statement, and a year later Sun was recalled. New Delhi conveyed to Beijing a message that unless Sun was recalled, the Indian Prime Minister would not send a final list of dates for his visit to China. The Prime Minister's Office held its ground despite China's initial refusal to concede. Delhi may seem to have been one up on the Chinese but it must be remembered that it could well be a case of two steps forward and one step backward. It is important to note that the envoy could not have taken a unilateral decision to claim the entire state of Arunachal Pradesh. Surely, there was some sort of official backing for him to make this provocative statement. Secondly, it took nearly a year for the Chinese to concede to the Indian demand for withdrawing him. Sun's statement could very well be the unstated Chinese policy on the border issue. India can ill-afford to ignore the Sun Yuxi factor.

The Nation needs to know: On the eve of the Indian Prime Minister's recent visit to China, India's External Affairs Minister Mr. Pranab Mukherjee candidly admitted in an interview to a TV news channel that Chinese incursions in the Tawang area of Arunachal Pradesh were taking place. He also added that though it was matter of concern, the incursions were not worrisome and that there was no reason to press panic buttons. The manner in which it was said gave the impression that it was China's prerogative to intrude and India's privilege to ignore it. This is only inference that can be drawn considering the fact that about 141 incursions had taken place in the past 12 months as of October 2007. It is quite disturbing as to why the government had chosen to play down the incursions. The interviewer also did not question the Hon'ble Minister about this. The incursions were highlighted by the MP from the area who repeatedly raised this issue in Parliament.

The Hon'ble Minister added that they (meaning the Indian government) took it up with the Chinese and that mechanisms were in place through which these types of problems were addressed. The nation is entitled to know, what are these mechanisms in the first place and if such mechanisms existed how effective have they been in dealing with the incursions. According to B Raman, there have been recurring instances of innumerable border intrusions by the Chinese troops. Two of these incidents are of great concern. The first was an intrusion into Bhutan and the second was about the Chinese raising an objection to the construction of two military bunkers inside Indian territory in Sikkim.

Apart from the incursions which are regularly taking place, the Indian Army is also concerned about an all weather highway being laid by the Chinese towards the Jechepla Pass in Myanmar. The pass provides direct entry into Arunachal and other sensitive eastern states. Farther west in Tawang, similar concerns have been raised about the pace at which China's network of roads and highways is being laid close to the Line of Actual Control. The Indian Prime Minister, after his recent trip to China is convinced that the border talks will make headway. However, it remains to be seen how sincere are the Chinese in negotiating a settlement.

Bibliography

B.R. Deepak: *India-China Relations In the First Half of the 20 Century*, APH, Delhi, 2001.

Bhawna Pokharna: *India-China Relations : Dimensions and Perspectives*, New Century Pub, Delhi, 2009.

Bidanda M Chengappa: *India-China Relations : Post Conflict Phase to Post Cold War Period*, Delhi, APH, 2004.

Calvin, James Barnard: *"The China-India Border War"*, Macmillan, New York, 1979

Haraprasad Ray: *Chinese Sources of South Asian History in Translation: Data for Study of India-China Relations Through History*, The Asiatic Society, 2004.

Kanti Bajpai and Amitabh Mattoo: *The Peacock and the Dragon : India-China Relations in the 21st Century*, Har-Anand, Delhi, 2000.

Kapur, Ashok: *Pokhran and Beyond: India's Nuclear Behaviour*, New Delhi: Oxford University Press, 2001.

Lamb, Alastair, *Incomplete Partition: The Genesis of the Kashmir Dispute 1947-1948*, Oxford:Oxford University Press, 2002

Lamb, Alastair: *The China-India Border: The Origins of the Disputed Boundaries*. L. Oxford University Press, London, 1964.

M.L. Sali: *India-China Border Dispute—A Case Study of the Eastern Sector*, APH, Delhi, 1998.

Neville Maxwell's: *India's China War*, Pantheon Books, USA, 1971

Perkovich, George: *India's Nuclear Bomb: The Impact on Global Proliferation*, Los Angeles: University of California Press, 1999

Shri Ram Sharma: *India-China Relations 1972-91*, Discovery, Delhi, 2003.

Snyder Glenn H.: *Deterrence and Defense*, Princeton: Princeton University Press, 1961.

Yu, Maochun: *The Dragon's War: Allied Operations and the Fate of China, 1937-1947*, Oxford, Lond, 1982.

Index

♦♦♦